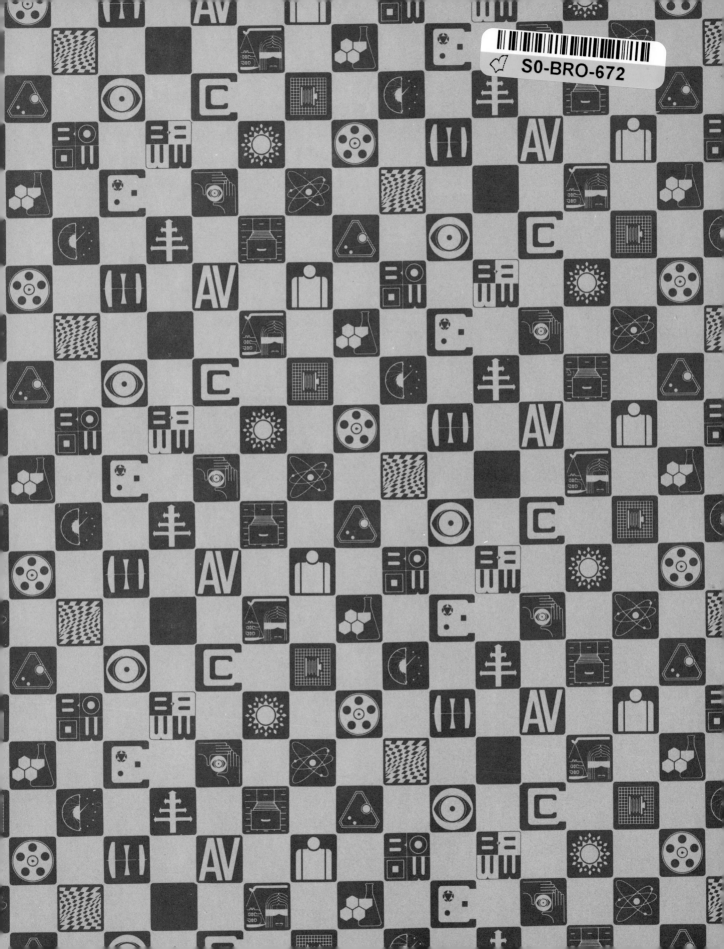

S0-BRO-672

Encyclopedia
of **Practical**
Photography

Volume **6**
Edit-Fla

Edited by and published for
EASTMAN KODAK COMPANY

AMPHOTO
American Photographic Book Publishing Company
Garden City, New York

Note on Photography

The cover photos and the photos of letters that appear elsewhere in this encyclopedia were taken by Chris Maggio.

Library of Congress Cataloging in Publication Data

Amphoto, New York.
  Encyclopedia of practical photography.

  Includes bibliographical references and index.
  1. Photography—Dictionaries. I. Eastman Kodak Company. II. Title.
TR9.A46   770'.3   77–22562

ISBN 0–8174–3050–4 Trade Edition—Whole Set
ISBN 0–8174–3200–0 Library Edition—Whole Set
ISBN 0-8174-3056-3 Trade Edition—Volume 6
ISBN 0-8174-3206-X Library Edition—Volume 6

Manufactured in the United States of America

Editorial Board

The *Encyclopedia of Practical Photography* was compiled and edited jointly by Eastman Kodak Company and American Photographic Book Publishing Co., Inc. (Amphoto). The comprehensive archives, vast resources, and technical staffs of both companies, as well as the published works of Kodak, were used as the basis for most of the information contained in this encyclopedia.

Symbol Identification

 Audiovisual

 Color Processing and Printing

 Picture-Making Techniques

 Biography

 Equipment and Facilities

 Scientific Photography

 Black-and-White Materials

 Exposure

 Special Effects and Techniques

 Black-and-White Processing and Printing

 History

 Special Interests

 Business and Legal Aspects

 Lighting

 Storage and Care

 Chemicals

 Motion Picture

 Theory of Photography

 Color Materials

 Optics

 Vision

Guide for the Reader

Use this encyclopedia as you would any good encyclopedia or dictionary. Look for the subject desired as it first occurs to you—most often you will locate it immediately. The shorter articles begin with a dictionary-style definition, and the longer articles begin with a short paragraph that summarizes the article that follows. Either of these should tell you if the information you need is in the article. The longer articles are then broken down by series of headings and sub-headings to aid further in locating specific information.

Cross References

If you do not find the specific information you are seeking in the article first consulted, use the cross references (within the article and at the end of it) to lead you to more information. The cross references can lead you from a general article to the more detailed articles into which the subject is divided. Cross references are printed in capital letters so that you can easily recognize them.
Example: *See also:* Zone System.

Index

If the initial article you turn to does not supply you with the information you seek, and the cross references do not lead you to it, use the index in the last volume. The index contains thousands of entries to help you identify and locate any subject you seek.

Symbols

To further aid you in locating information, the articles throughout have been organized into major photographic categories. Each category is represented by a symbol displayed on the opposite page. By using only the symbols, you can scan each volume and locate all the information under any of the general categories. Thus, if you wish to read all about lighting, simply locate the lighting symbols and read the articles under them.

Reading Lists

Most of the longer articles are followed by reading lists citing useful sources for further information. Should you require additional sources, check the cross-referenced articles for additional reading lists.

Metric Measurement

Both the U.S. Customary System of measurement and the International System (SI) are used throughout this encyclopedia. In most cases, the metric measurement is given first with the U.S. customary equivalent following in parenthesis. When equivalent measurements are given, they will be rounded off to the nearest whole unit or a tenth of a unit, unless precise measurement is important. When a measurement is considered a "standard," equivalents will not be given. For example: 35 mm film, 200 mm lens, 4″ × 5″ negative, and 8″ × 10″ prints will not be given with their customary or metric equivalents.

How Articles are Alphabetized

Article titles are alphabetized by letter sequence, with word breaks and hyphens not considered. Example:

> Archer, Frederick Scott
> Architectural Photography
> Archival Processing
> Arc Lamps

Abbreviations are alphabetized according to the letters of the abbreviations, not by the words the letters stand for. Example:

> Artificial Light
> ASA Speed

Contents
Volume 6

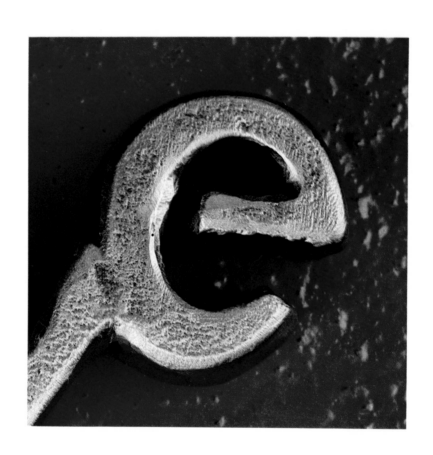

Editing Movies

Proper editing of a movie can mean the difference between a presentation that is quite ordinary and one that is exciting and interesting to see. Editing is the core of movie-making.

This article discusses how to create better movies through planning, and through careful selection and arrangement of movie shots and sequences. It explains how awareness of such things as motion and timing can help control the message a movie conveys. You can use these suggestions with movies already made as well as with new movies; they apply to any film size—super 8, 8 mm, or 16 mm.

First Phases of Editing

Basically, movie editing is *selecting* the scenes and *arranging* them within the body of the film. The first stages of movie editing begin with planning the movie.

Suppose you want to make a documentary film about a volunteer fire department. Begin by deciding which sequences will tell the story the way you want to tell it. Possible sequences might include fire-fighting equipment, training sessions, men on duty, actual fires, and social activities. When you select the different aspects of the volunteer fire department story that you want to photograph, and arrange these ideas in some sort of logical order, you are beginning to edit.

If you write a shooting script, you may rearrange some of the sequences and tentatively decide which shots will make up each sequence. You will decide what the shots should include, and whether a shot will be an extreme long shot, a long shot, a medium shot, a close-up, or an extreme close-up. This arranging and selecting is another form of editing.

The next phase of editing occurs in shooting the movie. Through the camera viewfinder, you select the strongest viewpoint for each scene. When it is convenient, do as much editing as possible in the camera. Carefully plan the action of your sequences, and when possible, photograph them in their final order. This saves time at later editing stages when all the shots are spliced in final order. When you edit in the camera, you become more acutely aware of

the continuity of the movie and the formation of the story line. You begin to "think sequences" and to form the story several shots ahead rather than to place emphasis on only one shot at a time.

Final Phases of Editing

After you have exposed the film, had it processed, and projected it (just to see how it looks), you are ready to begin working with your action editor and splicer. This viewing, cutting, and splicing comprise the final stages of editing.

During final editing, remember to handle the film with extreme care. Wear soft cotton gloves (many photo retailers stock inexpensive gloves for this purpose) and handle the film carefully. A scratch could mean a ruined scene.

The three most important elements of the final stage of movie editing are:

1. Screen movement.
2. Meaning.
3. Pacing.

Screen Movement. This is *all* movement on the screen—people walking, stretching, swinging; leaves tossing gently in the breeze; panning the camera slowly to take in all of a scenic vista. It is possible to make an already good sequence even better during editing by being critically aware of the effects of subject and camera movement.

A major element of screen movement is the direction of the subjects' travel. Direction of travel is important to the audience—they should feel that both the story and characters are logically moving through time and space. Keep direction of travel in mind while shooting, and remember to keep the audience clearly aware of the direction in which the subjects are moving. If you want the audience to think the subjects are getting closer to their destination, all of their movement should be in one direction on the screen. If they are moving left to right in one shot, and right to left in the next, the audience will think they changed their minds and reversed their direction. This could happen when you photograph a young couple walking down a path from one side of the path, and then moving to the other side of the path to complete the sequence. When the movie is projected, it will look as if they changed the direction in which they were walking. If you inadvertently create a situation such as this, you can minimize the error by editing in a cutaway shot. This filler scene is one related to the action in preceding and following shots, but is not directly a part of that action. When placed between unintentional direction changes, cutaways help divert the audience's attention from the original direction of travel, so they will tend to overlook the fact that the subjects are moving in another direction in the shot following the cutaway.

In the accompanying sequence, when the shot of the woman entering the room is spliced between the shots where the camera angle changes, the change of direction becomes less obvious. The cutaway shot side-tracks attention momentarily; when the man is seen once again, he is still working at the table. The editing covered what would otherwise have been a blunder.

Matched Action. Another element in screen movement is matched action. To keep the action moving smoothly on the screen, maintain the continuity of movement from one shot to the next. For example, consider the movement in a shot of a youngster playing with blocks. He extends his hand and places a block on top of the pile.

When you move in for a closer view of the action, simply ask the boy to repeat it for the close-up shot. That gives you two shots of the same action.

In splicing these shots together, you must cut to the close-up shot at precisely the same spot at which you leave the action in the medium shot. If the action overlaps on the screen, the boy's hand may reach out and place the block onto the pile twice. If there is a gap in the action, the boy's hand will appear to jump from one position to another. Either situation will jar the audience. You can avoid the

(Top row) Cutting directly between views from opposite sides of a performer (left, right) can disorient the viewer; the performer seems to jump to face himself on the screen. Inserting a cutaway to another performer (center) during editing shifts attention so that returning to the first performer from a new angle is not confusing. (Bottom row) General camera position for each shot is also shown.

930

Editing Movies

A jump cut occurs when performers have changed position while the camera was not photographing; cutaways and inserts can cover such jumps. The cutaway shot to the clock covers the man's change from a seated position to a standing one.

problem by viewing the two scenes very carefully in an action editor, and then cutting and matching the action correctly.

To cut on the action easily, make the cut from one shot to the next at the beginning or the end of the movement, rather than in the middle. It is easier to select and cut on the frame where, for example, the boy puts the block onto the pile, than it is to match the action in the middle of his reach for the block pile.

An unwanted type of cut that can easily creep into movies is a jump cut. A jump cut is a gap in the action from one shot to the next when neither the viewpoint nor the subject distance has been changed. Like mismatched action, this can be jarring because

the audience sees a person or object suddenly jump from one position to another. For example, imagine a movie sequence of a small boy coloring in a coloring book. The camera operator did not change the viewpoint or subject distance—but kept the camera in the same position during the entire 2-minute sequence. However, the camera was started and stopped several times throughout the boy's activity. On the screen, the child starts to color; suddenly, he "jumps" to the other side of the frame for a few moments; then his position shifts again and he is coloring a different part of the picture. Of course, we realize that during each interval the camera was stopped and the child shifted his position. But on the screen this appears as a glaring jump cut.

Editing Movies

If you inadvertently make a jump cut, you can reduce the visual jolt with a cutaway shot. Insert the cutaway between the two shots that make up the jump cut. This fills the apparent time gap and produces a smoother sequence.

It is always a good idea to shoot extra footage when you make a movie. A few cutaways in reserve may help cover an occasional mistake or let you discard some imperfect footage.

Meaning. The second consideration in final editing is screen meaning. After all the movement is edited to the best of your ability, make sure that the meaning it conveys to the audience is the one you intended. When all the shots are spliced together, do they tell the story in the best possible way? A good way to answer this question is to show the movie to an impartial panel. Family or a few friends will do nicely, provided they view the film with an unbiased eye. From the opinions of this preview audience, you will learn whether the film is assembled in a manner that tells the story clearly and interestingly. Editing is not complete at this point. There is still final polishing and tightening up to do, but you can proceed with the knowledge that the message is getting across. Previewing the film will also help the final polishing by giving you a feel for the pacing and story continuity of the film.

Changing the Meaning. You can alter the meaning of a movie by altering the order of the shots or sequences. For example, it is possible to take three very basic shots and connect them in a number of different ways. This offers the chance to create several different meanings. The accompanying doughnut sequence is an example.

Pacing. Pacing is the timing, or rhythm, of a movie. Each shot in the film should stay on the screen just long enough to support the action. If the shot is cut too quickly, the audience may become confused. If it stays on the screen too long, the audience may become restless or bored. So, correct film pacing is important.

Some film editors tighten up films by cutting the action immediately after the subject has either left the frame or completed a phase of action. To really accelerate the tempo, it is sometimes effective to cut the action a few frames *before* it has been completed.

The cutaway shot also plays an important role in the pace of a movie. Cutaways add variety, and variety almost invariably quickens the pace. In addition, a cutaway shot can indicate the passage of time —either rapidly or very slowly. The following are some examples:

1. When you shoot public activities, such as sports events or parades, shoot footage of the spectators, also. Later you can edit these shots into the movie to help control the pace. A rapid series of shots showing spectators jumping to their feet at a football game creates a feeling of fast action and excitement. You might also indicate passage of time by showing an excited child in one cutaway, and later splicing another cutaway shot of the child leaning against his father, sound asleep.

2. You can control pace by cutting away to the dial of a clock. If you insert this shot every so often in the sequence, it can indicate rapid or slow passage of time, depending on the time that has elapsed on the clock between cutaways.

3. Close-ups often make effective cutaways, and they add variety to increase the pace of a movie. When shooting a movie, make some extreme close-ups of subjects related to the action; such shots can come in handy as cutaways.

For every action, there is a reaction. Cutaway shots showing reactions to the main activity of the movie can be interesting and pace-controlling additions to a sequence. Effective reaction shots may even become the highlights of a sequence because they point up the effect or the dramatic impact of an action. You can increase suspense by splicing the reaction shot *before* you show the action.

Screen pacing also includes the use of parallel action—switching back and forth between two lines of action that are taking place at the same time. The way the pieces of parallel action are edited determines the pace. Switching from one short segment

Close-ups add variety and increase interest in a scene. Note that the camera pans in the first four pictures to follow the subject as he rises and moves into a close-up for a drink. The remaining individual shots are assembled by editing cuts to reestablish the situation and build pace with close-ups.

to another quickens the pace; long segments of parallel action slow the pace. Editing parallel action into a movie is also a good way to establish suspense. For example, switching between shots of a man climbing stairs and a secret agent trying to open a safe containing espionage plans can build up a lot of excitement and suspense.

Editing Sound Movies

A movie's major task of communication is accomplished by its pictures. But accompanying sound can make the total message far richer and more effective. It is easy to incorporate magnetically recorded sound in movies. Many modern super 8 cameras are equipped to record sound directly onto a magnetic stripe on the film as each shot is made. It is also possible to record sound onto the stripe after the film has been edited. Or, a stripe can be added to silent footage so that sound, music, and narration can be included. There are some important considerations in editing sound movies so that the aural portion matches and flows as smoothly as the visual portion.

Sound Editing Equipment. In addition to the film splicer and viewer needed for editing silent pictures, these items will be required: a film synchro-

Necessary items for editing sound film include a film splicer and viewer, editing gloves, marking pen, scissors, masking tape, extra reels, white leader, and film cleaner. A stopwatch is also useful to time sequences.

Most modern super 8 cameras are designed with microphones for recording sound while the picture is being shot. Photo by Stephen Stuart, Ad Team, Inc.

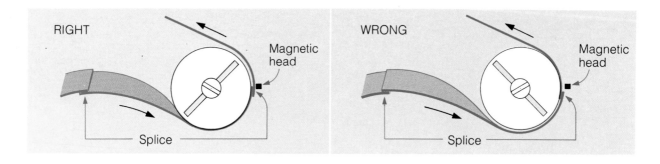

RIGHT

Magnetic head

Splice

WRONG

Magnetic head

Splice

To prevent catching at the splice and to minimize the loss of head contact with the sound track at splices, it is important that the splice be made with the leading piece of the film on the side of the splice that contacts the magnetic sound head, as shown at the left.

nizer, magnetic sound reader, and special rewinds with shafts that can accommodate two or more reels of film on each spindle. Several makes of film synchronizers are available commercially and may be rented or purchased. The long-shaft rewinds are available from professional motion-picture-equipment supply houses.

Splicing Magnetically Striped Film. Magnetically striped film can be spliced on any standard film splicer. The only difference in technique is that the striping, in addition to the film emulsion, must be removed in order to provide a good bond.

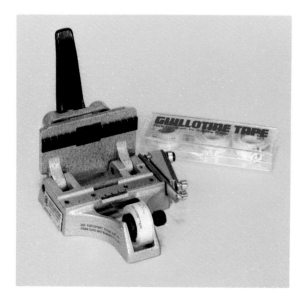

Film splicers are used to connect two pieces of film that were not photographed in sequence. Most splicers can be used for super 8 or regular 8 mm film, with or without sound.

The direction of splice overlap is especially important in the splicing of magnetic sound film. The overlap should be made so that it will not catch on the erase and recording heads of the projector and pull the splice apart. It is easy to determine the proper splice-overlap direction: one piece of film leads the other piece through the projector mechanism; the piece that follows should be on top of the one that leads. (The striped side is down when the film passes over the head. See the accompanying diagram.)

Removal of the magnetic stripe so that a proper splice can be made is no problem when film duplicates are being spliced. The film emulsion and the magnetic oxide stripe are on the same side of the film, and both are removed readily with the normal scraping operation used for removing the emulsion. Removing the stripe and film emulsion is a bit more difficult in the splicing of original footage. Here the emulsion layer and the magnetic stripe are on opposite sides of the film, and the ease of removal of the sound stripe depends upon the design of the splicing equipment used.

Some splicers permit turning the film over and affixing it on a new set of pins so that it is positioned

Editing Movies

for scraping from either side or either end, as desired. With other types of splicers, magnetic oxide can be removed from the film by hand-scraping with a single-edge razor blade or by applying film cement carefully and wiping.

To remove the oxide with film cement, place a drop of cement on the desired area to loosen the striping material, and wipe it away with a soft cloth. Care should be exercised to brush the film cement only on the section of the stripe to be removed. If all the oxide is not removed in the first try, the section should again be coated with cement and the process repeated.

Cutting Sound and Picture. There are two basic methods of recording sound and picture—single system and double system. In single-system recording, the sound is recorded directly on the film during shooting. Thus it is present at the time of editing and care must be taken not to accidentally remove necessary sound when unwanted picture footage is eliminated. In double-system recording, the sound is recorded on separate tape. The picture may be freely edited without danger of cutting any sound. The tape can be cut and spliced to match the picture either at the same time, or after picture editing has been completed.

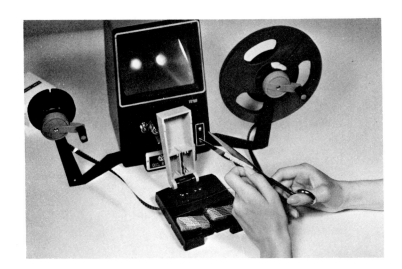

When editing film with camera-recorded sound, care must be taken not to accidentally remove necessary sound when eliminating unwanted footage. In addition, splicing tapes covering the sound stripe will degrade the quality of the sound in that area. Trimming approximately 1/16" from the edge applied to the striped side of the film will leave the sound stripe free of obstruction.

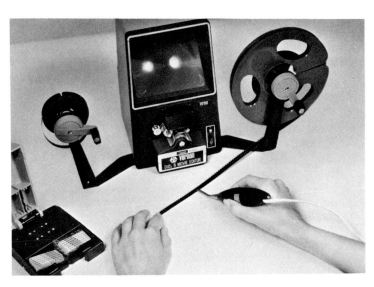

Unwanted sound on a stripe can be eliminated by moving a small electromagnetic tape eraser over the stripe.

Single-System Sound Editing

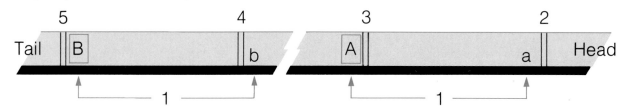

(1) In a single-system recording, the sound is located on the stripe ahead of the corresponding picture. Separation is 18 frames with super 8 film, and 28 frames with 16 mm film, equivalent to approximately 1 second of screen time. (2) At the beginning of a scene, the splice must occur just before the first sound. A splice at the picture (3) would cut the sound. Beginning picture portions (between a and A) must be silent action or fit with the sound from the end of the preceding scene. At the end of the scene, the splice must fall after the last picture frame (4). A splice made at the corresponding sound point (5) would eliminate the necessary picture. If the following sound (between b and B) is unsuitable for the picture at the beginning of the next scene, it must be erased.

Single-System Recording. Most super 8 sound cameras provide single-system recording. Because there is no room to locate the recording head directly alongside the picture gate in a camera or a projector, the sound that corresponds to any given frame is actually located many frames ahead of that point on the sound stripe. (See the accompanying diagram.) Therefore, at the beginning of a scene, the splice must occur just ahead of the *sound stripe location* of the first sound in the scene. If the splice is made at the picture frame that goes with that sound, the sound itself will be trimmed off.

At the end of a scene, the picture that corresponds to the final sound follows several frames beyond that point on the stripe. So, the splice must be made just after the *picture* frame. If there is unwanted sound on the stripe between the last sound scene and the actual end of the film, it can be erased by moving a small magnet over the stripe. A small electromagnetic tape eraser, or degausser, is especially useful for this purpose. Such instruments are available from dealers of tape recording supplies and equipment.

Double-System Editing. A common practice in adding sound to magnetically striped film is to shoot and edit the film first, have the magnetic striping added, and record the sound track. Such editing requires no special sound matching or cutting to fit the picture, because these operations are accomplished during recording. If the sound track is recorded on tape, then sound editing is needed in order to match or synchronize sound and picture prior to the final rerecording onto the finished film.

One of two approaches can be followed in matching narration and picture:

1. The narration can be cut and tailored to fit the previously edited film.
2. Scenes that have been purposely shot overlong can be cut to match the narration appropriate to them.

Both techniques require the same equipment and are done in a similar manner.

For this type of editing, it is necessary to have the narration recorded on perforated magnetic recording stock, several varieties of which are available. One kind resembles clear leader stock with the 100-mil magnetic oxide stripe running down one edge of it in the normal 16 mm sound-track position. Another variety resembles regular 1/4-inch recording tape, except that it is perforated along one edge and is a full 16 millimetres wide. Either type works very well for sound-track recording. Proceed as follows:

Set up the equipment for sound editing with the film viewer and sound reader located between the reels and in line with their particular take-up and supply reels. Locate the synchronizer next to the take-up rewind and thread the film leader through the viewer and the recording film through the reader. Pass both films through the appropriate sprockets in the synchronizer and onto their respective take-up reels.

Locate the beginning of the first line of the narration by cranking the sound track through the reader and listening for the beginning of the first word. Mark this spot on the track with a pencil and align it with the beginning of the proper scene in the synchronizer. This is done by releasing either the picture or track in the synchronizer and moving it ahead or back until the beginnings of the sound and picture are located on corresponding teeth of their respective synchronizer sprockets. The picture and the track should be locked in this relationship in the synchronizer and should not be released until the editing has been completed. To avoid trouble later on, if the film and track should get out of sync for one reason or another, put a punch mark in corresponding frames in the leaders of both picture and sound. The punching also serves as a cue mark in dubbing. From here on, it is merely a matter of:

1. Splicing in blank, unrecorded sound track to space out the narration for successive scenes and make scene and sound track of equal length, or
2. Cutting the scenes to fit the length of the narration.

It is possible to modify a silent super 8 viewer for sound unit editing. For left–right film travel, the sound head is located a distance equal to 18 film frames to the right of the viewer picture gate; this matches the separation in the camera, which recorded sound at a point 18 frames ahead of the frame in the camera gate. The same 18-frame displacement between sound and picture is built into sound super 8 projectors and viewers.

Sound super 8 film editing equipment can also be purchased from commercial suppliers.

The choice between these two methods depends primarily on the content of the scenes. If the scenes contain action that is longer than the commentary, it is best to space out the narration track to fit the picture. On the other hand, if the scenes are essentially static and are held together and given continuity by the narration, much better pace is achieved by shortening the scenes to fit the sound.

When narration is being synchronized to picture, it is not imperative that the voice and picture for a particular scene start on exactly the same frame. In fact, it is generally better practice to let the picture lead the voice by a few frames so that the audience will see the subject a moment before they hear the narration concerning it. In some instances, usually when introducing the next scene, the sound leads the picture.

After the editing has been completed, the sound track and picture can be threaded on two interlocked projectors and the sound dubbed onto the film. To provide good synchronization, start the punch mark in the leader of the picture at the aperture in the film gate of one projector, and the corresponding punch mark in the soundtrack leader at the magnetic record/play head on the sound drum of the other.

Sound from a separate track can be dubbed onto the film with a single projector by recording from the sprocketed sound original to tape on a regular tape recorder, and then dubbing it back from the tape to the picture on the magnetic recording projector. If these operations are done in one recording session, the tape recorder and projector will usually maintain satisfactory sync for films that involve only narration. However, if time is allowed to elapse between recording sessions, the transferring of sound is almost impossible, because of differences in operating conditions, to maintain satisfactory sync.

Editing Double-System Synchronous Voice and Coincident Sound. Cutting sound and picture to run synchronously in double-system sound recording is similar to cutting narration to fit the picture, except that sound and picture must be synchronized exactly. When a clapstick is used during shooting of the scene, no problems will be encountered in lining up scene and sound for exact sync in editing. It is only necessary to locate the frame in the picture where the clapstick came together at the beginning of the scene and line up that frame in the synchronizer with the corresponding loud clap on the sound track. All the scenes in the film can be synchronized in this manner and spliced together in proper order so that the clapstick sync of sound and picture line up perfectly on the synchronizer throughout the entire length of the film. Later on, the short lengths of film and sound track used for sync purposes at the beginning of each scene can be cut out. During cutting, care should be exercised to remove the same number of frames from both picture and track so that exact synchronization will be maintained.

When the sound from the edited track is transferred to the striped release print in double-system synchronous recording, it is imperative that interlocked projectors or a sprocketed film recorder be used. In the latter case, both the recorder and the projector should be driven by interlocked motors.

The procedures for editing coincident double-system sound are the same as those used in double-system synchronous sound editing. It should be noted, however, that since the picture and sound were not recorded with interlocked equipment (camera and recorder), there will be a tendency for the scenes to start in sync, then drift away from synchronization toward the end of each scene. If the scenes, as shot, were overlong and this lack of synchronism becomes noticeable, the addition or deletion of a few frames of blank film in the sound track can bring it back into proper alignment with the picture in the synchronizer. Sometimes it is possible to retard the picture, if it gets ahead of the sound, by using a manual speed-control accessory during the recording.

Synchronous Sound from Multiple Sources. Through the use of the sound reader and the synchronizer, it is possible to provide several separate sound tracks that are synchronized with the picture. In addition to the voice track, there might be one for sound effects and another for music. These tracks can be mixed and dubbed onto a master which, in turn, is dubbed onto the film. Such a technique is employed by major studios and by regular commercial producers, but it is generally thought to be beyond the scope of the magnetic recording projector.

Erasing and Removing Clicks. One disconcerting aspect of magnetic recording is the recording of clicks on the track. Although these may come from a variety of sources, their most common cause is switching from magnetic play to record mode. These switch clicks can be made almost inaudible if the amplifier volume is turned all the way down before the switch is made to record position, then brought back to normal recording volume before the next section of the track is recorded. The splicer is another source of clicks. If the splicer becomes magnetized, it will produce an audible click on the track. Splices that are too thick (improperly made) can cause an audible sound on playback because they prevent the track from contacting the magnetic head. Regardless of their origin, unwanted clicks, pops, or other noises on a magnetic sound track are a nuisance, and their elimination is desirable. Whenever possible, the instant-stop (cue, edit) control should be used for stopping the tape momentarily during a recording session. Use of this control reduces switch-clicking to a minimum.

The first step in the removal of clicks is to locate and mark their exact position. This can be done quickly and easily on the sound reader. They can be erased with a special magnetic-erasing pencil or a head demagnetizer. Instructions for use are included with such devices.

Most methods have their inherent difficulties. When work is being done near magnetic materials or a magnetic field, there is a chance that more noise will be created on the track than is removed. If other methods fail, the click can be removed by eliminating the magnetic oxide completely from the film at that point, using a drop of film cement or scraping and removing the oxide carefully with a razor blade. Even this will not be perfect, though, because the small amount of hiss or hum present on all magnetic tracks will be noticeable where the track interruption occurs. This, however, may be less annoying than the click.

• *See also:* A AND B ROLL EDITING; MAGNETIC SOUND FOR MOTION PICTURES; SOUNDSTRIPE; SPLICING FILM.

Further Reading: Adams, William B. *Handbook of Motion Picture Production.* New York, NY: John Wiley & Sons, 1977; Baddeley, W. Hugh. *The Technique of Documentary Film Production.* New York, NY: Hastings House, 1965; Clarke, Charles G. *Professional Cinematography.* Hollywood, CA: American Society of Cinematographers, 1964; Tremaine, Howard M. *Audio Cyclopedia,* 2nd ed. New York, NY: Howard W. Sams, 1969; Walter, Ernest. *The Technique of the Film Cutting Room.* New York, NY: Hastings House, 1968.

Electronic Flash

Electronic flash is the illumination produced when a gas-discharge tube is suddenly energized by high-voltage direct current. It is widely used for both color and black-and-white photography because it offers a number of advantages over conventional flash bulbs or cubes:

1. Electronic flash tubes have a useful life of many thousands of flashes. Although initially more expensive, they are much cheaper in the long run, and there is no need to repeatedly change them after each exposure.

2. Electronic flash duration is much shorter and reaches peak intensity as much as 1000 times faster than conventional flash. It can synchronize with all leaf-shutter speeds without exposure change. Equivalent exposures of 1/1000 sec. are common, and some units produce exposures of 1/10,000 sec. Consequently, electronic flash is widely used to stop fast action.

3. Electronic flash illumination has a color temperature of approximately 6000 K. That is so close to the balance of most daylight-type color film emulsions that corrective filtration is seldom required.

Electronic Flash Units

Electronic flash units are available in three basic types:

1. Miniature units with self-contained reflectors may be small enough to slip into a shirt pocket. They weigh so little that they may be mounted in the accessory shoe of small cameras. Most are powered by small batteries; some may also have ac adapters.

Electronic flash is widely used to stop fast action. This photograph, taken at 1/10,000 sec., shows a milk drop splashing from a height of about seven inches onto a plate covered by a thin layer of milk. Photo by Harold E. Edgerton.

Electronic Flash

(Above) Some pocket cameras have built-in electronic flash units. Photo courtesy Vivitar Corp. (Right) Miniature electronic flash units, designed for use with pocket cameras, may be small enough and light enough to carry in a shirt pocket.

Electronic Flash Circuits

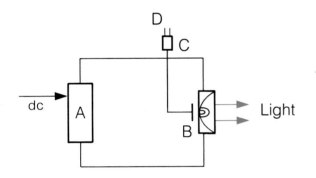

2. Portable professional units with integral reflectors are commonly hand-held or mounted on a bracket attached to the camera. Power may be from self-contained batteries, a portable accessory battery pack, or an ac adapter or power supply.
3. Studio units have high output, but are comparatively large and heavy. The flash head is separate from the power supply, so that it may easily be mounted in any position with a variety of reflectors—the folding umbrella-type reflector is widely used. The power unit is sizable and heavy; it operates on ac and is usually capable of powering two or more flash heads.

Whatever their size and power requirements, all electronic flash units have the same basic components: power supply, flash tube, and trigger and control circuits.

◄ *In a basic circuit, the capacitor (A) stores up low-voltage dc input to a level of several hundred or thousand volts, according to tube requirements. The circuit is completed through a flash tube (B) to produce light by sudden discharge when the trigger circuit (C) applies a voltage to the tube, which ionizes gas inside. The trigger circuit is connected (D) to the shutter sync contacts and to the open-flash or test switch.*

Power Supply. A capacitor or condenser stores up electrical energy supplied by batteries or by a rectifier connected to an ac power source. The batteries may be the disposable type, or rechargeable units such as nickel-cadmium cells. The capacitor requires only a low-voltage dc input, but it builds up a charge of hundreds or thousands of volts, as required by the flash tube. Most power supplies incorporate a ready light that signals when the capacitor charge has reached operating level. The time from the end of one flash until the capacitor has recharged sufficiently to power the next flash is called the recycling time. It may range from 6–10 seconds for low-voltage battery units, to only 2 or 3 seconds for ac-powered units. Some power supplies include smaller capacitors that may be switched into use to obtain ¼ or ½ power operation when maximum light output is not required. Recycling time is much shorter in reduced-power operation.

Portable electronic flash units may be either hand-held (left) or mounted on a bracket attached to the camera (right). Unit at left is powered by a portable accessory battery pack slung from photographer's shoulder; Metz 45 CT-1 unit at right may use self-contained regular alkaline or nickel cadmium rechargeable batteries, or an ac adapter. Photo at right courtesy Ehrenreich Photo-Optical Industries, Inc.

Flash Tube. An electronic flash tube is a hollow length of glass or quartz filled with xenon, krypton, or other rare gases. Tubes range in size from less than ¼-inch diameter and 1-inch length to about ½-inch diameter and 4- or 5-inch length. High-output tubes are commonly made in a spiral to concentrate light from a long-tube length in a small area. An electrode is sealed in each end of the tube. When a voltage high enough to complete a circuit through the gas is applied to the electrodes, the resulting energy discharge produces intense light for a fraction of a second. The kind of gas in the tube determines the color balance of the output; the gas pressure determines the voltage required to cause a flash. Since most tubes produce some ultraviolet energy and more blue light than green and red light, the light balance is bluish. Thus, self-contained electronic flash units usually use a warming reflector or a UV-absorbing plastic lens in front of the tube.

Direct flash from studio units or bare-tube setups may require UV filtration at the camera lens.

Special tubes include a circular or ring-like configuration. Such a tube is placed around the camera lens to provide directionless illumination, which is often desirable when photographing small objects at close distances.

Some heat is produced with each flash; however, the amount of heat is less than that of a conventional flash bulb, although a burn can occur. This usually happens only when something is touching the tube at the moment of the flash. However, too rapid refiring of a tube for a sustained period may cause sufficient heat buildup to affect the flash unit housing or wiring. Special tubes are available that are capable of being flashed repeatedly many times a second without excessive heat buildup; they must be powered by very high voltages applied through constant-recycling capacitors. The resulting *stroboscopic* illumination may flash at rates of from 2 or 3 times to more than 100 times a second. The term "strobe light" is sometimes incorrectly used when referring to the single-flash illumination produced by electronic flash units.

Trigger Circuit. The voltage required to cause a tube to flash is lowered when the gas is ionized.

The trigger circuit applies a momentary high voltage that ionizes the gas, making operation possible at lower supply voltages and capacitor – storage capabilities. During operation, the trigger circuit is connected to the synchronizing contacts in the camera or lens shutter. It usually includes a test or open flash switch so the unit may be fired without being

Studio flash units, such as those shown in the center of this photograph, are quite large and heavy; however, they have much higher output than smaller units. This Rollei E 5000 Studio Flash, which operates on ac. can power up to four lamp heads at one time. Also shown are a variety of studio reflectors: (left to right) boom light, standard reflector, fresnel spotlight with barn door, light bank, soft-light reflector, sun flood, special reflector with umbrella fitting, and broad flood reflector. Photo courtesy Ehrenreich Photo-Optical Industries, Inc.

A circus acrobat is caught in five phases of a single somersault through the use of multiple electronic flash triggered independently of the open camera shutter. Photo by Harold E. Edgerton.

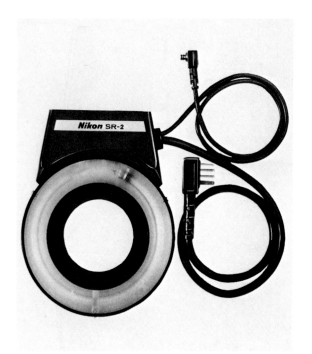

(Left) When mounted on a camera lens, a ringlight provides directionless illumination which may be especially useful when photographing small objects. This Nikon SR-2 unit has a light output selector which allows selection of full or ¼ output, depending on film speed and lens aperture. Photo courtesy Ehrenreich Photo-Optical Industries, Inc. (Right) Automatic or so-called computer flash units like this Vivitar 365 Auto/Thyristor Electronic Flash have light sensors (box at left) that read reflected light from the subject and cut off flash output as soon as enough has been produced for proper exposure. The sensor control is set according to the film speed in use; most can be used with several f-stops, for varying distances. Extension sensor permits more flexible use than sensor built into flash head. Photo courtesy Vivitar Corp.

connected to a shutter. If the high voltage required to flash the tube were put through the shutter contacts, it would burn them, shortening their life. A "slave" or remote control terminal is also common. It may be interconnected with another unit so they will fire simultaneously, or may accept an instant-response electric-eye sensor, which eliminates the need for connecting wires. Some portable electronic flash units have a built-in slave sensor.

Automatic Electronic Flash

In addition to a power supply, flash tube, and trigger circuitry, automatic or so-called computer flash units include control circuits that cut off the output as soon as enough light has been produced for proper exposure. The key to automatic control

is a sensor that receives light reflected back from the subject. It controls either a quenching circuit or a thyristor switching circuit.

In a quench-circuit flash unit, the sensor energizes a "black tube" that discharges the unused voltage in the capacitor without producing any additional light. The capacitor must recharge fully before the next flash can be produced. In a thyristor circuit, the flash tube is cut off without draining unused power from the capacitor. When the flash has been very brief, recycling time may be reduced by one-half or more because so much of the electrical charge remains in the capacitor.

The amount of light the sensor receives depends on the subject distance. Some sensors have high- and low-range capabilities, so they can be used with ei-

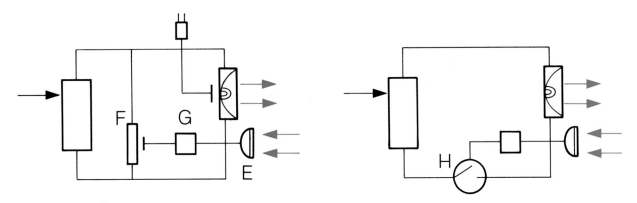

Automatic flash circuits incorporate a sensor (E) that receives light reflected from the subject when the tube fires. Ambient light levels are below the sensor threshold of response. If the sensor triggers the quench tube (F), the power is diverted so that no light is produced as the capacitor discharges the remaining voltage. Delay circuits (G) adjust the timing to the ASA speed of the film so the output will cease only after enough light for proper exposure has been delivered. If the sensor triggers the thyristor switch circuit (H), the power is cut off from the tube, but the capacitor is not drained of the remaining charge, so the recycling time is shorter. When automatic units are used in the manual mode, the sensor is switched off and the unit operates like the basic circuit.

ther of two basic *f*-stops for subjects from about 1 to 7 metres (3 to 22 feet). Setting the sensor control according to the film speed in use connects it to delay circuits so that it will trigger the quenching tube or the thyristor switch only after sufficient light for proper exposure has been produced.

Synchronization and Shutter Speeds

Some flashbulbs have long- peak- duration so that the shutter may open and close after the firing circuit has been completed. Because electronic flash tubes peak so much faster and so much more briefly than bulbs, the shutter must be fully open before the flash is triggered. This timing is provided by *X synchronization* in a shutter. Some shutters have separate M- (delayed-circuit) and X-sync settings or terminals; others have only a single synchronization, which is usually the X type. A check of the camera manual will indicate if this is the case. Using M synchronization with electronic flash will produce partial exposure or none at all, because the unit will fire when the shutter is not properly open.

Professional portable and studio electronic flash units usually connect to the X-sync terminal by lightweight cable. Many miniature flash units can either sync by cable connection, or through their mounting foot if the camera has a "hot" accessory shoe connected to the sync circuits. Many hot-shoe cameras provide only X synchronization; others

have an X/M control that must be set to the proper position.

Synchronization with Leaf Shutter. In a leaf shutter—the type built into lenses—X synchronization is possible at all speeds because the shutter opens fully in every case. The flash duration determines the actual length of the exposure. It is only necessary to choose a shutter speed fast enough so that existing light on the scene will not cause additional exposure or faint "ghost" images of moving subjects in the time after the flash has ended and the shutter is closing.

Synchronization with Focal-Plane Shutter. A focal-plane shutter does not open fully at all speeds. This kind of shutter has a two-piece curtain across the film plane. The first curtain opens to expose the film to light from the lens; the second follows a moment later to cover the film. At fast speeds, the second curtain begins moving after the first curtain has uncovered only a small portion of film. This forms a slit that moves across the film, letting light strike each portion very briefly. Because electronic flash is so short, it would expose just the narrow strip of film directly behind the shutter slit if used at high speeds. For this reason, X synchronization is possible with focal-plane shutters only at speeds slow enough so that the first curtain has completely uncovered the film before the second curtain begins moving. With most shutters, this is a speed of 1/50

Electronic Flash Synchronization

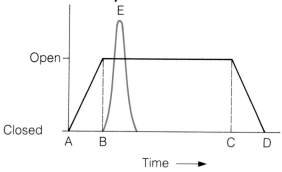

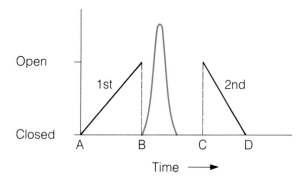

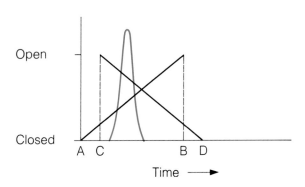

X-synchronization completes the circuit to fire a flash as soon as a shutter is fully open. In a leaf shutter (top), the blades move to open (A-B) or to close (C-D) in a very short time. The length of time the shutter is fully open (B-C) decreases as the speed setting is made higher, but is always longer than the duration of the electronic flash (E). In a focal plane shutter (center), at slow speeds, the first curtain opens fully (A-B); then the second curtain moves to close the film gate (C-D). The electronic flash must fire during interval (B-C) when the film is completely uncovered. At fast speeds of a focal plane shutter (bottom), before the first curtain has completely uncovered the film (B), the second curtain begins to cover it (C). No matter when the electronic flash fires, some portion of the film is covered.

Most portable electronic flash units have handy exposure dials that give the correct f-number to use, based on the film speed and flash-to-subject distance.

or 1/60 sec., or slower. Some small cameras with focal-plane shutters that travel vertically rather than horizontally provide X synchronization at speeds up to about 1/125 sec. The maximum X-sync speed is often marked in color on a shutter-setting dial, or indicated by a dot or lightning-bolt arrow between two speeds. Slower speeds may also be used, but, as with leaf shutters, they can produce ghost images if the ambient light level is high.

Exposure

Because exposure time is determined by the duration of the flash itself, the amount of exposure the film receives depends on the lens aperture and the flash-to-subject distance. When the flash unit is at the camera position, or is kept in a fixed location, the *f*-stop setting is the only exposure control available.

With an automatic flash unit, proper exposure is achieved in the following way:

1. Set the unit for the ASA speed of the film in use.
2. Set the camera to X sync, connect the flash unit, and set the shutter to an X-sync speed (1/60 sec. or slower in most small cameras).
3. Set the camera lens to an *f*-stop suitable for the distance range of the subject or action.

GUIDE NUMBERS FOR ELECTRONIC FLASH

Film Speed (ASA) for Daylight	BCPS Output of Electronic Flash Unit									
	350	500	700	1000	1400	2000	2800	4000	5600	8000
10	13	16	18	22	26	32	35	45	55	65
12	14	18	20	24	28	35	40	50	60	70
16	17	20	24	28	32	40	50	55	65	80
20	18	22	26	32	35	45	55	65	75	90
25	20	24	30	35	40	50	60	70	85	100
32	24	28	32	40	50	55	65	80	95	110
40	26	32	35	45	55	65	75	90	110	130
50	30	35	40	50	60	70	85	100	120	140
64	32	40	45	55	65	80	95	110	130	160
80	35	45	55	65	75	90	110	130	150	180
100	40	50	60	70	85	100	120	140	170	200
125	45	55	65	80	95	110	130	160	190	220
160	55	65	75	90	110	130	150	180	210	250
200	60	70	85	100	120	140	170	200	240	280
250	65	80	95	110	130	160	190	220	260	320
320	75	90	110	130	150	180	210	250	300	360
400	85	100	120	140	170	200	240	280	340	400
500	95	110	130	160	190	220	260	320	370	450
650	110	130	150	180	210	260	300	360	430	510
800	120	140	170	200	240	280	330	400	470	560
1000	130	160	190	220	260	320	380	450	530	630
1250	150	180	210	250	300	350	420	500	600	700
1600	170	200	240	280	340	400	480	560	670	800

Many automatic flash units offer a choice of two or more *f*-stops, with the larger stop providing a greater distance capability. So long as the subject remains within that range, no change in the camera settings will be required. A dial or table with this information is usually included in the unit.

Guide Numbers

Exposure with a non-automatic unit or with an automatic unit in manual mode is determined from a guide number. Most units carry tables of guide numbers for the most common film speeds. These numbers relate light output to film speed; they are used to determine the *f*-stop required for proper exposure. The method is to divide the guide number (GN) by the flash-to-subject distance. Many units have built-in dial calculations that perform this division for you.

Example: GN for ASA 25 film: 44. Flash-to-subject distance: 11 feet. $44 \div 11 = 4$. Set the lens at *f*/4.

Whenever the distance between the flash and the subject changes, a new lens aperture setting must be calculated from the guide number. No adjustment is required if the camera-to-subject distance changes, but the flash distance does not. A convenient way to determine the distance is to focus sharply on the subject from the flash position and read the distance from the lens focusing scale.

The accompanying table gives guide numbers for portable electronic flash units of various outputs used in average-size rooms with white walls and ceilings. (The additional exposure required for larger rooms or darker surroundings is best determined by test or by using a flash meter.) The output is given in beam or effective candlepower-seconds (BCPS, ECPS), which takes into account the built-in reflectors of such units.

To find the *f*-stop for proper exposure, divide the guide number for the appropriate film-speed/flash-output combination by the flash-to-subject distance in feet. For distances in metres, multiply the

make such tests, along with methods to compute or adjust guide numbers for a variety of situations and setups.

Flash Exposure Meters

An electronic flash meter may be used to determine exposure with any kind or size of unit. It is particularly useful when two or more units or flash tubes are used to light a subject, especially when the units have different outputs or are used at different distances.

A flash meter is usually an incident light meter that responds only to a sudden, large increase in the level of illumination. A typical meter is used in the following manner. With the flash units in place, the meter is set to the appropriate film speed and is held in the subject position with its receptor pointed toward the camera position. When the flash is fired, the meter responds to the peak intensity of the light and provides a direct reading of the *f*-stop to be used.

Flash Setups

The methods of using flash illumination for various subjects and to create various effects are essentially similar whether electronic or bulb flash is used. Light placement, the use of reflected or "bounce" flash, combining flash with sunlight, and related subjects are covered in FLASH PHOTOGRAPHY.

Development Times

Electronic flash may be so brief that the regular black-and-white films show a reciprocity effect. In typical flash units where the exposure time is 1/1000 sec. or longer, no additional exposure is needed, but a slight (10 percent) increase in developing time is helpful to produce negatives of normal contrast. At 1/10,000 sec., a half-stop increase in exposure is needed, with a 15 percent increase in developing time. In rare instances, flash exposure times up to 1/100,000 sec. are encountered; a full-stop increase

guide number by 0.304 before dividing. To determine guide numbers for a BCPS output not given in the table, use the formula:

$$\frac{GN}{(feet)} = \sqrt{0.05 \times BCPS \times daylight\ ASA\ speed}$$

Studio-type and other large electronic flash units are often rated in watt-seconds, which expresses their energy storage/discharge capacity. Because they are used with a variety of reflectors and often may be combined in banks of multiple units, ECPS ratings or single guide numbers cannot be given. Instead, it is necessary to determine exposures or guide numbers for various conditions by practical tests. The article GUIDE NUMBERS explains how to in exposure and 20 percent increase in developing time should be given. Many Kodak films do not require any adjustment when exposed by electronic flash. However, Kodak Tri-X pan (roll and 135), Panatomic-X, and Plus-X pan films should be developed for 10 percent more time when electronic flash is used.

With color films, the brief duration of electronic flash may cause some color shift. Because color processing is essentially invariable, compensation is achieved by filtration, sometimes along with a larger aperture setting. It is essential to consult the data sheet or instructions for the color film in use to determine what adjustment, if any, is required for electronic flash.

Filters with Color Films

Pictures taken with electronic flash and daylight-type color film will usually have good color balance without the use of filters over the camera lens. However, flash units do vary; some may produce illumination that results in pictures that are slightly bluish. A yellowish filter such as a No. 81B light balancing filter will improve the color balance in such a case. A No. 81B filter requires an exposure increase of one-third stop.

Causes of Light Loss

Recycling Time. After an electronic flash unit has fired, it takes several seconds for the condensers in the power pack to recharge. Most electronic flash units have a ready-light that comes on after about 10 seconds (depending on the unit) to indicate that the unit is ready to flash. But at this point, the unit may provide only about 65 percent of the total light output because the ready-light does not necessarily indicate when the condensers in the unit are *fully* charged. Recycling time for full light output varies in practice and depends on the type of power pack, type and condition of batteries, and other factors. An ac-powered unit will usually recharge more quickly than a battery-powered unit.

To get more consistent photographic results, wait until the unit has recycled completely before taking the next picture. Allow at least 30 seconds between flashes, because it takes that long for the condensers in the typical unit to recharge fully. Pictures taken more rapidly than this may not get full light output from the flash unit. This can cause un-

derexposed pictures, depending on the exposure latitude of the film.

Weak Batteries. As the batteries in a flash unit lose power with use and age, the recycling time increases. When the battery power drops below the required level, the unit will lose light output even though it may still flash. The remedy, of course, is to make sure the batteries are in good condition by recharging them if they are the rechargeable kind, or by purchasing new ones.

De-forming of Condensers. Another factor that can weaken batteries and cause a loss of light output is the tendency of electrolytic condensers to "deform" after a month or so of inactivity. When this happens, it will take an extra-long time to "re-form" the condensers and bring them back up to a full charge. "Re-forming" the condensers electrically builds up the insulating layer that separates the metal foil from the electrolyte. This reforming puts a considerable drain on the batteries. If possible, use ac rather than battery power. It is a good idea to re-form the condensers by letting them recharge from the power line for an hour or so whenever the unit has been out of use for several days. This method helps insure that the flash unit will produce full light output.

• *See also:* ECPS; FLASH PHOTOGRAPHY; GUIDE NUMBERS; LIGHTING; RECIPROCITY EFFECT.

Electron Imaging

Conventional photography relates to the visible, plus very limited regions of the ultraviolet and infrared regions of the electromagnetic spectrum. Photographic materials of special design are also capable of directly recording other portions of the electromagnetic spectrum as well as high-energy particles, including accelerated electrons. A single electron may make approximately ten silver halide grains developable, whereas approximately ten light photons must be absorbed by a single halide grain to make it developable.

An important characteristic of exposure by electrons is that contrast continues to increase with negative density; therefore, contrast can be built into a negative by increasing electron exposure or by development activity in the darkroom. Sheet, plate, and roll films are all used in electron microscopy. Some photographic materials are specially designed for electron microscopy; while others, although intended for other applications, have desirable characteristics for some electron microscopy needs. The electron micrograph negatives are processed and printed in the normal fashion.

It is customary with electron micrographs to indicate the total magnification of the print as viewed. A magnification of one hundred thousand diameters would be indicated $100,000\times$. Magnification may also be indicated on the micrograph with a measured scale such as 10 μm. This technique is particularly valuable when the magnification is not fixed as occurs when projecting slides or when the viewer is not accustomed to converting from magnification labels to microscopic scale.

The high efficiency of electron exposure combined with advanced technology for focusing and deflecting electrons allows rapid conversion of electrical signals to excellent photographic records using direct electron exposure. Television recordings, computer output, microfilm, computer micrographics, automated micrography, and satellite photography are examples of applications of this technology, which is known as electron beam recording. Direct electron imaging with a transmission electron microscope is discussed in the article ELECTRON MICROGRAPHY.

Electron Beam Recording Apparatus

The apparatus for electron beam recording is in principle similar to that of the cathode-ray tube, where the phosphor screen has been replaced by the photographic material. A high-resolution electron gun is used to generate a beam of electrons that is focused with electromagnetic lenses onto the photographic film. A beam deflection and control system is used to determine the position and intensity of the beam on the film, which is held in a suitable transport device. The entire system operates in a vacuum.

Relationship to Color

The concept of color does not apply to direct electron imaging, but the input electrical signal to the electron imaging system can be related to color as has been done in satellite photography. The satellite imaging system has a multispectral analyzer so that signals from separate spectral bands (green, red, near infrared, and infrared) can be used to produce individual electron beam recordings. The separate spectral bands enhance land and water characteristics that are important for subsequent agricultural, ecologic, geologic, hydrologic, metrologic, and other investigations.

Photoresists

In addition to conventional silver halide emulsions, photoresists have been developed that directly record electron images. This type of electron imaging is important in the fabrication of high-density solid-state devices for the electronics industry. The interaction with electrons changes the solubility of the photoresist when placed in particular solvents. The remaining photoresist protects the underlying substrate from subsequent treatment that the exposed portion receives. By repeating this process a number of times, complex circuitry and devices of remarkably small dimension can be produced.

• *See also:* ELECTRON MICROGRAPHY.

Electron Micrography

Anton van Leeuwenhoek's invention of the light microscope in 1675 generated great excitement that through the centuries has resulted in the fine light microscopes available today. Although new and improved methods of making specimen detail visible have and will continue to be produced, the light microscope has a fundamental limitation determined by the relatively long wavelengths of visible light. The finest optical instruments are not capable of separating two adjacent objects less than 0.1 to 0.2 micrometres apart. The combination of de Broglie's theory that moving electrons could be assigned very short wavelengths and Busch's demonstration that magnetic or electrostatic fields could be used as lenses for an electron beam led in 1932 to Rudenberg's patents and Knoll and Ruska's description of the first electron microscope. By the 1970s, resolving powers over a thousand times that of the light microscope were allowing images of molecules and single atoms to be recorded with the electron microscope.

Transmission Electron Microscope

The transmission electron microscope (TEM) is similar in concept to the light microscope, but the

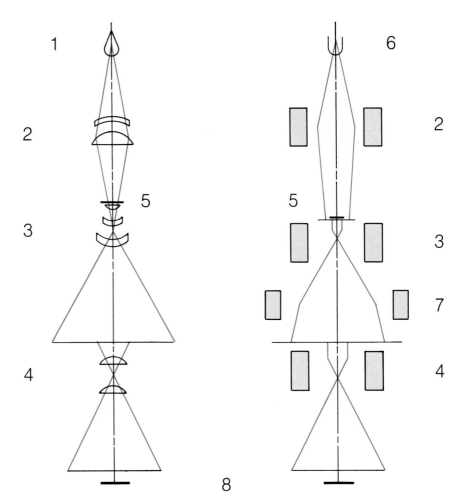

This is a simplified drawing illustrating the similarity in basic configuration between the light microscope and the transmission electric microscope: (1) Light source, (2) Condenser lens, (3) Objective lens, (4) Projector lens or eyepiece, (5) Specimen, (6) Electron source, (7) Intermediate lens, (8) Final image.

mechanical components of each instrument have little resemblance. Both have an illumination source, with one using light from an incandescent lamp, and the other using electrons generated from cathodes made of materials such as tungsten or lanthanum hexaboride. The electrons are accelerated to thousands and even millions of volts, depending on the specimen and the information desired. The light microscope uses glass lenses of fixed focal length that require an actual change in lens when a different focal length is desired. The electromagnetic lenses in electron microscopes are fixed, but the focal lengths may be varied by adjusting the current passing through the lens windings. In this way, the magnification can be varied from a few hundred up to hundreds of thousands of times by simply manipulating a control knob. The electron path is influenced by

interaction with only the field of an electromagnetic lens and not by transmission through a material, as is the case with the transmission of light through a glass lens. The electron microscope objective lens approximates a stopped-down lens in conventional photography. The result is that the electron microscope has a great depth of field, which allows specimen structures of varying heights to be in focus even at high magnifications. The image in the electron microscope is made visible for focusing and observation when the electrons strike a phosphor screen. A record of the image can be made by direct electron exposure of photographic film. The depth of focus in a transmission electron microscope can be a metre or more; therefore, the camera plane need only be in the general proximity of the focusing screen. The entire electron beam from source to specimen to

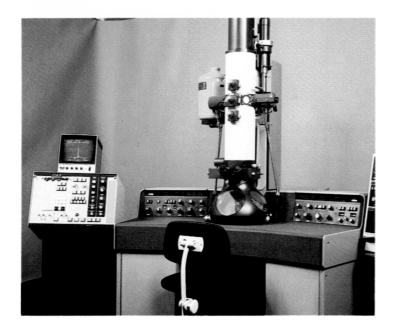

The Philips EM 400 TEM/STEM, which is representative of the latest generation of electron microscopes, can resolve specimen features separated by only a few ten-thousandths of a micrometre. An EDAX® x-ray analyzer system is shown (at left) coupled to the EM 400, thereby adding the capability for determining the elemental composition of samples as small as a few thousandths of a micrometre.

camera is kept at a vacuum of 10^{-6} torr or better. The specimens must generally be considerably thinner than one micrometre (.000039 inches) if high-quality images are to be produced. Contrast in the specimen is proportional to its physical density and thickness.

Uses of the TEM. The TEM is used in medicine, biology, geology, metallurgy, materials sciences, and other disciplines where there is a need for the fine detail resolvable with this technique. The preparation of specimens for viewing in the microscope can require much time and skill. An example is tissue, which as found in the animal or human is neither thin enough for viewing nor able to withstand the vacuum in the microscope. The tissue must first be treated to remove the water, stained with heavy atoms for contrast, fixed and embedded in order to maintain the original structural orientation, and finally thin-sectioned. Thin-sectioning or ultramicrotomy is a technique that uses diamond, or specially broken glass knives, to produce thin slivers of the specimen only a few hundredths of a micrometre thick.

Photographic records of what is viewed in the microscope are called electron micrographs. Electrons can be used for direct imaging on photographic emulsions. The high-energy electrons used in TEM make the photographic emulsion respond differently than with lower-energy light photons.

Scanning Electron Microscopy

Another type of electron microscopy called scanning electron microscopy (SEM) records electron images indirectly. An electron beam as small as 0.0015 micrometres is systematically scanned across the specimen. As the beam interacts with the specimen, some electrons are reflected, additional electrons are generated, characteristic x-rays are emitted, and other phenomena occur that with suitable detectors can produce an electrical signal. This signal is used to control the intensity of a cathode-ray tube (CRT), which is scanned synchronously with the electron beam. In this fashion, a point-by-point image of the specimen is developed on the CRT screen.

The reflected electrons or the newly generated electrons called secondary electrons are used to produce images of the specimen surface that have great detail and depth of field. Because the signal is generated by information from the specimen surface, as is also true with most visual observations, scanning electron images are generally straightforward in their interpretation. The reflected electrons produce images that appear as though they were illuminated with specular light, whereas the secondary electrons produce images that appear to be diffusely lighted.

The SEM is used in many of the same disciplines as the TEM where its surface information complements that obtained with transmitted electrons. The ease of sample preparation combined with a magnification range from tens to tens of thousands of diameters makes the SEM a valuable development and quality-control instrument in many industries. Another approach called scanning transmission electron microscopy (STEM) uses the scanning electron beam but generates the image from an electrical signal produced from transmitted electrons.

The scanning electron micrograph is produced by photographing the CRT display tube using conventional techniques. Instant photography is widely used for this application. Conventional photographic materials are also used.

• *See also:* BIOMEDICAL PHOTOGRAPHY; CLINICAL PHOTOGRAPHY; DENTAL PHOTOGRAPHY; MEDICAL PHOTOGRAPHY; PHOTOMICROGRAPHY; RADIOGRAPHY; SCIENTIFIC PHOTOGRAPHY; STEREO PHOTOGRAPHY; THERMAL PHOTOGRAPHY; ULTRAVIOLET AND FLUORESCENCE PHOTOGRAPHY.

Further Reading: Glauert, A.M., ed. *Practical Methods in Electron Microscopy,* vols. 1–4. Amsterdam, Holland, and London, England: North Holland Publishing Co., New York, NY: Elsevier Publishing Co., 1972–77; Hall, C.E. *Introduction to Electron Microscopy, Second Edition.* New York, NY: McGraw-Hill Book Co., 1966; Hayat, M.A. *The Principles and Techniques of Electron Microscopy, Biological Applications, Volume 1.* New York, NY: Van Nostrand Reinhold Co., 1970. Hirsch, P.B. and A. Howie, R.B. Nicholson, D.W. Pashley, and M.J. Whelan. *Electron Microscopy of Thin Crystals.* London, England: Butterworth and Company, 1965; Rogers, A.W. *Techniques of Autoradiography.* Amsterdam, Holland, and New York, NY: Elsevier Publishing Co., 1973; Thorton, P.R. *Scanning Electron Microscopy.* London, England: Chapman and Hall, Ltd., 1968.

Electrophotography

Electrophotography combines the interaction of light, matter, and externally applied electric forces to form images. Among the several subdivisions of electrophotography (for example, electrostatic electrophotography, electrolytic electrophotography, photoelectrophoresis), electrostatic electrophotography is by far the best known.

In the version of electrostatic electrophotography known as xerography (*xeros* = dry), a thin layer of a photoconductive insulating material (amorphous selenium, zinc oxide in a binder, or a solid solution of an organic compound) is charged with ions or electrons in the dark, exposed to a pattern of

(Left) Transmission electron micrograph of silver halide grains at 12,000X magnification.
(Right) Scanning electron micrograph of the head of an ant at 50X magnification.

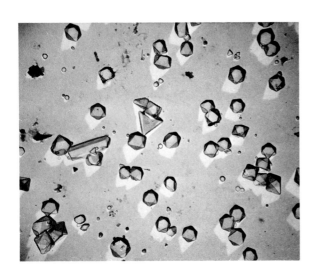

light, and developed with small charged particles of matter called toner. The toner particles may be fixed to the photoconductive insulator (for example, by heat) or may be transferred to another material (paper) so that the photoconductive insulator can be reused. The xerographic process is used extensively in offices where there is a need to make large numbers of copies quickly and inexpensively.

Photoelectrophoretic processes are still in the experimental stage. Like xerography, they involve relatively high voltages and low current flows. Their distinguishing feature is that the photoconductor is particulate and is an integral part of the toner; a most interesting consequence of this is that multicolored images can be formed from a single exposure to light if the photoconductive toner is a mixture of differently colored particles.

Electrolytic electrophotography (employed for many years in microfilm reader-printers) involves relatively low voltages and high current flows. A photoconductive layer, of somewhat lower electrical resistance than that employed in the electrostatic process, is made conductive by exposure to light; a visible image is formed by electroplating metal ions onto the layer in the areas of exposure.

Most electrophotographic processes have a sensitivity that is substantially closer to that of silver halide photography than to that of processes like diazo or blueprint, because the absorption of each photon in the photoconductor can lead to a very large number of light-absorbing atoms or molecules in the image. The amplification factor associated with this phenomenon can be as high as a million or so in electrophotography, whereas it is limited to unity in most other non-silver processes.
• *See also:* XEROGRAPHY.

Elon Developing Agent, Kodak

Elon is a trademark of Eastman Kodak Company for the developing agent monomethyl p-aminophenol sulfate. It is commonly known as Metol, and has been offered by other manufacturers under a variety of trademarks, including Photol, Pictol, and Rhodol.
• *See also:* DEVELOPERS AND DEVELOPING; METOL.

Emulsion

A photographic emulsion consists of crystals of light-sensitive compounds evenly distributed throughout a medium that can be coated in a uniform layer on a suitable base material. The light-sensitive crystals in all conventional emulsions are silver halides—compounds of silver with bromine, chlorine, and/or iodine. Silver halide emulsions are inherently sensitive to ultraviolet radiation and some wavelengths of blue light. They can be made sensitive to other colors of light and to near-infrared radiation by the addition of spectral sensitizing dyes. Gelatin is universally used as the medium that holds the crystals in suspension.

Conventional emulsions are all manufactured in essentially the same way, but controlled variations in procedures and in the choice and proportions of ingredients are made to produce emulsions with different characteristics. The inherent characteristics of an emulsion are speed (sensitivity to light), granularity ("graininess"), spectral (wavelength or color) sensitivity, and contrast.

Almost all conventional photographic films and print materials, whether color or black-and-white, use the same basic kind of "developing-out" silver halide emulsion. In such an emulsion, exposure produces an invisible latent image that the chemical process of development converts to a visible image composed of dark metallic silver. If the image is a negative, subsequent processing steps may change it to a positive silver image, or a positive or negative color dye image. A few materials have "printing-out" emulsions that produce visible, dark silver images directly from the action of exposure, without the need for development.

Gelatin emulsions are commonly coated onto cellulose acetate, plastic, glass, or paper materials. The coating may be a single thin or thick layer, or multiple layers of different speeds and/or spectral sensitivities. Multi-layer emulsions are essential for selective-contrast black-and-white materials, and for all color materials.

Evolution of Emulsions

The earliest photographic processes did not use emulsion-coated materials. The daguerreotype

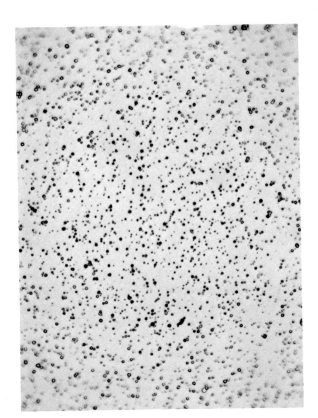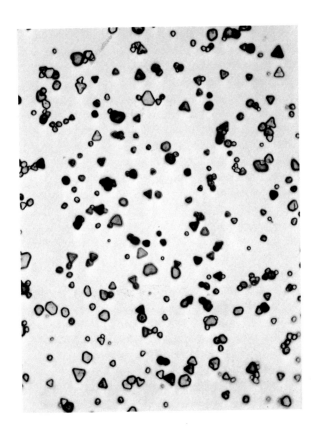

(Left) When silver halides first form during emulsion manufacture, they are fine and evenly distributed. An emulsion containing only such grains has high contrast and resolution, low speed, and little or no appreciable graininess. Magnification: 2500X. (Right) As an emulsion ripens, fine grains may be dissolved and redeposited on others, building up grain size, but reducing the evenness of distribution. An emulsion with predominantly large silver halide crystals has low contrast and resolution, high speed, and significant graininess. Magnification: 2500X.

formed an image directly on the silver surface of a metal plate. The talbotype used paper in which the surface fibers were impregnated with light-sensitive compounds.

The first emulsion-like coating in photography used albumen (egg white) as a binding medium. A process for negatives on glass was introduced by Abel Niépce de Saint-Victor in 1848. The albumen coating contained potassium iodide; it was sensitized by a solution of silver nitrate just before use. Albumen-on-glass negatives were vastly superior to paper (talbotype) negatives in terms of resolution, contrast, and printing transparency. However, exposures from 5 to 15 minutes were required, which made portraits impossible, and the albumen coating was fragile. It tended to crack, reticulate, and flake

off after a short while. Printing paper using albumen to achieve a glossy surface was introduced by Louis Desiré Blanquart-Evrard in 1850. A coating of albumen and ammonium chloride was sensitized just before use by floating the paper on a silver nitrate solution. This kind of paper remained the standard printing material until almost the end of the nineteenth century.

Collodion, a viscous liquid that dries to a tough, flexible, transparent film, replaced albumen for the production of glass-plate negatives in 1851, when the "wet-plate" process was published by Frederick Scott Archer. A coating of collodion and potassium iodide was flowed onto a glass plate and then sensitized in silver nitrate. The plate had to be sensitized, exposed, and processed while the collodion was still tacky, or "wet"—a period of about 20 minutes. Otherwise, the collodion would dry to a waterproof coating that prevented developer and fixing solutions from contacting the exposed crystals. A similar coating was used to produce positives on glass (ambrotypes) and on metal (ferrotypes, tintypes). Collodion was superior to albumen in all respects and became the universal medium for glass-plate negatives for the next 25 or 30 years. A dry collodio-bromide (collodion plus silver bromide) emulsion was invented in 1864 by Sayce and Bolton. It was used for the manufacture of dry plates for negatives and for printing paper. However, neither of these products was widely used largely because they were far less light-sensitive than the wet plate and albumen paper.

The gelatin-silver halide emulsion was invented in 1871 by Richard Leach Maddox. As described in the following section, gelatin has almost ideal qualities for use as the binding medium of an emulsion. It made possible dry plates of greater speed, which replaced the collodion processes almost immediately because of the vastly greater convenience. Gelatin emulsion printing paper was commercially introduced in 1885, and nitrate-base film in 1889. Almost all films today are coated either on acetate or polyester bases. Today's emulsions have speed, contrast, fine grain, and spectral sensitivity characteristics unimaginable in Maddox's time, but they are basically the same as his combination of gelatin and silver halides.

Gelatin

Gelatin is a protein substance prepared from the skins, bones, hides, cartilage, and related tissue of mammals, especially cows and pigs. The raw material is treated for a period of up to several months with lime to clean it and promote tissue breakdown. It is then washed in mild acid, and slowly cooked until it is reduced to a jellylike mass. It can be used in this state, or can be dried, powdered, and reconstituted with water for use when required.

Gelatin is a colloid, a substance that in its liquid state does not pass through a permeable membrane. When set on a suitable base, a layer of gelatin is colorless, flexible, and will not react with photographic solutions or the silver compounds it contains. When immersed in cool-water solutions, it will not dissolve, but can absorb up to ten times its own weight in water. In this way, chemicals in processing solutions can reach the halide crystals and act upon them. During absorption, the gelatin softens and swells but does not allow halide crystals to be washed out of place. Upon drying, it shrinks back to its original size and shape, returning all crystals or their corresponding silver or dye deposits to their original positions so that the image is undistorted. A gelatin emulsion can be wetted and dried repeatedly without affecting the image. Its surface can be made smooth or textured.

Although soft and susceptible to damage when wet, a dry gelatin emulsion can be freely handled with reasonable care. Hardening agents such as potassium alum are often included in processing solutions to provide extra protection when the emulsion has dried. Special treatment during manufacture can produce emulsions that will withstand temperatures of 38 C (100 F) or more without dissolving, as required in many color and high-speed processes.

Gelatin treated with potassium dichromate (bichromate) or a related compound will harden to a high degree of insolubility upon exposure to light. Such coatings form the basis of the gum bichromate and dye transfer processes, and are used in photomechanical reproduction.

Silver Halides

A silver halide is a salt composed of silver and a halogen: chlorine, iodine, or bromine. The halide cannot be formed by the direct combination of silver and a halogen. Instead, a solution of silver nitrate ($AgNO_3$)—produced by dissolving pure silver in nitric acid—is mixed with a solution of a sodium, ammonium, or potassium halide such as potassium bromide (KBr) or sodium chloride (NaCl). A typical reaction is:

$$AgNO_3 + KBr \rightarrow \underline{AgBr} + KNO_3$$

That is: silver nitrate plus potassium bromide yields a precipitate of silver bromide, and potassium nitrate in solution.

The precipitated halide is in the form of very fine crystals—as many as 3,000,000,000 per square centimetre in a fine-grain emulsion. Certain inherent

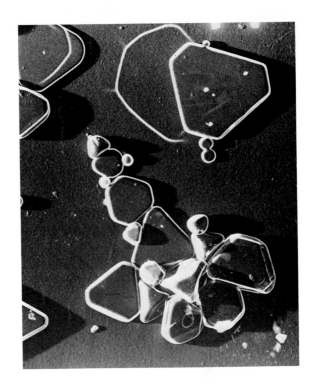

As silver halide crystals grow in size, they take on a characteristic six-sided shape. This electron micrograph shows carbon replicas of emulsion grains magnified 20,000 times. This replica technique retains the shape of the crystal after the silver has been removed by a hypo fixing bath so that surface detail can be studied.

emulsion characteristics are directly related to crystal size or the related size of the developed silver grains. A fine-grain emulsion has slow speed and produces images of high contrast and high resolution. A high-speed emulsion has a higher percentage of large crystals, which produce images of lower contrast and reduced resolution.

Spectral sensitivity is not related to crystal size. All photographic silver halide emulsions are sensitive to ultraviolet and blue wavelengths. During manufacture, sensitizers may be added to extend response into the green and red wavelengths, and into the infrared, as required. At the same time, crystal size can be controlled and modified to produce a combination of desired characteristics.

Silver bromide is the principal compound in film emulsions and high-speed enlarging paper; high-speed film emulsions also have a small percentage of silver iodide. Silver chloride is used in slow-speed (contact) developing-out papers and in printing-out paper emulsions. A combination of silver chloride and silver bromide is used in nearly all enlarging paper emulsions.

Emulsion Manufacture

The gelatin used for emulsions must have greater purity than that used for foods; even minute traces of unwanted substances can affect photographic characteristics. Usually many different batches of gelatin are continuously blended to provide large quantities of uniform material.

To produce an emulsion, a one to ten percent solution of gelatin in water is prepared in a vat. A high percentage of gelatin is used to produce a slow, fine-grain emulsion; a lower percentage is used for higher-speed emulsions. The basic halide—potassium bromide in the case of film emulsions—is dissolved into the gelatin solution; then the silver nitrate solution is stirred in. The speed with which the nitrate is added and the proportions of the ingredients directly affect the kind of emulsion produced.

An excess proportion of halide is required to make a developing-out emulsion; an excess of silver nitrate will produce a printing-out emulsion.

As the silver halide is formed, it precipitates in billions of tiny crystals with very little sensitivity. The gelatin in the solution keeps the crystals suspended and dispersed without clumping. When mixing is complete, the solution is brought to a specific temperature—often about 32 C (90 F)—and held for up to several hours for "ripening." During this time, the tiniest crystals dissolve and are redeposited onto others to form larger crystals with a variety of sizes. This process builds the grain characteristics of the emulsion, and increases its speed as the crystal sizes increase.

More gelatin is added toward the end of the ripening period to bring the mixture to the desired consistency, and traces of sulfur, gold, or other elements are added. These additives are responsible for the formation of "sensitivity specks" in the growing crystals. The sensitivity specks act as collection points around which the latent image builds during exposure, and they become attack points for developer action.

Emulsion

The ripened mixture is allowed to set to a jelly. Then it is shredded into noodles for washing to remove the alkaline nitrate salt (potassium nitrate in a film emulsion) and other free chemicals formed during earlier reactions.

The final stage is "digestion." The noodles are melted and the mass again held at a fixed temperature for after-ripening. There is little additional crystal growth, but significant increases in speed and changes in contrast characteristics are produced. At this time, dyes that extend spectral sensitivity are added, along with other compounds such as stabilizers to improve keeping qualities, hardeners, and plasticizers, which increase flexibility after drying.

When fully digested, the emulsion is coated onto the base material. This is usually accomplished by a flow nozzle that deposits a bead of emulsion across the width of a continuously moving roll of paper or film base. The coated material immediately passes over chilled rollers or into a cold chamber to quickly set the emulsion in a uniform layer. When the emulsion is completely dry, the film or paper is cut into standard sizes and packaged.

The manufacture of modern emulsions is extremely complex and requires precise control of many factors. However, it is possible to produce a simple emulsion with only a few chemicals and ordinary kitchen and darkroom equipment; the method is explained in the article EMULSION MAKING. Discussion of various non-silver halide materials or specialized processes are covered in separate articles; consult the index for the name of the process or procedure.

• *See also:* BLACK-AND-WHITE FILMS; BROMIDE; CHEMISTRY OF PHOTOGRAPHY; COLOR FILMS; DEVELOPERS AND DEVELOPING; DEVELOPMENT; DIFFUSION TRANSFER PROCESS; EMULSION MAKING; EXPOSURE; FABRIC SENSITIZER; FILMS AND PLATES; GELATIN; GRAININESS AND GRANULARITY; LATENT IMAGE; PAPERS, PHOTOGRAPHIC; WEDGE SPECTROGRAM.

Further Reading: Carroll, B.H. et al. *Photographic Emulsion.* (Focal Library Books) Belmont, CA: Pitman Publishing Corp., 1967; Duffin, G.F. *Emulsion Chemistry.* (Focal Library Books) Belmont, CA: Pitman Publishing Corp., 1966; James, R.W. *Photographic Emulsions: Recent Developments.* (Chemical Technology Review Series: No. 21) Park Ridge, NJ: Noyes Data Corp., 1974.

Emulsion Making

The light-sensitive surface of photographic films and papers is called the emulsion. Basically it consists of light-sensitive silver halide crystals suspended in gelatin. To make consistent emulsions of the right characteristics for each photographic purpose is usually beyond the ability of the individual experimenter. However, being able to make and coat an actual emulsion that does record images can be useful, especially for demonstration or educational purposes. This article details how an emulsion can be made.

Materials

Ingredients. The two principal ingredients of a photographic emulsion are gelatin and silver halide. The silver halide is made from three chemicals. To make the emulsion, you will need the following ingredients: gelatin, silver nitrate, potassium bromide, and potassium iodide.

For the gelatin, use clear food gelatin, the nonflavored kind, sold in grocery stores. Food gelatin is not as photographically pure as the gelatin used by photographic manufacturers, so a few blemishes may occur in the pictures. The chemicals are available at large photographic stores, at some drugstores, and from chemical supply houses, or they can be ordered by photo dealers.

Emulsion Support. In order to coat the emulsion on a support, you will need thin glass plates of the proper size to fit the camera you use. The glass should be clear and of good quality; it should have no obvious flaws, and it should not produce distortions when you look through it.

The thickness of the glass should be $\frac{1}{16}$ inch or slightly less so that it can be used in the film holders described in the section in this article on taking pictures. You can obtain glass from hardware stores or glass supply firms. Have it cut to size for your camera. If the camera accepts 4″ × 5″ sheet film or plates, you can use Kodak projector slide cover glass, 3¼″ × 4″ (precleaned). This is the right size for use in 4″ × 5″ film holders, since the glass has to be smaller than the film the holders are designed to accept, as explained later. This glass is .050 ($\frac{1}{20}$) inch thick and is available through photo dealers.

The glass must be clean and free of fingerprints so that the emulsion will adhere properly. If the glass needs cleaning, wash it in warm water with dishwashing detergent, and rinse it thoroughly with clean water so that the detergent will not contaminate the emulsion.

Film base is not recommended as the support for a homemade emulsion. It is difficult to coat the emulsion evenly on film base by hand; special equipment is required to obtain a uniform coating. Glass plates are much easier to coat evenly by hand.

Equipment

The equipment required to make an emulsion and coat it on plates is as follows:

1. Three 1-litre (or 1-quart) stainless steel, glass, or plastic containers for mixing solutions,
2. A 2-litre (or 2-quart) stainless steel or glass container for mixing emulsion,
3. A stainless steel spoon or an electric food mixer with stainless steel beaters,
4. A 7.5- or 11-litre (or 2- or 3-gallon) stainless steel or plastic pail for washing the emulsion,
5. A large pan, such as a dishpan,
6. Scales for measuring chemicals, calibrated in grams or in ounces and grains,
7. Darkroom graduates, 1-litre (32-ounce) size and 25-millilitre size,
8. Two pieces of cheesecloth about .7 metres (2 feet) square, available at department stores and other stores that sell fabrics,
9. Thin glass plates on which you will coat the emulsion,
10. A darkroom thermometer with a range of 2 to 55 C (35 to 130 F), such as a tank and tray thermometer,
11. A safelight equipped with a Kodak safelight filter, No. 1A (light red), and a 15-watt bulb,
12. A clock or timer,
13. Rubber gloves,
14. A darkroom apron.
15. A viscose sponge,
16. Black masking tape,
17. Black paper large enough to cover the top of the emulsion container,
18. A cardboard box that has a lid and is large enough to accept the container of emulsion,
19. Metal or glass plates for chilling purposes. Plates about ¼ inch thick are best, but thinner ones can be used. They should be larger than the glass plates used as the emulsion support.

This photograph was taken on an emulsion made according to the instructions in this article. Blemishes such as appear here may result from using food gelatin, which is not as pure as the gelatin used by film manufacturers. While homemade emulsions are not recommended for general photographic purposes, knowledge of their preparation is useful for demonstration or educational needs and experimental images.

Emulsion Making

Emulsion Formula

The following solutions are for making photographic emulsions:

Solution A

Water at room temperature	530.0 ml
Gelatin	40.0 g

Solution B

Water at about 140 C (105 F)	360.0 ml
Gelatin	10.0 g
Potassium bromide	32.0 g
Potassium iodide	0.8 g

Solution C

Water at room temperature	400.0 ml
Silver nitrate (see warning)	40.0 g

WARNING: Silver nitrate is a poisonous and caustic chemical that causes burns. Do not get it on the skin or in the eyes. In case of contact with the eyes, immediately flush with water for at least 15 minutes; get medical attention.

ANTIDOTE: If swallowed, give a tablespoonful of salt in a glass of warm water and repeat until vomit fluid is clear. Have the person lie down and keep warm. Give milk or egg whites beaten with water. Call a physician at once.

Silver nitrate will produce brown stains on hands or clothing. To prevent stains on hands, wear rubber gloves. A plastic darkroom apron will help keep stains off clothing.

Mixing the Emulsion

1. **Solution A.** Soak 40 grams of gelatin in water at room temperature. Use a glass, plastic, or stainless steel litre (or quart) container and enough water to cover the gelatin. Soak the gelatin until it is thoroughly softened. Let it soak while carrying out the following steps.

2. **Solution B.** Use another litre (or quart) container to dissolve 10 grams of gelatin in 360 millilitres of warm water at about 40 C (105 F). Stir with the stainless steel spoon or an electric mixer at medium speed.

3. While stirring Solution B, add the potassium bromide and potassium iodide and continue stirring until they are dissolved. Then put this solution in the 2-litre (or 2-quart) stainless steel or glass container and raise the temperature of the solution to 55 C (130 F). Maintain the solution at that temperature, preferably by using a water bath. To do this, run hot water at 55 C into the dishpan and set the emulsion container in the hot-water bath. Make sure the water bath does not overflow into the emulsion container.

4. **Solution C.** In a 1-litre (or 1-quart) stainless steel, glass, or plastic container, dissolve the silver nitrate in 400 millilitres of water at room temperature.

In the next step, the emulsion becomes light-sensitive. So the remainder of the procedure must be carried out under a safelight equipped with a Kodak safelight filter No. 1A (light red) and a 15-watt bulb at a distance no closer than 1.4 metres (4 feet).

5. Add Solution C to Solution B at the rate of 20 millilitres every 30 seconds for 10 minutes while stirring constantly. Maintain the temperature of the emulsion at 55 C (130 F) for an additional 10 minutes to allow ripening. Then let the temperature drop slowly to about 40 C (105 F) by taking the emulsion container out of the water bath.

6. Take Solution A and pour off any excess water from the gelatin. Add the swelled gelatin to the emulsion. Mix thoroughly by stirring rapidly while cooling the emulsion. Use a water bath at 2 to 7 C (35 to 45 F) for cooling. Ice water is good for this purpose.

Continue to stir the emulsion until it becomes thick and begins to set up. Then use black paper to cover the container and seal it around the edges with tape so that light and air cannot enter. If the container is glass, put it in a cardboard box that has a lid, and seal the box with black tape so that it is lighttight.

Then put the emulsion in a refrigerator for 2 to 4 hours until it has set up firmly. Or leave it in the refrigerator overnight and continue the experiment the next day. Be sure to use a lighttight and watertight container, and store it at 2 to 7 C.

To complete the next two steps, you will need about 15 to 19 litres (4 or 5 gallons) of cold water that has been cooled to a temperature of 2 to 7 C. You can put ice cubes in the water to cool it.

7. Under the safelight illumination, scrape the set emulsion onto the cheesecloth and form it into a ball by gathering the cheesecloth around the emulsion. Hold the emulsion ball under *cold* water at 2 to 7 C (35 to 45 F) in the 7.5-litre (2-gallon) pail, and twist the ball to force the emulsion through the cloth. This produces emulsion "noodles" or shreds; the cold water helps to keep the shreds separated. Pour off the water, using a clean piece of cheesecloth to strain the mixture so as not to lose the shreds.

Pour approximately 3 litres (3 quarts) of cold water, at 2 to 7 C (35 to 45 F), onto the shreds and leave it for 2½ minutes. Pour off 2 litres (2 quarts) and add 2 litres more water. Repeat this process five times to wash out excess potassium bromide, potassium iodide, and potassium nitrate that have formed.

8. Drain the excess water from the emulsion shreds; then heat the emulsion to 55 C (130 F) and hold it at that temperature for 15 minutes for further ripening. You can put the emulsion container in a hot-water bath for heating. Then slowly cool the emulsion to 40 C (105 F). Keep the emulsion at this temperature for coating.

Coating the Emulsion

Prepare a supply of metal or glass plates about ¼ inch thick by chilling them in a refrigerator. These chilled plates will cool the thin glass plates after they have been coated with emulsion. The chilled plates help the liquid emulsion adhere to the emulsion support.

Under safelight illumination, pour about 4 millilitres of the emulsion onto a clean and level 3¼" × 4" thin glass plate that you are using for the emulsion support. Spread the emulsion with the tip of your finger to form a uniform coat. This is not too difficult, because the emulsion has a tendency to form an even coating. Wear rubber gloves to keep the emulsion off your hands. Be careful not to get the emulsion on the back of the plate being coated. If this happens, wipe the back of the plate with a damp viscose sponge, holding the plate level. Otherwise the plate may stick to the surface you place it on.

Lay a chilled metal or glass plate on a *level* surface and place the coated plate, emulsion side up, on the chilled plate until the emulsion sets and is

dry. This will take several hours, depending on the air temperature and the humidity. Keep the area totally dark while the plates are drying.

Taking Pictures

You will need a camera such as a view camera or a press camera that accepts sheet-film holders or plate holders. New plate holders are not available from most photo dealers, but you may be able to find some used ones.

If you use sheet-film holders, the glass plates should be somewhat smaller than the size of film the holders are designed for. The glass should lie flat in the film holder between the two film-retaining channels along the sides. The glass will be too thick to fit under the retaining channels the way film does. Put the plate in the holder with the emulsion side up, and use black tape on the edges of the plate to hold it in place. The glass must be thin enough to provide sufficient clearance under the dark slide so that the film holder can be closed properly. Glass ¹⁄₁₆ inch or less in thickness should provide enough clearance.

When you take pictures on glass plates loaded in sheet-film holders, the surface of the emulsion will not be in the correct plane for sharp focus. To correct for this, first focus the camera normally, then rack the lens outward *slightly*—the same distance as the thickness of the glass plate you are using. This brings the image into sharp focus on the plate. This focus correction is not necessary with plate holders.

Exposure. The emulsion you have made is not as light-sensitive as that on most manufactured films; it will require much more exposure than normal. Since that will call for slow shutter speeds or even time exposures, put the camera on a firm support such as a tripod to hold it steady.

Outdoors in bright sunlight, the approximate exposure for a front-lighted, average subject is 1 second at $f/5.6$. The sensitivity of the emulsion can vary due to variations in the emulsion-making procedure and variations in the gelatin used. For more assurance of a properly exposed picture, bracket the exposure. Take one picture using one stop more than the suggested exposure and take another one using two stops more exposure than suggested. Then take a picture at one stop less than the suggested exposure and another at two stops less.

Another type of camera you can use for taking pictures on these plates is a pinhole camera. Such a camera is an interesting experiment in itself because it can be made out of ordinary, readily available materials.

When you take pictures with a pinhole camera using the plates you have made, the exposure times will be very long. Using a camera constructed according to the directions in the article, PINHOLE CAMERA, an exposure of approximately 8 minutes should produce proper exposure for a frontlighted, average subject in bright sunlight.

Developing. To develop the plates, use any of the active, fast-working film developers, such as Kodak HC-110 developer, dilution A; Kodak Dektol developer, diluted 1:1; or Kodak developer DK-50. Develop the plates in a tray, emulsion side up, at 20 C (68 F) for 4 minutes in HC-110 developer, dilution A; for 2 minutes in Dektol developer, diluted 1:1; or for 5 minutes in Developer DK-50. Rock the tray continuously during development to provide agitation. Since the emulsion is very fragile, handle the plates carefully, keeping them separated to avoid scratching the emulsion surfaces.

After development, rinse the plates in a tray of water or in Kodak indicator stop bath or Kodak stop bath SB-5 at 18 to 24 C (65 to 75 F) for about 30 seconds with agitation. Next fix the plates for 5 to 10 minutes at 18 to 24 C in Kodak fixer or fixing bath F-5. Agitate the plates frequently during fixing.

Wash the plates for 20 to 30 minutes in running water at 18 to 24 C. After washing, treat in Kodak Photo-Flo solution for 30 seconds to minimize drying marks. Dry in a dust-free place.

After the plates are dry, you can make contact prints or enlargements from them.

• *See also:* EMULSION; FABRIC SENSITIZER; PINHOLE CAMERA.

Enlargers and Enlarging

Enlarging is projection printing—an image is optically projected onto print material for exposure. As the term implies, enlarging is primarily used to obtain images larger than those recorded on the film. It is essential in obtaining prints of adequate size from small-format films, and it makes possible the selection of only a portion of the entire picture on the film. Enlarging equipment and techniques may also be used to obtain reduced-size images, if desired.

The equipment required for projection printing includes an enlarger equipped with a good quality lens, a timer that will switch the printing light off at the end of a selected interval, an easel to hold the print material, and a magnifier for critical focusing. In addition, filters are required for printing on selective-contrast black-and-white papers and on color papers. A constant-voltage transformer or voltage regulator is also valuable to keep the light output constant and to avoid shifts in the color balance of the exposing light in color printing. Of course, such darkroom equipment as trays, tube processors, and chemicals are required for processing the exposed enlargements.

This article covers the fundamental aspects of the equipment and procedures used for enlarging. Additional detailed information will be found in the entries listed at the end of this article.

Enlargers

An enlarger consists of a baseboard, a vertical column, and a head assembly. (There are some horizontal enlargers; they are used primarily for special-purpose printing in commercial photolabs.) The easel that holds the printing material rests on the baseboard; the head assembly moves up and down the column to vary the size of the projected image. The head assembly includes a lamphouse that provides the exposing illumination, a negative stage that receives a holder with the negative (or transparency) to be printed, and a lens mounted on a bellows for focusing the image. While most modern color enlargers incorporate a filtration system in the lamphouse, they may also be used for black-and-white printing.

The main differences between enlargers are their size, type of illumination used, and the method of diffusing the light to get even illumination on the easel. Moreover, while most enlargers are focused manually, some focus automatically as the head is raised or lowered. Most modern enlargers are of the vertical type, and are designed to expose one sheet of paper at a time. There are also various types of continuous-roll machines employed in mechanized printing and processing systems.

Enlarger Sizes. Enlargers are made in a range of sizes that correspond to the principal negative

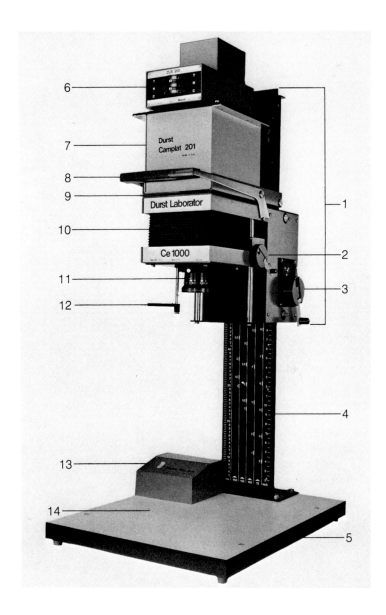

A typical color-b/w vertical enlarger. (1) Head assembly, (2) Focus control, (3) Vertical position control, (4) Vertical column, (5) Baseboard, (6) Filtration system, (7) Lamphouse, (8) Lamphouse raise–lower control, (9) Negative stage, (10) Bellows, (11) Lens, (12) Viewing, focusing swing-away filter, (13) Timer, (14) Easel placed here. Photo courtesy Ehrenreich Photo-Optical Industries, Inc.

formats, namely, 35 mm to 8″ × 10″. However, special enlargers are available for subminiature negatives and microfilms. Sizes larger than 8″ × 10″ are also available.

If your enlarging work consists mainly of printing from small negatives, do not buy a large-format enlarger on the assumption that you may occasionally need the extra size. Although you can enlarge small negatives, such as 35 mm, on an 8″ × 10″ enlarger, the greater time and effort needed would make the work uneconomical.

Enlarger Illumination. The principal differences in illumination are the light source and the method of light diffusion used to obtain even illumination at the easel.

Light Sources

Tungsten Lamps. These provide the most suitable enlarger illumination for general use. Tungsten illumination is compatible with practically all papers including variable-contrast and color papers.

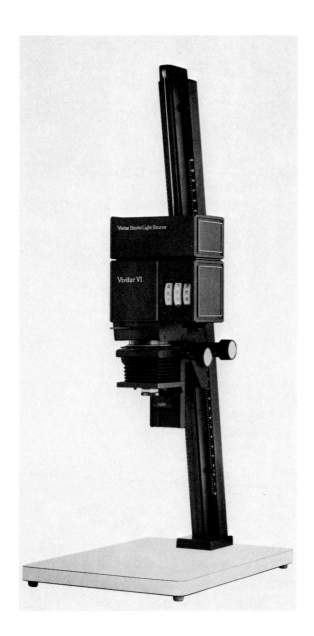

(Left) The Vivitar VI Condenser enlarger contains a Dioptic light source which delivers two to three times as much light on the baseboard as similar wattage enlargers. This facilitates composition and focusing, even with dense negatives or slides. (Below) The Minolta Color Enlarger uses diffuse illumination, which tends to minimize scratches, grain, and the effects of negative retouching.

Tungsten lamps for enlarging are of a special type known as photoenlarger lamps. Following is a list of photo enlarger lamps and their approximate wattage:

Photo Enlarger Lamp No.	Wattage
211	75
212	150
213	250
302	500
521	1000

The higher power lamps, such as Nos. 302 and 521, are generally used in big enlargers that employ ground-glass or opal-glass diffusion. The smaller lamps are used in condenser-type enlargers that accommodate negatives up to about 4″ × 5″. Remember that these lamps, particularly the small ones, lose light output and change in color temperature due to discoloration of the glass envelope after a period of use. These changes are not very important in black-and-white printing, but if your exposures seem to be increasing, use a new lamp.

Tungsten-Halogen. In a suitably designed lamp-house, these lamps provide an excellent source for enlarging. Their color temperature is similar to that of ordinary tungsten lamps. The halogen gas sealed in the lamp reduces blackening and maintains the color temperature for the life of the lamp.

Fluorescent Light. Some enlargers employ fluorescent tubes, sometimes referred to as cold light. This diffuse illumination yields somewhat low contrast in printing. Its principal use is in portrait work. The soft nature of this light tends to subdue retouching, blemishes, and grain. Fluorescent light is not suitable for color printing, nor is it ideal for use with selective-contrast paper. For these papers, the light should be balanced with suitable filters. For details, see the instruction sheet that accompanies the papers.

Mercury-Vapor Tubes. Mercury-vapor light is an excellent light source for use with ordinary black-and-white papers because of its coolness and great intensity. Although unsuitable for color printing and for selective-contrast papers, it is particularly suited to photomural work with normal black-and-white papers. Focusing must be done with care, because while relatively strong actinically, this type of light is weak visually, making the image difficult to see. Some mercury light sources have other gases in addition, making the light stronger visually.

Optical Systems

To obtain an evenly exposed print, the enlarger must provide even illumination on the easel. This is difficult to achieve, but in a well-designed enlarger the difference in intensity between the center and the edges of the focal plane is reduced to the minimum. There are three principal methods of obtaining even illumination:

1. By diffusing the light source with a material such as ground or opal glass,
2. By reflecting the light toward the negative from an integral diffusing surface,
3. By using optical condensers.

Ground-Glass Diffusion. The ground-glass diffusion system is generally used in big enlargers because it avoids the weight and cost of optical condensers. Since diffuse light tends to minimize small scratches, grain, and the effects of negative retouching, it is very desirable, if not essential, for good-quality portrait printing. On the other hand, this illumination reduces the apparent sharpness in enlargements.

Four types of enlarger illumination systems are shown here: (A) ground-glass diffusion, (B) integrating reflector diffusion, (C) optical condensers with opal bulb, and (D) optical condensers with point light source.

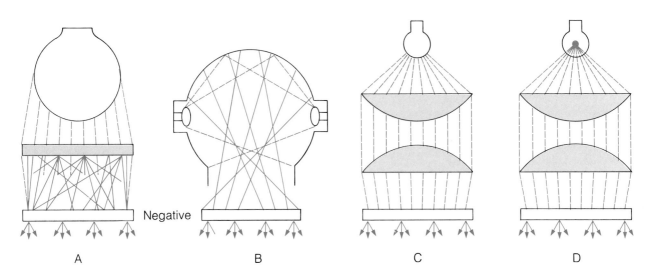

Negative

A   B   C   D

Another disadvantage of ground-glass diffusion is the difficulty in getting even illumination over the whole area of large negatives. This method often produces a relatively intense spot in the center of the field. The deficiency can be corrected by using an extra diffusing sheet that has been ground or sandblasted in the center only.

Opal-Glass, or Flashed-Opal-Glass Diffusion. This is sometimes used as the diffusing medium. It diffuses the light to a greater extent than does ground glass, and hence tends to show less of the hot-spot effect. Since it does not have a ground texture, there is no danger of a texture showing in the prints. Because it is so highly diffusive, it provides less illumination to the easel than ground glass does.

Diffuse enlarger illumination yields lower print contrast than the condenser type. This difference may amount to as much as one grade of paper. Contrast also varies according to the fineness or coarseness of the diffusing material. The coarser the texture, the higher the contrast will be. If you use a coarse ground glass, make sure that the texture is not brought into focus when the lens is stopped down to a small aperture. Otherwise, the prints will have an unpleasant mottled texture.

Integrating Reflected Diffusion. This system is widely used in color enlargers with built-in filtration because it assures that all portions of the light reaching the negative stage are uniformly colored. The diffusing reflector may be a sphere with a lamp at either side, or a flat surface at a 45-degree angle to a side-mounted lamp. In either case, tungsten-halogen lamps are used because in addition to their constant color-temperature output, they provide the intensity required to compensate for that lost to filtration and reflection.

Condenser Enlargers. There are basically three types of condenser enlargers:

1. Specular
2. Semi-specular
3. Semi-diffuse

The specular type of enlarger has a nearly point-source bulb and polished condensing lenses. It provides the highest degree of contrast of all types of enlargers and the greatest apparent sharpness in en-

largements. It also exaggerates dust, negative scratches, and grain. This type of enlarger is very sensitive to the alignment of the bulb with the condensers, and the bulb must be carefully adjusted both vertically and horizontally to provide even illumination. As a consequence, not many are made, and they usually are for the enlargement of small negatives.

The semi-specular type of condenser enlarger uses an opal enlarging bulb with polished condensers. This is the most common type of condenser enlarger. It provides adequate sharpness without excessive enhancement of grain, dust, and scratches.

The semi-diffuse enlarger is similar to the semi-specular type, except that (usually) the top condenser surface is ground instead of being polished. It gives results partway between those of a semi-specular enlarger and a diffusion enlarger. This type is least sensitive to the adjustment of the lamp position.

When black-and-white negatives are being printed, the degree of specularity affects the contrast of the prints being made. Specular enlargers produce prints with higher contrast than do diffuse enlargers. The semi-specular and semi-diffuse enlargers produce an intermediate contrast. This is the result of the Callier effect.

With color negative and transparency printing, there is no such effect because dye images produce practically no Callier effect when they are enlarged.

Lenses for Enlarging

Since both the negative to be enlarged and the printing paper are two-dimensional, flatness of field is a very important characteristic of a good enlarging lens. That is, the lens should yield critical sharpness out to the edges of the print, even when wide open.

Enlarger lenses differ from camera lenses in that they are designed to work best at short lens-to-subject distances. In enlarging, the negative is the subject; the easel is at the focal plane. Although good enlarging lenses yield satisfactory definition over a fairly wide range of magnification, say 2 to 10 times, they give peak performance within fairly narrow limits. Since most enlarging is done at magnifications between 2 and 6 times, enlarging lenses are computed accordingly. Therefore, if you need critical sharpness at 10 or 12 times magnification, as you

Types of Enlargers

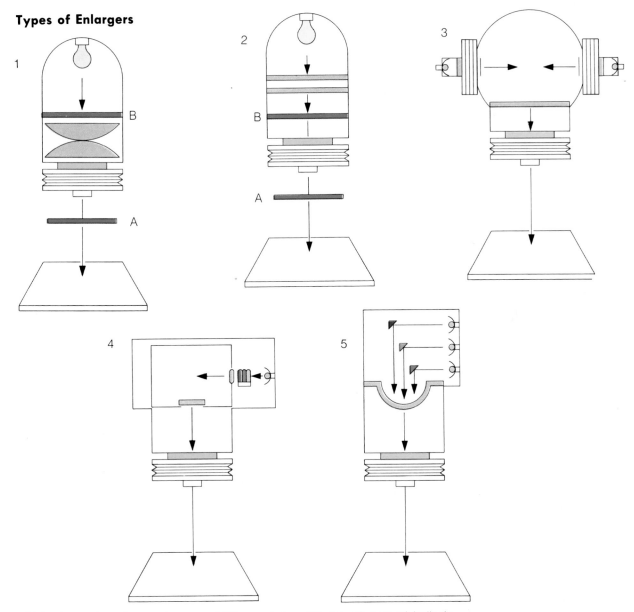

(1) Fundamental condenser enlargers and (2) ground-glass diffusion enlargers originally designed for black-and-white printing require that filtration be placed under the lens (A) for printing selective-contrast papers or for color printing. Later models have a drawer or compartment to permit filters to be placed in the lamphouse (B). In color printing, gelatin color correction (CC) filters must be used at A; less expensive acetate color printing (CP) filters may be used at B. (3) The integrating-sphere diffusion color enlarger has twin light sources, two sets of graduated, dial-in filter wheels protected from the light sources by heat-absorbing glass, and a built-in UV filter above the negative. (4) The latest models of subtractive color-printing enlargers have intensely bright tungsten-halogen light sources coupled with dichroic glass printing filters, which are non-fading. The filter segments move in and out of the light beam on carefully calibrated cams, which permit accurate repetition of filter-pack combinations. (5) The additive color enlarger has three tungsten-halogen lamps, coupled with red, green, and blue dichroic glass mirrors, to expose prints with a single exposure. Built-in rheostats control lamps so the red, green, and blue light can be adjusted to attain the proper color printing light.

do in making big enlargements from miniature negatives or blowups from microfilms, use a lens computed for this higher range of magnification.

Evenness of Illumination. Given a well-designed lamphouse and condenser system, a good enlarging lens throws an almost even circle of illumination on the easel. Unevenness in a diffusion enlarger is usually caused by inadequate diffusion. Placing the bulb as far as possible from the ground or opal glass helps minimize the hot spot. An additional layer of diffusing material, slightly spaced from the original layer(s), will help in evenness, but will lower the illumination so that exposures will take longer.

If there is a hot spot in the illumination of a condenser enlarger, it means that the vertical adjustment of the lamp is incorrect. Condenser enlargers are designed so that the image of the bulb should be focused on, and fill the enlarging lens with light. Obviously, changing the focal length of the enlarging lens requires adjusting the position of the bulb for maximum performance. Placing a piece of ground glass (or tissue paper) in the position of the enlarging lens will show what the best position is. Some enlargers have interchangeable condensers for different formats within their different focal-length enlarging lenses, while others have indexed lamp positions.

All lenses have some illumination falloff from the center to the edges of the field—it is intrinsic in their design. This falloff should not be confused with the illumination hot spot.

You can check the evenness of illumination with a light meter and no negative in position. Use an incident-reading meter, or take reflected-light readings from a sheet of white paper placed on the baseboard (read from an angle that avoids the meter shadow). The difference between the center and the edges of the lighted area should be less than a half-stop when the lens is closed down two or more aperture settings from wide open.

Focus Shift. A feature of many otherwise excellent enlarging lenses is a shift in focus when the aperture is changed. If you suspect that your lens behaves in this way, make the following test. With the aperture wide open, use a focusing magnifier to focus a fairly grainy negative. Observe the sharpness of the grain as you stop the lens down one or two stops. If the grain loses definition, focus with the lens stopped down to the aperture you intend to use for exposure. When using filters under the lens, focus with them in place to insure maximum sharpness.

Focal Length of Enlarging Lenses. In enlarging, magnification is governed by the focal length of the lens and by the lens-to-easel distance. With vertical enlargers, the lens-to-easel distance is limited by the height of the column on which the enlarger head travels. The focal length is determined by the size of the negative to be enlarged. For the best overall sharpness and evenness of illumination, the focal length of the lens should approximately equal the diagonal measurement of the negative to be enlarged. This rule holds for high magnification, but in practice a slightly shorter focal length can be tolerated. (See the accompanying table.)

Greater magnification for a given lens-to-easel distance can be obtained with a relatively short-focal-length lens, but it covers a smaller area. Therefore, you can use it only to enlarge a small negative or part of a larger one. For example, if you use a 4" × 5" enlarger, a standard lens will probably have a focal length of about 5½ inches. Auxiliary lenses of 4-inch and 3-inch focal lengths would greatly extend the range of magnification of which the enlarger is capable. Shorter-focal-length lenses will not cover the complete 4" × 5" negative. The 3-inch lens will cover about a 2¼" × 2¼" area, while the 4-inch lens will cover about a 2¼" × 3¼" area.

In an automatic focusing system, the enlarger must remain in critical focus throughout its travel. This depends on precise construction and on the mechanism being matched correctly with the focal length of the lens. Although similar lenses may be rated at the same focal length, they are, in fact, very rarely exactly the same. For this reason, lenses for auto-focus enlargers are not interchangeable.

FOCAL LENGTH OF ENLARGING LENSES

Negative Size	Focal Length
Subminiature (Minox, size 110)	25 mm
Single-frame 35 mm, Robot, and Instamatic® size 126	35 mm
Double-frame 35 mm	50 mm
4 × 4 cm to 6 × 6 cm	75 mm
6 × 7 cm to 6 × 9 cm	90–105 mm
3¼" × 4¼" to 4" × 5"	135–160 mm

Many enlarging lenses are equipped with click-stops; this makes it easy to set the lens at any aperture in the dark simply by opening it to the widest position and counting clicks as the lens is then stopped down. Some modern enlarging lenses have illuminated *f*-numbers that make aperture setting even easier. Most enlarging lenses give optimum performance closed down two or three stops from wide open, although most high-quality lenses give very satisfactory performance wide open.

Negative Carriers

Enlargers have removable negative carriers so that the image may be positioned accurately in the carrier opening. A carrier is usually composed of two plates that are hinged together at one side to open like a book, or that have a pin-and-hole registration system. Glassless carriers simply have openings cut in the center of the plate; they grip the film by pressure on the edges outside the image area. They are excellent for small-format films, but generally allow large-format negatives to sag out of the focal plane of the lens, or to buckle or "pop" out of focus as they absorb heat and expand during an exposure. Glass-type negative carriers may use a single piece of glass in the lower plate to support the negative, or may sandwich the film between two pieces of glass. They provide negative flatness throughout the exposure, but present four additional surfaces that must be absolutely clean and dust-free. Further, they can form Newton's rings that show in prints.

Negative carriers are available with openings to match all standard-image formats. Stray light from outside the image area can cause veiled highlights and reduced contrast in a print. For this reason, it is best to use a carrier with an opening only as large as the negative area being printed. Alternatively, a larger opening can be masked down with strips of black paper laid against the base side of the film. Some carriers have built-in adjustable blades or accept inserts for masking. It is also fairly easy to make a carrier with any desired size and shape of opening by using a standard carrier as a guide for cutting pieces of mounting board or other stiff, opaque material. For permanent use, they should be of metal.

An opening just slightly larger than the full-frame area of a negative will produce a print with a black line around the image. Enlarged cut-out carriers are available for some formats. It is also possible

to file the opening of a standard metal carrier to the required size. The finished edges must be absolutely smooth to avoid scratching the film, and they should be beveled and blackened to eliminate reflections into the image area.

Tilting Negative Stage

Some enlargers are made with a mechanism to tilt the negative carrier and sometimes tilt the lens board as well. If only the negative can be tilted, then the paper easel must be tilted also. With this capability, a negative that shows perspective distortion due to camera tilt can be rectified in printing by tilting some part of the enlarger system.

If only the negative carrier, or only the easel, is tilted, usually it is not possible to attain sharp focus over the entire picture area. However, where only a modest degree of correction is required, the depth of field obtained by stopping down the lens to a small aperture may achieve overall sharpness. This means longer exposures in printing. Where extreme correction is required, or where long exposures are undesirable, it is possible to secure sharp focus over a tilted negative or paper plane by also tilting the lens board. Or, if the lens board cannot be tilted, the negative and the paper easel may be tilted. In short, with the three elements in an enlarger setup—negative plane, lens plane, and paper plane—tilting *any two* of the three will secure both perspective correction and uniform focus at the same time. The method is explained in detail under "Perspective Correction" in the section on enlarging techniques in this article.

Focusing Aids

The projected image must be critically focused to obtain the best quality enlargements. This is not only a matter of the sharp definition of details, but of tonality as well. An out-of-focus dark area spreads into neighboring light areas, and light areas spread into dark. The result is muddied tones with reduced contrast. Similar problems arise with color images.

Since the image in a black-and-white negative is composed of grains of silver, the sharpest picture is obtained when the grains themselves are sharply focused. This cannot be judged accurately by eye; a magnifier is required. "Grain focusers" for enlargers are essentially low-power microscopes for examining the projected image on the easel, or a portion of the image intercepted by a small mirror in the

focuser. They are designed for viewing at an angle so that the viewer's head does not get in the way of the image light.

An out-of-focus image in the focuser looks like mushy grains of oatmeal. As the focusing control of the enlarger is adjusted, the pattern changes to sharp, clear grains like sand or a salt-and-pepper mixture when the image reaches the best possible focus. Critical focus should be rechecked before each exposure because negatives expand or contract between exposures, and focus adjustments may be disturbed during the normal activity of printing. When printing filters are used under the lens, focusing should be done with the filters in place.

Timers

A very important enlarging accessory is a timer. Consistent, repeatable exposures are the key to high-quality results, especially in color printing. It does little good to make a test exposure of 15 seconds, for instance, if the final exposure is likely to vary from 13 to 18 seconds. The shorter the exposure time, the more important the timing accuracy becomes.

Because attention during an enlarging exposure must often be paid to burning-in or dodging, or other manipulations, a clock with a sweep second hand or an audible-beat device such as a metronome is not very practical—it is too easy to lose track of the time. An electrical switch timer that can be set

to turn off the enlarger light after a desired number of seconds is the best solution. Some timers have a clock-like face with a movable pointer that is turned to the desired exposure. When a start button is pushed, the enlarger light is turned on and a spring mechanism moves the pointer back to zero, where the enlarger is turned off.

When a variety of times are used—for instance, for a set of test strips—it may be difficult to reset the timer to exactly the same position that produced the best exposure. In addition, mechanical limitations, especially as the timer ages, make it unlikely that a setting of 20 seconds, for example, will be exactly four times as long as the exposure given by the 5-second setting. An easy way to avoid such variations is to accumulate exposure in "bursts" by setting the timer to a short interval and pushing the start button repeatedly to add up to the desired time. With a 5-second setting, four exposures will total 20 seconds again and again, with no significant variation. This method also makes it easy to time burning-in or dodging. If an area needs to be dodged for, say, 10 seconds, it is far easier to do that for two of the four 5-second bursts, than to try and determine 10 seconds out of a continuous 20-second exposure.

Many new models of timers have solid-state circuits that time exposures electronically, avoiding the vagaries of mechanical systems. They provide extreme accuracy at all settings, and may be set for intervals of a tenth of a second in some cases.

Most timers of either type are designed with receptacles for connection with both the enlarger and the safelight, so that when the enlarger light goes on, the safelight is automatically turned off. A separate control switch makes it possible to turn the enlarger on continuously for focusing or other image adjustments.

Easels

Another essential piece of equipment that will be needed is a paper easel. This is a device that holds the paper flat on the baseboard of the enlarger. It usually has masking devices of one sort or another to produce a white margin on the print.

Single-size easels are both inexpensive and convenient to use when prints are always in the same format.

An adjustable easel is more flexible because it allows adjustment both of the image area and width of the white border. Generally, setting the position of the paper clamp adjusts the width of the margin, while sliding the masking bands adjusts the image area. So to make a print on 8″ × 10″ paper, with a ¼-inch white margin all around, the paper clamp (or corner guide) is set to ¼ inch, and the masking bands to 7½ and 9½ inches, respectively, thus allowing for the ¼-inch margin on the opposite edge as well. For ½-inch margins, the corner guide is set to ½ inch and the masking bands to 7 and 9 inches. Other sizes are done the same way. (*See:* EASEL.)

Print Exposure Meters

There are various measuring devices that can minimize the need to make any test strips at all.

They read the projected image on the easel in much the same way that an exposure meter for camera use reads the light from the subject. A spot-reading meter measures the brightness of selected portions of the image, usually a highlight and a shadow. An integrating meter uses a diffuser to blend all the intensities together for a single, average reading.

The amount of light available for measurement is much less than for a normal exposure meter, so enlarging meters have to be a good deal more sensitive than camera meters. The simpler ones use various methods to avoid this problem. The main difficulty with enlarging exposure meters is that the exposure of paper for a print has to be much more precise than exposure for film in a camera; papers have nearly no latitude.

This means that it is not possible simply to look up a paper speed, set it on your meter, and proceed to read the correct exposure for a print. In nearly all cases, it is first necessary to make tests with a given paper and arrive at a meter calibration setting for that paper and contrast grade. Separate calibrations

(Left) Easels are required to hold the paper flat on the baseboard of the enlarger. (Right) The EPOI MM7 Color Analyzer is one type of print exposure meter designed for color printing. An electronic f-stop feature permits increasing or decreasing the sensitivity range by the equivalent of five f-stops. This model is capable of taking both average and spot readings of the projected image. Photo courtesy Ehrenreich Photo-Optical Industries, Inc.

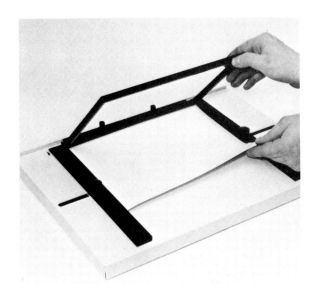
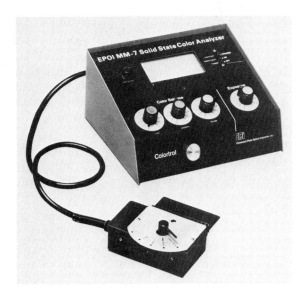

are required for other papers and contrast grades. Buying paper in large quantities reduces the necessity of calibrating the meter at frequent intervals.

Enlarging Papers and Chemicals

Papers are available in standard sheet sizes and rolls, and in a variety of surfaces, textures, and emulsion types (for example: glossy, lustre, silk, etc.). The choice of a paper involves both physical and expressive considerations. (*See:* PAPERS, PHOTOGRAPHIC.) Black-and-white papers may be available in separate grades of contrast (1 to 5, soft to hard) or as selective-contrast papers. Kodak Polycontrast paper is a selective-contrast paper, as is Kodak Ektamatic SC paper. This kind of material can produce prints of different contrasts when exposed through filters of certain colors. Kodak Polycontrast printing filters have numbers (1 to 4) that are roughly equivalent to the same graded degrees of contrast. Some warm-tone black-and-white papers intended primarily for portraits are available in only one contrast grade.

Papers for color printing are available only in a single contrast grade, because acceptable color negatives cannot vary in the way that black-and-white negatives do. Color reversal papers permit making prints directly from color slides. Panchromatic papers such as Kodak Panalure and Panalure portrait papers make it possible to obtain full-range black-and-white prints from color negatives.

Conventional black-and-white papers are usually tray-processed in developer, stop bath, and fixer. Stabilization papers contain developing agents in their emulsions. They are commonly passed through a processor that develops the image with an activator, and makes it semi-permanent with a stabilizer; tray processing with a conventional developer may be used instead. In either case, subsequent fixing and washing will make the image permanent. Another type of paper is available for activation processing. The paper has developing agents incorporated in the emulsion so that it develops when placed in an activator. Such processors as the Kodak Royalprint processor then fix, wash, and dry the prints rapidly to optimum stability levels.

The chemicals required for proper processing of color papers are specified in the instructions that accompany the paper. The number of solutions and the processing steps differ for negative and reversal printing papers, and the developers must be carefully designed for a particular emulsion to produce the best results. Processing may be by tray or by drum or tube processors; see the various articles on color printing.

Some papers are made using a conventional paper base, while others, called water-resistant papers, are made on a resin-coated paper base. Conventional (or fiber-base) papers take longer to process, wash, and dry than do water-resistant papers, but they are available in a larger choice of surfaces and can be used to make prints that have a longer life.

ENLARGING TECHNIQUES

Basic Procedures

The fundamental steps in making an enlargement are as follows.

Clean the dust from both sides of a selected negative; a blast of air from a squeeze-bulb syringe or a pressurized can, or a soft brush work best. Place the negative in the carrier and insert the carrier in the enlarger so that the emulsion faces the lens.

Turn out the white light (leave safelights on, if any), turn on the enlarger, and adjust the size and sharpness of the image projected on the easel. Move the enlarger head up to make the image larger, down to make it smaller. Focusing will change the image size somewhat, so two or three adjustments may be necessary. A scrap piece of white paper will make the image easily visible.

Adjust the easel blades to take in the desired portion of the image. If this is the first time the negative is being printed, begin with the full image, without cropping; it is generally easier to decide cropping by looking at a positive test print than by looking at the projected negative image.

Focus critically on the image grain without moving the enlarger head. Close the lens down two or three stops to its optimum aperture.

Turn out the enlarger light. Under safelight (or total darkness with some color materials) make a series of test exposures. Be sure to use the suggested basic filter pack for a color print. Use a single 60-second exposure on a full sheet of paper through the Kodak projection print scale, or make test strips (*See:* TEST STRIPS.) on one or more pieces of paper. Use various exposure times for black-and-white

(Left) Using the Kodak projection print scale on top of the print paper, a 60-second test exposure is made. (Right) The final print is then exposed at the indicated number of seconds which appeared in the best sector—in this instance, 24 seconds.

tests; use a constant time and change the *f*-stop setting for color tests in order to avoid reciprocity effects. Make sure each piece of paper is placed emulsion-side-up in the easel.

Process the tests. Look at them under white light to determine whether the contrast grade seems suitable to the subject, and which exposure time is best. In black-and-white, if everything looks gray and muddy, use a higher contrast for the next test; if everything looks "soot-and-whitewash" harsh, use a lower contrast. If all the tests are too light, make another series with the lens set one *f*-stop wider; if they are all too dark, close down one stop for the next set of tests.

When an exposure has been selected, expose a full sheet of paper. Process this workprint and evaluate it for overall quality, possible cropping, and local exposure control. As explained in separate articles,

local control is achieved by burning-in an area with additional exposure to bring out details or make the area print darker, or by dodging (holding back some light) during part of the overall exposure to make it print lighter.

In color printing, evaluate the color balance in this print and determine what filter pack adjustments are required; see the articles on color printing.

Open the lens to full aperture, refocus critically, then stop down to the working aperture again. Make a print incorporating all the modifications decided upon from the workprint. Process and evaluate it.

Refocus and expose another print with any further modifications that seem necessary. Continue refining subsequent prints until the desired quality is achieved. Reserve final judgment until a seemingly satisfactory print has dried completely. The expressive quality of a print often changes with drying; it may be necessary to try again in another printing session. Prints dry down; that is, they look darker when dry than when wet. The amount of white light falling on a print affects its apparent density. The light used to judge the density of a print should have about the same intensity as the light under which it will be displayed.

Exposure in Printing

Because the exposure latitude of photographic papers is quite small, the best-quality prints are those that attain the desired density in the development time recommended for the paper used. As a practical matter, however, small errors in exposure sometimes must be tolerated for the sake of economy in time and material. Minor errors can be compensated by slightly more or less development, depending on the type of paper.

Grossly overexposed and underdeveloped prints are often mottled, and lacking in shadow contrast and a good gradation of tones in the highlights. Underexposed and overdeveloped prints usually lack detail in the highlights, and they often show chemical fog or yellow stain. Incidentally, it is not good practice in professional printing to resort to the use of hot developer, strong developer, rubbing the print with warm hands, or breathing heavily on the print to get detail in light areas. These expedients consume time and stain as many prints as they save. It will be obvious after the development time is three-fourths gone that the print is not correctly exposed. Don't waste any more time on it; make corrections on the next exposure.

To some extent, exposure is related to developer temperature. It will save much time and effort by keeping the developer at the recommended temperature—usually 20 C (68 F) for black-and-white.

Another factor that makes exposure more unpredictable than it need be is varying developer activity, caused by exhaustion or contamination. Therefore, do not overwork the developer or allow it to be contaminated by other chemicals, particularly by hypo.

Voltage Fluctuation

Exposures in printing can be affected considerably by variations in the voltage of electric current applied to the printer or enlarger lamp. Light output may drop as much as 30 percent with a 10 percent

drop in voltage. Also, when the voltage changes, so does the color temperature of the light. As voltage drops, the light becomes more yellow, a color to which black-and-white printing papers are less sensitive. Of course color paper is even more noticeably affected, because both print density and color balance change.

Sudden changes in voltage are usually due to switching on or off equipment such as studio lights, drying machines, and the like. Slowly changing voltage is more often due to variations in the incoming supply. The current applied to an enlarger lamp can often be regulated by use of a constant voltage transformer or voltage regulator. However, take the advice of an electrician before you buy equipment of this kind. It may be that your wiring is inadequate for its load or that a more even distribution of the load among the various circuits would be a solution to the problem.

Photometry in Black-and-White Printing

An electronic densitometer equipped with a suitable probe can be used to find the exposure required for a particular negative. Readings of the negative density are taken from the projected image directly on the enlarger easel. This system is known as on-easel photometry; it is used with considerable success in color printing to determine both exposure and the filter pack required by a negative.

1. Successful on-easel photometry depends largely on the ability to recognize the most suitable density to read. This requires experience. Photometry provides only a basic exposure. Local control of exposure for other parts of the negative may also be needed.
2. The exposure required by high-contrast papers is critical. Unless correct density is read, the print will be grossly underexposed or overexposed.
3. For subjective reasons, all black-and-white prints are not exposed to have the same density. Consequently, personal experience must often override the exposure indicated by the instrument.
4. Abnormally high or low contrast in the negative affects the indicated exposure. Generally, you must apply corrections for such negatives.

Enlargers and Enlarging

To use a photometer successfully in black-and-white printing, observe the following points:

1. Take every possible step to make sure that negatives are developed to a uniform contrast. Maintain constant developer activity and temperature, as well as proper agitation during development. Use as few different kinds of film or developer as possible.
2. Keep the print developer at a constant temperature. Do not overwork the bath, and protect it from contamination by splashes of other chemicals and by hypo on the hands. These precautions remove one serious variable factor.
3. Use as few different papers as possible. A selective-contrast material, such as Kodak Polycontrast paper, is particularly suitable. A selective-contrast paper is especially useful in printing varied negatives on a single roll of paper. The contrast of the paper can be adjusted to suit that of the negatives by use of filters. In operating the photometer with selective-contrast paper, determine the exposure required for white light (no filter) and then apply the appropriate correction for the filter in use.
4. Because the response of a photometer to light of varying intensity may not be the same as that of a photographic emulsion, adjust the print exposure by altering the lens aperture rather than by changing the exposure time.
5. Most modern photometers are equipped with CdS photoconductive cells, which are sensitive to the safelight. For this reason, do not allow the direct rays from a safelight to fall on the enlarger easel. Even a shadow cast by the operator's body or a reflection from a white lab coat may affect the accuracy of the readings.

Perspective Correction

Often, a picture may be taken with the camera pointed upward, for instance, at a tall building. The result is almost always a steep convergence of the vertical lines of the building, making it look as if it is leaning backwards. This effect can be corrected in printing by using an enlarger with a tilting negative carrier. However, in correcting one type of distortion, it is quite possible to introduce a different type. Distortion correction often has uses in commercial photography, as well as in producing expressive effects.

To see how this works, try a dry run first. Find a negative that has converging verticals (or even a normal negative if nothing else is available, just so it has some marked vertical lines in it). Start with easel and negative carrier parallel to one another, and insert the negative in the carrier. Focus the image on a sheet of white paper in the easel, and then proceed as follows:

1. Raise the enlarger head until the desired image size is reached.
2. Focus the image on a sheet of white paper on the easel.
3. Tilt the easel to a position such as the one shown in the accompanying diagram—left side higher than the right.
4. The image will now be out of focus. Refocus so that the image is sharp in the center of the easel. Both edges will be out of focus.
5. Tilt the negative carrier in a direction opposite to the tilt of the easel. Watch the image while tilting; if it goes out of focus, stop and refocus it again for the middle.
6. When the correct angle is reached, the image will be sharp not only in the middle, but all the way across its width. A slight touch-up of focus may be needed at this point, but if the angle is right, the focusing should result in uniform sharpness from one side to the other. Close the lens aperture at least two stops to increase overall sharpness.

Exposure Compensation

When printing with tilted negative and easel, one end of the image will be bigger than the other. As in any enlargement, the bigger image requires more exposure. If a print is made without compensation, the larger end will be underexposed.

The correction is simply a matter of dodging. The easiest way to do it is to make an exposure test at the larger end of the image. If this is correct, then the smaller end will be getting too much exposure, but can be held back easily with a straight dodger during the exposure.

For most precise results, it may be best to make a separate exposure test at each end of the image. If it turns out that the larger end needs 20 seconds, and the smaller end 13 seconds, simply dodge the smaller end of the image for 7 seconds while making the exposure.

Since the change in exposure is uniform from one end to the other, it would seem necessary to dodge progressively, with the most holdback at the smaller end, and then gradually less and less across the print area. This can be done without too much trouble, but in most instances it will not be necessary. If the smaller end of the image is dodged for the proper time, no great or sudden change in density will be noted at the transition point, especially if the dodger is kept in motion as recommended.

Deliberate Distortion

When the easel is tilted to correct a tilt in an original image, other things happen at the same time.

Take the case of a building photographed with the camera pointing upward. When this is corrected by tilting the easel, the top and bottom of the building become equal in width, but the height of the building increases at the same time. The original camera tilt not only caused the image to converge, but also to foreshorten at the same time; correcting the tilt at the easel also corrects the foreshortening.

However, this compensation is not automatically correct. It is correct only when the extension of the enlarger lens is the same as that of the camera lens when the picture was taken. If the enlarger lens happens to be of the same focal length as the camera lens, and is extended the same amount, it will produce a print the same size as the original building, which is impractical. But if the enlarger lens has a slightly shorter focus than the camera lens, when it is extended for a reasonable size enlargement, it will also produce the proper size correction when used with a tilted negative and easel.

As a numerical example: If a building is photographed at a fairly large distance with a 4-inch lens, a 3-inch enlarger lens at $3\times$ enlargement will produce correct proportions, as will a 3½-inch lens at $7\times$, and so on. If the image of a building is rectilinear, few persons will notice that the height of the image is incorrect. But the general principle has other uses: In general, if the enlarger lens has a longer focus than the camera lens, the image will be somewhat stretched; if it has a shorter focus than the camera lens, the image will be shortened.

This principle can be used to make prints that are deliberately extended or compressed. In fashion photography, for instance, a favorite trick is to photograph the model from a low angle, then to rectify the image in an enlarger with a long-focus lens and a tilted easel. The resultant image makes the model appear taller and thinner than he/she actually is.

Since the method works just as well sideways, this trick can be used in photographing automobiles. Instead of making a picture square to the side of the car, it is photographed at an angle, generally in front. The converging image is then straightened out in an enlarger with a long-focus lens and a tilting mechanism, and the end result makes the car appear considerably longer. The expressive possibilities of this type of deliberate distortion are limitless.

• *See also:* BLACK-AND-WHITE PRINTING; BLACK-AND-WHITE PRINTS FROM COLOR FILMS; BURNING-IN; CALLIER EFFECT; COLOR PRINTING FROM NEGATIVES; COLOR PRINTING FROM TRANSPARENCIES; COMBINATION PRINTING; DARKROOM, AMATEUR; DARKROOM, PROFESSIONAL; DICHROIC FILTERS; DODGING; DRUM AND TUBE PROCESSING; EASEL; MULTIPLE PRINTING; PAPERS, PHOTOGRAPHIC; PRINTING, PHOTOGRAPHIC; STABILIZATION PROCESS.

Further Reading: Bullock, Wynn et al. Edited by Eleanor Lewis. *Darkroom*. Rochester, NY: Light Impressions Corp., 1977; Feininger, Andreas. *Darkroom Techniques: The Darkroom, Film Development, Basic Photo Chemistry*. Vol. 1. Englewood Cliffs, NJ: Prentice-Hall, Inc., 1974; Spillman, Ronald. *Darkroom Techniques*. Dobbs Ferry, NY: Morgan & Morgan, Inc., 1975; Spoerl, Alexander. *Enlarging Techniques*. New York, NY: International Publications Service, 1973.

(Below) The parallel lines of the original scene tend to converge because the camera was tilted upward. (Right) The convergence may be partially corrected by tipping the enlarging easel so that the foreground portion of the image is closer to the enlarger lens than the top of the picture. Note that this tends to elongate the building vertically.

(Right) Further tilting of the easel creates greater elongation which, however, may not be apparent to a viewer unfamiliar with the original. Fashion photographers use such tricks to make a model appear taller and leggier.

Equipment Cases

There is a wide variety of cases intended to protect cameras, lenses, and other equipment while they are being carried or transported. Cases should be selected both for convenience of use and for the protection they offer to the equipment.

Equipment and accessories need three kinds of protection:

1. *From outside sources.* This is a matter of the strength of the outer shell of the case; the security of the closure against dirt, dust, and moisture; and the quality and amount of cushioning within.
2. *From the case itself.* A lined, padded interior and provision for holding items securely in place will help avoid damage caused by the case body.
3. *From other pieces of equipment.* Separators, divided cushioning, or individual pouches are required when two or more items are carried in a single case.

Soft Cases

Materials such as leather and flexible plastic are suitable for individual and small all-purpose cases that are to be carried by the photographer. Many are equipped with straps that go over the neck or shoul-

Small cases for individual pieces of equipment such as cameras, lenses, and light meters may be made of soft leather or flexible plastic. Designed to be carried separately or with other equipment in a larger bag, these cases may be equipped with neck or shoulder straps, or they may be designed to attach to the belt. (Left) This small, soft-leather case will hold a camera body with attached lens. Photo courtesy Ehrenreich Photo-Optical Industries, Inc. (Center left) Lens cases of different sizes. Photo courtesy Service Manufacturing Co., Inc. (Bottom left) A small case designed to be attached to the belt may be used for light meters or mini-format cameras.

der; others are drawstring or zipper pouches intended to be carried in a larger case.

General-purpose carrying cases, so-called gadget bags, are extremely convenient for small-format equipment such as 35 mm cameras, lenses, and accessories. The type that has a waist strap in addition to a shoulder strap can be carried with a minimum of jostling or bouncing. Zipper closures are more convenient and secure than snaps, but are likely to have a short life if not of the heavy-duty type. Lift-out trays, two-section covers, or exterior pockets are very useful for small, non-fragile items such as extra rolls of film. Gadget bags made of soft material, and into which camera, lenses, films, etc., are crammed, are hazardous to equipment.

Rigid-Body Cases

Cases made of hardened fiberboard, lightweight metal, or wood must be used for large pieces of equipment, and in all instances where equipment will be handled by someone other than the owner during shipping or transport. The outer material should be thick enough to be sturdy under all handling conditions, otherwise it will be useless. Overall

interior plastic foam padding, which can be cut as required to receive individual items, provides excellent protection. Or, shaped and cushioned compartments or cradle-like rests can be used, if each item can be firmly fixed in place. Interior compartments or cases made of materials such as rigid plastic that can crack under impact should be avoided.

Construction Details

A flimsy case is a waste of money. In soft cases, look for double-thick materials held together by double-stitched seams with reinforcing rivets at stress points. Avoid cases assembled with adhesives that can lose strength with age. Zippers, snaps, or buckle-closures must be heavy-duty and securely attached. Straps that pass under the entire body of the case provide the best support. Attachment rings or tabs on the side of a case can pull out or tear with the strain of repeated use. A smooth, lined interior helps avoid damage and is easy to clean.

The materials of rigid cases must remain rigid under the impact of severe handling. They should be assembled with rivets, welds, or screws at all corners

Bags for small-format equipment should be made of stiff material for support and protection of their contents. (Below) This model has a separate lift-out tray and a soft interior pocket for non-breakable items. (Right) Zipper closures and an exterior pocket are useful features. Photos courtesy Service Manufacturing Co., Inc.

and along all seams in order to have adequate strength. Hinges, fasteners, and handles are often weak points; they must be substantial and securely attached. They should lie flat, or preferably, be recessed into the body of the case to avoid damage from other cases sliding against them. Locking fasteners are necessary if cases are to be handled by various people. A truly waterproof seal between cover and body is essential for cases that are to be shipped or used in bad weather. A light-colored exterior helps reflect heat from sunshine; interior insulation is necessary in hot climates.

Using Cases

Decide how much equipment will be required for a job or trip, and select a case of adequate size; excess size increases bulk and weight, which decrease convenience. It is seldom practical to carry more than two or three individual items hanging from straps; they can bounce, tangle, and generally interfere with the act of taking pictures.

Plan the arrangment of items in the case so that the most used are the most accessible. Lift-out dividers or trays make it easier to get at other items. Be sure that both ends of the lenses are capped, that camera lens mounts are protected with body caps, and that delicate items are individually protected in the packing arrangement.

Avoid excess weight. Even a moderate load becomes tiring after an hour or so. It is far less fatiguing to carry a small case by a waist strap than by a shoulder strap. Use collapsible luggage-transporters for medium-weight cases, and wheeled dollies or hand trucks for bulky and heavy cases.

Keep case exteriors and interiors clean and dry. Vacuum or wipe out the interior after each major use. Inspect for damage or wear at intervals.

• *See also:* CAMERA AND LENS CARE.

Rigid-body cases must be sturdy enough to withstand handling by persons other than the owner. (Left) Interior of this case by Fiberbilt Photo Products is compartmentalized by a patented system of movable, interlocking partitions that may be adapted to individual needs. Photo courtesy Ikelheimer-Ernst, Inc. (Right) Plastic foam padding, cut to fit individual pieces, will hold items firmly in place. A foam-rubber top lining gives additional protection. Photo courtesy Service Manufacturing Co., Inc.

 **Errors in Processing**

Negatives, transparencies, or prints sometimes reveal the results of imperfect or improper processing. The evidence may be spots, stains, discoloration or improper color balance, missing or obliterated image, physical distortion or damage, too much or too little contrast, or a wide variety of other faults.

A common source of many faults is careless or improper physical handling of the sensitive material. The remedy is obvious: proper attention to careful handling. However, many faults are caused by problems with the processing solutions. These solutions may be contaminated, exhausted, improperly mixed, or used at the wrong temperature, to list just a few possibilities.

Black-and-White Materials

Often the cause of a particular problem in processed material is very difficult to identify conclusively. The accompanying tables describe some of the most common faults in black-and-white processing and suggest appropriate cures or corrective action where possible.

Dark or black streaks in the negative may be caused by light leaks in the camera or processing tank.

PROCESSING ERRORS: BLACK-AND-WHITE NEGATIVES

Problem	Probable Causes
Dark or black streaks with shaded edges	Caused by uneven development, possibly due to slow or incomplete filling of small developing tanks. Sometimes due to negatives sticking together when sheet films are processed in a tray. May also be due to a light leak in the camera.
Irregular dark blotches with sharp edges	Caused by splashing or spattering developer on dry film awaiting development.
Irregular dark streaks, not completely opaque	Caused by chemical contamination of developer or dirty tank, reel, or other utensil.
Straight dark streaks combined with overall fog	Generally caused by light-fogging before development, which may be due to light leaks in the darkroom while tanks are being loaded.
Light streaks running from highlights (commonly known as "bromide drag")	Caused by diffusion of bromide from highlight areas during development, especially when sheet film is being processed in hangers; due to insufficient agitation.
Dark, straight streaks running inward from edge of negative	These streaks usually coincide with perforations on 35 mm film, or with the holes in developing hangers for sheet films; they are caused by developer surging through the holes during agitation. Agitation should be gentle and not continuous.

Errors in Processing

Problem	Probable Causes
Light, roughly circular or irregularly shaped streaks	Often caused by accidental splashes of hypo on undeveloped film.
Lightning streaks, forked or branching and very sharp	Usually caused by discharges of static electricity while the film is being unrolled. In extreme cases, flashes of blue light can be seen while handling the film spool. To avoid this, unroll very slowly and carefully. Keeping the humidity in the darkroom fairly high will minimize static charges.
Irregular shrinkage of negative	This usually occurs when sheet films are dried in the developing hangers; some parts of the film stick to the hanger while others are free. Always remove film from hangers for drying.
Aerial fog	This is an overall fog that occurs on a negative. Caused by excessive exposure to air during development. Such fog cannot occur if film remains completely submerged at all times. Where conditions require hangers or reel to be out of the developer for much of the time, aerial fog can be prevented by the addition of 2 parts per million of Pinakryptol Green to the developer (make stock solution of 2 grams of Pinakryptol Green to a litre of water; add 1 ml of this solution to each litre of developer).
Dichroic fog	This fog appears green on the surface of the negative, but red when one is looking through the negative. Caused by traces of hypo, ammonia, or excess sulfite in developer or by exhausted fixing bath. Sometimes caused by growth of algae in developer tank, especially in hot weather. Tank should be emptied, cleaned, and sterilized with Clorox solution before refilling. Dichroic fog can also be caused by developers that contain silver halide solvents. Use of other developers corrects this.

Miscellaneous fog
  Fog on old film
  Developer fog
 	
  Fog from contaminated developers
  Overdevelopment fog
 	
  High-temperature fog
 	
  Fog from unsafe light conditions
	Fog increases with the age of the film; its formation is accelerated by poor storage conditions.
	Incorrectly compounded developers may cause developer fog; if in doubt, try a freshly mixed sample of the same formula.
	Traces of sulfides, hypo, salts of copper and tin, the latter in tiny amounts that may be leached from solder joints in equipment; all can produce fog, especially on color products.
	Since fog increases with the amount of development, overdevelopment and attempts to push underexposed negatives may cause fog.
	Excessively warm developers can cause fog; special formulas for tropical use usually contain extra bromide or other antifoggant.
	Illumination from an unsafe safelight can cause fog of the normal type if it strikes the film before development begins. If film is exposed by light after development has begun, the result can be partial or complete image reversal.

Contrasty negatives, lacking in shadow detail	Caused by forcing development in an attempt to save an underexposed negative. There is no remedy for this error if shadow detail is essential; otherwise, the negative can be printed on very soft paper, or reduced in a superproportional reducer.
Contrasty negatives with full shadow detail	Due to overdevelopment of normally exposed negatives. If only slightly overdeveloped, they can usually be printed on soft papers; extremely overdeveloped negatives may need reduction in a superproportional reducer.
Contrasty negatives, highlights blocked	Caused by overexposure and/or overdevelopment. There is no remedy for blocked highlights, but reduction in a proportional reducer may improve printing quality somewhat.
Flat negatives, lacking in shadow detail	Caused by underexposure and/or underdevelopment. Intensification may make the negative printable, but nothing can restore missing shadow detail.
Flat negatives, ample shadow detail	Caused by underdevelopment of a normal exposure. Try to print on hard paper; if contrast is still not sufficient, then intensify the negatives.
Flat negatives, highlights blocked	Caused by overexposure and underdevelopment. The only remedy here is to print on hard paper, but there is no way to restore highlight detail.
Image reversal	Usually caused by exposure to light after development has begun. The safelight should be checked. Occasionally, reversal can be caused by a contaminated developer.

(Top left) Streaks or spots on the edge of the film usually correspond to the perforations on 35 mm film. They may be caused by the improper seating of the film in the apron. If they are parallel streaks, like the teeth of a comb, improper agitation is the probable cause. (Top right) Overall grayness, or fog, is the result of light striking undeveloped film. This may be caused by light entering the darkroom, either from outside or from an unsafe safelight. (Above left) Dense, contrasty negatives are usually the result of overexposure and/or overdevelopment. (Above right) Underdevelopment is usually the cause of thin, transparent negatives, if they were properly exposed. It will compound the error of underexposure. (Right) Large clear spots on the negative, with no picture detail, usually represent undeveloped areas caused by the developer not reaching the film surface.

PROCESSING ERRORS: BLACK-AND-WHITE NEGATIVES (continued)

Problem	Probable Causes
Uneven density	May be caused by excessively slow filling of tank, or incomplete filling, followed by vigorous agitation. The cause is either inadequate or excessive agitation. There is no remedy.
Overall milky-gray or cream-colored tone	Due to incomplete fixing; negative should be treated again in fresh fixing bath.
Gray or cream-colored spots	Caused when emulsion is not cleared by fixer either because film layers touched and prevented fixer from reaching the film surface, or because the fixer is exhausted. Can be removed by treatment in fresh fixing solution.
Large clear spots in image area	Undeveloped areas, usually caused by film layers touching so that the developer does not contact some sections, which are then cleared during fixing. There is no way to restore the missing image.
Black spots	May be caused by foreign matter that becomes imbedded in the emulsion during drying. Also, could possibly be caused by chemical dust settling on the film before processing.
Drying marks (water spots)	Lighter spots with gray halos can be caused by drops of water drying on the back of the film. Dark spots with small white centers are caused by water drops that are on the emulsion side of the film during drying. Spots of the same density as the negative, but with a sharp outline, are caused by water dropping on the negative after it has dried.
Fading	Brown, yellow, or sepia tones in a negative, appearing some time after processing, are usually caused by insufficient fixing or incomplete washing. Note that fixation is complete only when the negative has cleared except in a fresh fixing bath; in partly used baths, film should be allowed to fix for twice the time it takes to clear.
Fingerprints	The cause is obvious. If fingerprints are dark, fingers were probably wet with developer. Light fingerprints may be caused by handling film with slightly greasy fingers before processing. Light fingerprints with stain are usually due to handling film with hypo-contaminated fingers.
Mottled appearance	May be due to lack of agitation in developer or fixer; a more likely cause is the use of outdated film or film that has been stored at too high a temperature.
Very small, clear spots; very narrow or clear wiggly lines	Very tiny clear spots are usually the shadows of dust specks, caused by a dusty camera or dusty film holders. Clean all equipment periodically with a vacuum cleaner.
Large clear spots	Generally caused by air bubbles in developer. The tank should be agitated vigorously when first filled; a few sharp raps on the table top may help to disperse any air bubbles.
Yellow spots	Caused when air bells in hypo, or gas bubbles from stop bath, prevent fixation. If caught right away, these spots can be removed by refixing.
Blisters	These look like small bubbles when film is wet and like small craters when it is dry. Caused by warm water flowing directly onto the film emulsion during washing or, more often, by gas generated when the film is placed in an acid rinse after being in a developer containing sodium carbonate. A developer that does not contain this substance should be used, as well as a stop bath that is not too acidic (mix by measurement, not by guessing).
Brittle, buckled film	Film twists and buckles if attempts are made to dry it very rapidly, with excessive heat, in very dry air, or after excessive hardening in fix.
Creeping or running of emulsion	Caused by too rapid drying by heat, especially when film has not been adequately hardened during processing.
Reticulation	This refers to wrinkles and cracks in the emulsion that form a leather-like pattern. Usually caused by sharp changes in temperature between processing steps such as a cold rinse between warm developer and fixing bath, or too cold wash water. Can also be caused by pH shock; that is, by going directly from a very alkaline solution into one that is very acidic, or vice versa.

Errors in Processing

PROCESSING ERRORS: BLACK-AND-WHITE NEGATIVES (continued)

Problem	Probable Causes
Crystalline surface	Drying a negative without proper washing causes a deposit of hypo crystals on the surface. If caught right away, the negative can be rewashed and no permanent damage will result.
Silvery deposit on negative	Usually due to traces of sulfides in processing solutions. Sometimes due to silver sludge in developers, such as *Kodak D-76* developer, that have been overworked. These deposits are usually easy to wipe off while the film is still wet, but cannot be removed once the film is dry. (*See:* DICHROIC FOG.)
Green slime on negative	Usually due to the use of wash tanks that have become coated with deposits of algae from the water supply. Tanks should be washed; if used continuously, they should be scrubbed down frequently and sterilized with a Clorox solution periodically. Slime can usually be wiped off while the negative is still wet, but cannot be removed once it has dried.
White powdery deposit	This is usually aluminum sulfite and is due to lack of acid in the fixing bath; such a deposit seldom occurs with modern fixers that contain a boric-acid buffer.
Blue-green stain	If completely transparent, probably caused by using a chrome-alum fixing bath at high temperatures. When it is an overall stain, it will have no effect on printing and can be ignored.
Blue spots and stains	Small blue spots are due to iron in the water; they frequently occur when a negative is treated in Farmer's reducer that is near exhaustion.
Green, pink, and lavender stains	These are usually not very intense and are caused by traces of the antihalation layer of the film, or of the sensitizing dye used in making the emulsion. Even if overall they can be ignored; they have little or no effect upon printing.
Milky green stain	Usually caused by carry-over of developer into a chrome-alum fixing or stop bath.
Milky yellow stain	May be caused by insufficient fixing, or by films sticking together in the fixing bath. Sometimes caused by a deposit of colloidal sulfur that occurs because of excessive acid in the fixer. If it is due to incomplete fixing, the negatives can be refixed; if it is due to a sulfur deposit, it can sometimes be removed by treating the negatives in a strong sodium sulfite solution at about 45 C (100 F) after prehardening with formaldehyde.

PROCESSING ERRORS: BLACK AND WHITE PRINTS

Problem	Probable Cause
Black lines or streaks	These are abrasion marks on the paper that are caused by pressure or rubbing. They occur mostly on glossy papers. Unexposed paper should be handled with care to avoid this.
Gray cast over entire print	This cast is referred to as fog. Usually caused by unsafe darkroom illumination, occasionally by improperly compounded developer, or outdated paper. In the last case, outdated paper can sometimes be salvaged by adding a small amount of antifoggant such as benzotriazole or 6-nitrobenzimidazole nitrate to the developer.
Excessively contrasty tones: black, white, and harsh grays	Caused by a paper grade that is too hard for the negative in question. If a softer paper is not available, softer prints can sometimes be made by using a water bath prior to development of the paper, or by transferring the paper to plain water after development has begun.
Flat quality, low in contrast	Caused by a paper grade that is too soft for the negative in question. There is seldom any way to increase the contrast of a paper to any useful extent. Make another print using paper of a higher contrast grade.
Print too dark and flat	Caused by overexposing paper and/or using too soft paper.

Errors in Processing

Problem	Probable Cause
Print too dark, normal contrast	Grade of paper is correct. Problem caused by overexposing print.
Print too dark and contrasty	Caused by attempting to print up highlight detail from contrasty negative on paper that is too hard for subject.
Print too dark and foggy	Generally caused by forced development combined with overexposure.
Print too light, no highlight detail	Caused by underexposing either normal or hard paper.
Print too light, but ample highlight detail	Caused by using a paper grade too soft for the negative in question and cutting short exposure time to keep highlights clear or underdeveloping.
Prints all right in developer, but too light after fixing	Due to bleaching in hypo bath, which may occur because fixer is too strong or too warm, or because print is left in fixer too long. Overfixing is an easy error to make when a rapid (ammonium thiosulfate) fixer is used on papers.
Round, sharp-edged, white spots	Due to air bubbles in developer that occur because the print is developed face down, or because of insufficient agitation. The print should be turned over several times during development. Also caused by paper being splashed with drops of fixer prior to development.
Round, sharp-edged dark spots	Caused by air bells in hypo; developer in paper continues to develop in these areas after it has stopped in the remainder of the print. A stop bath between developer and fixing bath should always be used to avoid this. Prints should be agitated in the fixer.
Round, irregularly shaped, sharp-edged, brown or yellow spots, appearing some time after drying	Due to hypo remaining in the emulsion because of air bells or prints sticking together in the wash water.
Small, sharp brown spots	Probably caused by bits of iron rust in the wash water; if this trouble prevails it will be necessary to install a water filter in the darkroom water supply.
Fading of entire print on aging	Always due to incomplete fixing and/or incomplete washing. For maximum permanence, use the two-bath system of fixing, wash through a number of separate changes of fresh water, and use a hypo eliminator and a toner or gold protective solution. Use of a hypo clearing agent shortens the necessary wash time.
White fingerprints	Caused by handling the print with hypo-stained fingers before development.
Black fingerprints	Caused by handling the paper with developer-stained fingers before development.
Yellowish fingerprints	Caused by handling prints with hypo on fingers, after washing but before or during drying.
Small, white spots on print	Probably due to dust on negative or negative-carrier glass.
Small, black spots on print	Probably caused by printing a negative that has small dust spots or pinholes in the image.
Mottled gray print	Usually caused by using old paper, or paper that has been stored in damp or humid conditions. Add antifoggant to developer (benzotriazole or 6-nitrobenzimidazole nitrate). Could also be caused by gross underdevelopment.

PROCESSING ERRORS: BLACK AND WHITE PRINTS (continued)

Problem	Probable Cause
Greenish blacks	Occurs mainly with slower types of enlarging paper, and warm image-toned contact papers. Due to excessive potassium bromide in the developer, or to overexposure of the paper followed by shortened development.
Irregular purple spots	Caused when prints stick together in the hypo, and the developer continues to act in some areas. May be avoided by using an acid stop bath, with proper agitation, between developer and hypo.
Yellow stains appearing during development or immediately after placing print in fixer	This effect is usually caused by too warm a developer, contaminated developer, or failure to use stop bath between developer and fixing. When it occurs during development, it is usually due to forcing an underexposed print, or rubbing its surface with fingers in an attempt to bring up detail in one area. Yellow stains can also be caused by exposure of the print to air during development, especially in hot weather.

Color Materials

Relating visible imperfections in color films and papers to causes is very difficult, and in some cases impossible. Furthermore, there are many materials and processes, and what applies to one product and one process will probably not apply to another. Sometimes poor results are due to exposure problems that either occur in a camera or are caused by an enlarger; sometimes such results are due to poor storage conditions or processing errors.

In small-scale processing, color processing solutions are normally used once and discarded. By mixing solutions accurately, using careful processing techniques, avoiding contamination of chemicals, and following the instructions for times, temperatures, and agitation, one can avoid most processing errors. For some of its color processes, Kodak does have process error charts in instruction sheets or in data books, but there is none for color negative processes because it is exceedingly difficult to see color error in color negative images.

For large-scale processing, Kodak publishes a series of process-monitoring manuals. In process monitoring, densitometry is used to control a process. Process-control strips are processed along with regular film or paper, and certain areas on the processed strips are measured on a color densitometer. The readings are compared to a standard, and the differences are plotted on an ongoing graph. The plotted points form lines that run between limit lines when the process is under control. When the process gets out of control the lines form a pattern. Information in the manual, along with sample patterns given on wall charts, help the user interpret the patterns with respect to probable cause. In this way, potential process difficulties can often be found and corrected before valuable films or prints are ruined.

• *See also:* AERIAL FOG; ANTIFOGGANT; DEVELOPERS AND DEVELOPING; DICHROIC FOG; DIRECTIONAL EFFECTS; FOGGING; FUNGUS ON FILMS; RETICULATION; STAINS, REMOVAL.

Further Reading: Eastman Kodak Co. *Introduction to Color Process Monitoring.* Rochester, NY: Eastman Kodak Co. Happe, I. Bernard. *Your Film & the Lab.* (Media Manuals Ser.) New York, NY: Hastings House Publishers, Inc., 1975; Jacobson, C.I. *Developing: The Technique of the Negative,* 18th rev. ed. (Amphoto-Focal) New York, NY: Hastings House Publishers, Inc., 1972; Litzel, Otto. *Darkroom Magic,* 2nd ed. Garden City, NY: Amphoto, 1975; Mason, L.F. *Photographic Processing Chemistry.* New York, NY: Halstead Press, Division of John Wiley & Sons, Inc., 1975.

Evans, Ralph M.

(1905–1974)
American physicist

A pioneer in the development of color photography at Eastman Kodak Company, Evans' career was devoted chiefly to the study of color photography, its visual effects and subjective perception. In his early career at Kodak, he was responsible for the application of the Kodachrome film process to motion pictures and to applications of Kodachrome sheet film to professional and commercial use. He became assistant superintendent of color processing and development at Kodak Research Laboratories and then superintendent in charge of color control (later the photographic technology division), with the responsibility for standards and quality of all photographic products. Evan's work was widely published, and he was the holder of numerous patents in color photography.

Evidence Photography

Photography serves as a tool of police and other investigators to make a record of the scene of a crime or other incident, to show particular items of evidence and their relationship to the scene, and to make close-up records of significant portions of the scene. Some items of evidence are transient or perishable and must be recorded at the scene. Others can be removed to the laboratory where they can be examined at leisure and photographed with special techniques. Usually, a photographer can record and preserve essential information using straightforward photographic techniques. However, he or she may find that special lighting, close-up photography, or photography with infrared, ultraviolet, or x-radiation can reveal further information.

Classifications of Evidence Photographs

Photographic *replication,* or copying of a two-dimensional object, comes closest to picturing the real object. Photographs made at normal distances from scenes, people, or objects are *representations;* that is, they represent the three-dimensional world in two dimensions. Further *extension* of photographic technique divorces the images produced from a reality that is easily interpreted by a layman. Extension is implicit in such techniques as photomacrography, photomicrography, or aerial photography. Finally, a photographic method may be used to record invisible radiation: infrared, ultraviolet, x-ray. The result of such methods is photographic *analysis* of information.
1. Replication: copies and blueprints.
2. Representation: scenes, people, and close-ups.
3. Extension: photomacrography, photomicrography, and aerial photography.
4. Analysis: infrared, ultraviolet, and x-ray photography.

Photographs in Government

There is now little argument as to the validity or utility of photographs to demonstrate facts in the courtroom. Commonly, photographs of scenes or of common objects are simply supported as being adequate representations by an investigating officer or reliable witness. Usually the photographer does not even have to appear. (*See*: TESTIFYING IN COURT.)

Most clearly defined and understood of photographic evidence is the simple pictorial representation. Such a photograph may show a crime or accident scene, details of the scene, or the victim. These photographs, when viewed to give proper perspective, can be easily understood and fairly evaluated in the context of the average viewer's experience. The only issue with such photographs may stem from the question of whether they are a fair and accurate representation of the scene as it appeared to the investigator.

It is on this point that the photographer's effort is judged. The interpretation of "fair and accurate" may be contested in a case. But, if the photographer has produced a properly exposed, well lighted, technically correct photograph, it will be more readily accepted by the court.

Color Photographs

Color photographs are now widely taken as the norm by the public at large. Accurate color photographs are more realistic and thus, unless otherwise objectionable, better evidence than black-and-white photographs.

Where actual colors are in question, an expert may be required to discuss the accuracy of photographic rendition. Under normal circumstances, however, the fidelity of color materials is sufficient, and the color photograph reproduces the scene more realistically than does a black-and-white print.

Photographs and Expert Testimony

Some types of photographic evidence may require expert interpretation and supportive testimony to define the value of the exhibit. Such materials include larger-than-life-size photomacrographs, photographs taken through the microscope, photographs taken by invisible infrared or ultraviolet radiation, radiographs, and photographs with changes in tone reproduction affected by filters.

(Right) A black-and-white photograph fails to show the distinctive color of the tool box or the red paint scraps adhering to the crowbar.

Color photographs tend to be more realistic and therefore easier to understand. Where color itself contains the important information, a black-and-white photograph simply cannot do the job.

In the field or in the laboratory, investigators and forensic scientists may either make their own photographs or rely on a photographic technician. At other times, a professional photographer may be called upon to assist. Whatever the division of labor, both the scientist and the photographer should have an understanding of the capabilities of various photographic techniques.

Obtaining Photographic Evidence

While the photographer is usually a technician working under the direction of an investigating officer, he or she should take the initiative to learn the elements of the case. With this preparation, independent judgment can be used to assess the requirements for photographs, angles of coverage, appropriate supplementary lighting, close-ups, and other technical factors. Frequently, further information and leads are developed by subsequent study of photographs of a crime or accident scene made by an expert photographer.

In trying cases, the attorney must relate particular details of a scene to the locale. It is therefore imperative that the photographer obtain overall pictures of a scene that can be related to a close-up. This connection is so important that it should not be sacrificed for expediency or other reasons. A wide-angle lens will give adequate scene coverage when it is impossible to move to a vantage point where a normal lens would suffice.

When taking the overall shots of the scene, the photographer should try to avoid inclusion of extraneous people, automobiles, or other confusing elements. Such elements not only may mislead a jury considering a case but also may obscure important detail. Investigating officers will usually cooperate in clearing the scene for these overall views.

Where the topography of a scene is important, an aerial photograph may be the best way to show this. Since aerial photography may be expensive or inaccessible for departments without their own plane or helicopter, improvisation may be required. Tall, adjacent buildings may provide an adequate view. An aerial ladder or articulated boom lent by the fire department may provide a suitable elevated viewpoint.

The photographer should not attempt to recreate the scene if conditions have changed before he or she arrives. Repositioning vehicles or having an officer assume the apparent location of a body that has been removed is *not* helpful. There is no assurance that the repositioning is accurate, and the photographs are open to attack as "contrived." The photographer should picture the scene *as he or she finds it.*

Close-ups of physical evidence, weapons, automobile damage, body wounds, and other details should be made on the scene and before the evidence is moved. Some details will, of course, require laboratory treatment and lighting, but the on-scene shot will establish the original condition and position of the object.

Color photographs show the subject differentiated from backgrounds that may appear similar in black-and-white photographs. In practically every case, such differentiation provides useful, additional information. As for black-and-white materials, the lighting and exposure for color photographs are important. Deep shadows should get supplemental

Aerial photographs made with conventional films and cameras are useful to present a clear picture of a crime scene. Whereas high altitude pictures require special films and techniques, as well as the use of a plane or helicopter, oblique views, taken from high buildings or fire-department equipment, may be entirely satisfactory.

Evidence Photography

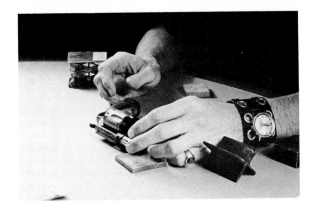 

It is a good practice to photograph dusted fingerprints before attempting to lift them, because the lift might distort or destroy the prints. (Top left) The photographer arranges a revolver to get a photograph of a print on the cylinder. (Top right) For identification of the weapon and for accurate measurement, the original evidence tag and a dated, initialled scale are placed next to the gun. (Bottom left) After the evidence technician lifts a fingerprint from the cylinder, he will make a record of the lift. (Bottom right) Lifted fingerprints can be photographed individually on a copying setup designed for this purpose. Photos courtesy of Chicago Police Department.

Photographing Trace Evidence. The following are methods of photographing trace evidence.

Blood. Blood oxidizes and turns brown. Frequently the crime laboratory will remove the blood from a weapon to analyze it, and there might be objections to a weapon being offered in evidence after it has been cleaned. A photograph of the origi-nal condition of the weapon may overcome an objection that is raised.

Use color film, especially with old, dry blood, which may not record satisfactorily in a black-and-white photograph. Bloodstains are frequently found where a background of similar color makes it difficult to photograph. There are several methods of differentiating such stains; and in very difficult cases,

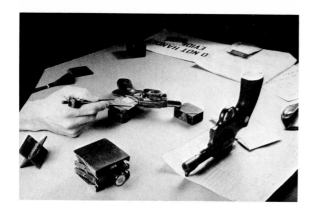

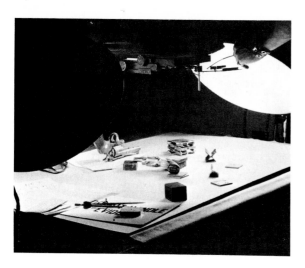

all should be tried because each method may contribute some information.

The objective in photographing blood is to separate the bloodstain and the surroundings as much as possible. A Kodak Wratten filter No. 25 (red) and panchromatic black-and-white film may lighten the blood more than its surroundings. A Kodak Wratten filter No. 47 (blue) may darken the blood more than the background. The use of a very low grazing light, especially in photographing fabrics, will sometimes record bloodstains because of the difference in reflectivity between the blood and the nap of the fabric.

Fresh blood, and sometimes oxidized blood, will fluoresce when illuminated with ultraviolet light. Use a panchromatic film and a filter such as a Kodak Wratten filter No. 2A over the camera lens. Turn off the room lights. Since only the area that fluoresces will record with this arrangement, make a second negative with flash from exactly the same camera position to show overall detail. A positive transparency made from the ultraviolet negative and superimposed over the standard print shows the exact location of the blood spot.

Footprints* and Tire Impressions. Imprints of shoes and tires are often found at the crime scene. Although these may be reproduced by plaster casting, they should be photographed first. Place the camera on a tripod with the film plane parallel to the ground. In the case of footprints, include a ruler beside the print and adjust the camera to obtain as large an image as possible. In the case of tire prints, select a length of track for best tread pattern, especially areas that reveal defects, such as cuts, which may help to identify an individual tire. Photograph in sections a sufficient length of tire tracks to correspond to the circumference of each wheel.

---

*The term footprint is used to define print impressions made by either the shod or unshod foot.

Evidence Photography

Dusty Shoe Prints. Occasionally dusty shoe prints are found on a newly waxed floor or on paper strewn on the floor. Although these may be visible to the eye by use of cross-lighting, floor color, printing (such as newsprint), or the pattern on the linoleum may make them extremely difficult to photograph. Sometimes a dusty shoe print can be lifted by using a black rubber matrix material with a tacky surface. If the print lift image is weak, use an extremely high-contrast film for maximum contrast. When a suspect is found, photograph his shoe or a dusty print made from it. If the negatives of the original dusty print and of the suspect's shoe print are identical in size, it should be possible to superimpose the two negatives, or positives made from them, to show that the two match in every respect.

Paint Chips One of the most exacting photomacrographic assignments for the forensic photographer is demonstrating that two paint chips originally came from the same object. The evidence can be photographed to show how the two pieces fit together or to show exact matching equivalence of paint layers in the chips.

Evidence that two paint chips were once joined is offered in the accompanying illustration. Here, the two edges were photographed to demonstrate that the paint layers were exactly the same. Since this record was made at a camera magnification of $30\times$, there was very little depth of field available. Therefore, the chips had to be presented perpendicular to the subject-lens axis.

When the chips were placed vertically under the camera, the highest edge of one chip was at the same level as the highest edge of the other. The lighting was established with the 30-watt filament at 45 degrees above the chips in line with the space between.

(Left) This edge view of two paint chips shows the matching paint layers. The drawing at right shows how the paint chips were held to make this photograph.

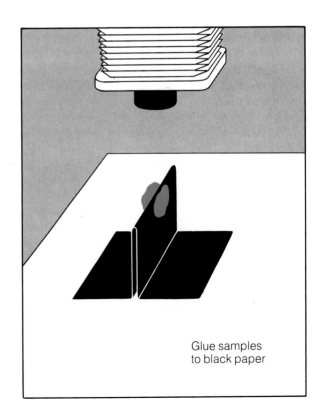

Glue samples
to black paper

Fingerprint Photography. The latent fingerprint is often the most convincing evidence that the suspect was present at the crime scene. Without photography, such evidence would lose much of its effectiveness.

Since the latent fingerprint is easily destroyed by handling and by exposure to weather, fingerprints at the crime scene should be photographed promptly. Often fingerprints are found on objects that can be taken to the police laboratory. The procedures used in fingerprint photography may also be applicable in photographing palm prints, sole prints, glove impressions, and similar patterns. (Fingerprint photography is the subject of a separate article.)

Preparing Photographs for Court Exhibit

Photographic Prints. There are two choices for presenting photographic prints as evidence. Large display prints can be made and shown on an easel that is placed so that judge, jury, attorneys, and a witness can see the exhibit. This is most useful where a witness may have to give detailed testimony about attributes of the photograph. Large prints also provide dramatic impact precisely because of their size. This may give rise to objections upon introduction of such exhibits.

A second method of presenting prints that is more widely used and easier to accomplish is production of a number of duplicate prints of moderate size that can be held in the hand and viewed while a witness is giving testimony. Enough prints must be provided so that the judge, both attorneys, the witness, the court clerk, and the jurors can view the prints without passing them from hand to hand. Usually one print for every two jurors is sufficient. Prints to be hand-held for viewing should be enlarged according to the guide for true perspective at normal viewing distances. (*See:* PERSPECTIVE.)

The best way to make sure that all prints are alike is to make them all at the same time. While it is always best to anticipate the required number of prints, reprints are sometimes needed. Reprints are more easily matched to the first prints if data on magnification, filtration, and processing are logged at the time of initial processing.

Since the photographic exhibit is actually a visual aid for the court, it is often permissible to use markings to assist the jurors in understanding points of proof. Arrows or lines connecting significant points in the subject matter with identifying numbers or letters are the most common markings. Any writing placed on the exhibit should be free of opinions or issues. Finally, the witness who is using the exhibit should be prepared to explain all markings made on the photographs. If the photographer has any doubt about the admissibility of certain writings or markings, the exhibit should be prepared in two forms—one with and the other without the markings. The use of transparent overlays is helpful for this purpose.

Composite Exhibits. With certain restrictions, such as those just given, many of the common visual-aid techniques can be used in exhibits if they provide accurate information to assist the jury in understanding points of evidence. Clarity and usefulness are the essential qualities of an effective court exhibit. The form that the exhibit takes will depend on the nature of the points of evidence—these may be similarities or dissimilarities.

To make a composite exhibit, photograph the subjects with identical lighting and enlarge to the same degree. Then mount them side by side on one board so that the significant areas are adjacent or in corresponding positions and properly aligned. Lines and symbols can be drawn in to identify points of similarity or difference. An appropriate legend can also be included to explain the symbols. The composite picture is now rephotographed and copies made. These final prints are mounted and the print data inscribed on the backs. Relative size can be shown by including a scale in each of the original photographs. This technique is especially useful for fingerprints, shoe marks, and similar impressions. Handwriting and typewriting comparisons and other document exhibits can also be made in this manner.

Another technique for illustrating similarities is to place part of one photograph above and in careful alignment with another so that the eye is led from a point of similarity in the upper photograph to the corresponding point in the lower. The procedure for this type of exhibit is also applicable to shells, firing pin indentations, tool marks, and matching pieces such as broken ornaments or glass fragments.

To show that two objects have identical outlines, a positive transparency of one can be placed over a similar transparency of the other, adjusted so that the outlines coincide, and viewed in front of a strong light source. This technique of illustration is especially useful in proving forgery by tracing; the fact that the questioned signature is an exact duplicate of another signature can be demonstrated convincingly. The method is applicable also to hit-and-run cases involving broken segments, where one piece was found at the scene and another in the suspect's possession. By fitting one transparency over the other, the identity of the curve of the fracture is shown clearly. An alternative method is to prepare two slides and project them on one screen so that the image of one lies directly over the other.

The use of a slide projector is usually admissible in court as a method of presenting photographic evidence. This procedure is especially convenient if the photographs have been made in the form of color transparencies. Many medical examiners and coroners prepare a set of color slides as a routine part of the autopsy. These slides are then available for court demonstration in the event that a criminal trial later requires testimony of the autopsy surgeon on the cause and manner of death.

• *See also:* CLOSE-UP PHOTOGRAPHY; CRIME PHOTOGRAPHY; DOCUMENT EXAMINATION BY PHOTOGRAPHY; FINGERPRINT PHOTOGRAPHY; FIRE AND ARSON PHOTOGRAPHY; INFRARED PHOTOGRAPHY; PERSPECTIVE; PHOTOMACROGRAPHY; PHOTOMICROGRAPHY; SCIENTIFIC PHOTOGRAPHY; SURVEILLANCE PHOTOGRAPHY; TESTIFYING IN COURT; TRAFFIC ACCIDENT PHOTOGRAPHY; ULTRAVIOLET AND FLUORESCENCE PHOTOGRAPHY.

Further Reading: Eastman Kodak Co. *Photographic Surveillance Techniques for Law Enforcement Agencies.* Rochester, NY: Eastman Kodak Co., 1972. Mandel, Mike and Larry Sultan. *Evidence.* Santa Cruz, CA: Clatworthy Colorvues, 1977; Scott, Charles C. *Photographic Evidence.* St. Paul, MN: West Publishing Co., 1969;

Existing-Light Photography

Photography by existing or available light means using only the light that happens to be on the scene. This includes the light from table and floor lamps, ceiling fixtures, fluorescent lamps, spotlights, neon signs, windows, skylights, candles, fireplaces, and any other light source that provides the natural lighting of the scene. Existing light is the type of light found in homes, schools, museums, churches, restaurants, theaters, and auditoriums. Outdoor scenes at twilight or after dark are also considered to be existing-light situations. Daylight pictures, while technically made with existing light, are usually not considered to be within the scope of this category.

Existing-light photography produces pictures that appear natural. Even a skillfully lighted flash or photolamp picture may look artificial and contrived by comparison with a good existing-light picture. Existing-light photography provides opportunities to make pictures that are dramatic, creative, soothing, romantic, or even harsh and pitiless. Also, existing-light photography allows greater freedom of movement, because it does not require extra lighting equipment. It is as easy to photograph distant subjects as it is to photograph nearby subjects, because camera-to-subject distance does not affect exposure as it does when you are using flash. Also, existing light is less expensive than flashbulbs.

Equipment and Film

You will need a camera with an *f*/2.8 or faster lens, and a shutter with a "B" or "T" setting for time exposures. Long exposures are required in some types of existing-light photography, such as when taking pictures of fireworks displays. For exposures longer than 1/25 or 1/30 sec., place the camera on a firm support. A tripod is ideal, but a tabletop, hand railing, wall, or similar steady surface can be a good substitute. A cable release will prevent jiggling the camera when the shutter is released.

A camera with an *f*/2.8 or faster lens combined with a high-speed film will let you photograph many subjects without a camera support. You can hand-hold a camera when using shutter speeds of 1/25 to 1/30 sec. or faster. For sharp pictures, hold the camera steady as you gently squeeze the shutter release; this minimizes camera movement. Picture-taking using a hand-held camera offers more flexibility than when using a camera support. You can shoot faster, more easily, and less obtrusively in order to capture natural, candid expressions.

Since many existing-light scenes have low light levels, it is usually desirable to use a high-speed film. However, where the existing light is brighter (near windows or a skylight, for example) or when the camera is on a tripod, you can use a medium-speed

Existing light may be used to create many moods. Here, soft colors from a fading sky give the impression of calm and tranquility to this quiet harbor scene.

film. For those situations that do not require a high-speed film, you can successfully use slower-speed color films with ASA ratings from ASA 25 to 80, or ASA 125 black-and-white films.

Using a high-speed film for existing-light picture-taking has many advantages. More film speed helps get enough exposure for hand-held shots of dimly lighted scenes; permits using faster shutter speeds for stopping action; enables you to use telephoto lenses, which require higher shutter speeds for hand-held picture-taking; and allows a smaller lens opening to gain greater sharpness of near and far objects in the same picture—more depth of field.

Very often in existing-light picture-taking with color film you need all the film speed you can get. Many processing labs offer special processing services that can increase the speed of most color films up to 2½ times.

Taking Pictures Indoors

For color pictures of indoor existing-light scenes that are illuminated by tungsten light, use tungsten film. For indoor pictures where windows or skylights are providing the light, use daylight film; you can also use tungsten film with a No. 85B filter under these circumstances. An exposure meter is a great help in determining indoor exposures. This is especially true in a home or museum where you can easily approach your subject to make an exposure-meter reading. If the background includes a bright window or light that would influence the meter reading, take a close-up reading of just the principal subject.

Pictures taken indoors in existing daylight are especially pleasing because of the soft, diffuse quality of the lighting and the squint-free expressions subjects will have. They are easy to take because there is usually more light than with other kinds of existing light. Open all the window drapes in the room and pose the subject so that diffuse daylight illuminates the front or side of the face. Avoid poses that put too much of the subject's face in shadow, unless you want a special effect such as a silhouette. You can also photograph a subject in direct sunlight coming through a window. There will be plenty of light, but you may find that the picture will be very contrasty.

Some artificial lighting is also quite contrasty. For example, subjects that are close to lamps will be well illuminated, while other areas in the room will be comparatively dark. Turning on all the lights in the room will make the light more even and will provide more light for taking pictures.

To minimize contrasty artificial lighting in interior pictures, bounce fill light off a white ceiling. A simple way to do this in an average-size room is to position one or more reflector photolamps near the camera and aim them at the ceiling. Tilt the lamps slightly so that the light will strike the ceiling between the camera and the subject. Adding bounce light means you will not be making true existing-light pictures, but this light will reduce the contrast of the existing lighting without spoiling its natural

The soft quality of daylight coming through a window is ideal for portrait photographs. Shadows are muted and the effect is generally flattering. In this photograph, some of the window light has been bounced off a reflector behind and to the right of the subjects for additional fill light.

When the main light source in the room is from fluorescent lamps, color rendition will be on the greenish side.

Use of daylight film and filters will render the color more natural. (See the article on Fluorescent Light Photography.)

appearance. In addition, the extra light may let you use a shutter speed fast enough for hand-held shooting. Since bounce light makes the lighting more uniform, you can photograph a subject moving around the room in the general vicinity of the bounce light without changing shutter speed or lens opening.

Fluorescent lamps in a room may cause poor color rendition in color pictures, since most fluorescent illumination is deficient in red. When fluorescent lights provide the main light source, use day-

light color film. The results will probably still look greenish, but with tungsten film they would be decidedly blue. With daylight fluorescent bulbs and daylight film, a CC40M plus CC30Y filter will improve the rendition; with cool-white bulbs, a CC30M filter will usually suffice. The CC30M filter requires an increase in exposure of two-thirds stop, while the CC40M plus CC30Y filter requires a one-stop increase in exposure. When fluorescent lamps are providing most of the light, you can minimize their effect by aiming reflector photolamps at a white ceiling.

When the subject includes both very bright areas and large, very dark areas, such as an indoor ice show or any other event where spotlights are used, an exposure meter is not much help. The meter sees the large dark areas surrounding the bright areas, and the meter needle barely moves. Actually, there is plenty of light on the spotlighted subject. An exposure of 1/60 sec. at $f/4$ with Ektachrome 200 (daylight) film, or its equivalent, is effective. With the carbon-arc spotlights usually used in theaters and auditoriums, daylight film gives better results than tungsten. For black-and-white prints, use

Photographs taken at night require slow shutter speeds with a firmly supported camera. The trails of light created by moving traffic add interesting patterns.

Existing-Light Photography

Tri-X pan film or its equivalent, ASA 400 at 1/125 sec. between $f/4$ and $f/5.6$.

Taking Pictures Outdoors at Night

An excellent time to shoot "night" color pictures outdoors is just before complete darkness, when some rich blue (or orange) still remains in the sky. The deep color of the sky at dusk provides a dramatic background. For outdoor picture-taking at night, the choice of either daylight film or tungsten film is a matter of personal taste. Pictures taken on tungsten film may look more natural, while pictures taken on daylight film will have a warmer, more yellow-red appearance. Both types of film produce pleasing results.

When the subject is evenly illuminated and you can get close enough to take an exposure-meter reading, do so. Many floodlighted buildings, statues, and store windows are subjects of this type. Night sporting events are also usually evenly illuminated. Before you take your seat at the event, take an exposure-meter reading from a position close to where the action will take place, and set the lens opening and shutter speed accordingly. Use as high a shutter speed as possible to help stop the action.

In many modern sports stadiums, mercury-vapor lamps illuminate the outdoor playing field. These lights have a slightly blue-green appearance compared to conventional tungsten lamps. With mercury-vapor lighting, color pictures will be better on daylight film, although they will probably look bluish-green because the lights are deficient in red.

One of the most exciting and colorful subjects to photograph outdoors at night is an aerial fireworks display. Put the camera on a tripod, aim it in the direction of the display, and focus the camera on infinity. Set the lens opening, and with the shutter set on "B" or "T," keep the shutter open for several bursts.

Bracketing. To be sure of getting a properly exposed picture of an especially important subject, bracket the exposure. Take one shot at the suggested exposure, one at one-half the exposure, and another one at twice the suggested exposure. If it is a case of "now or never," take two more pictures—at one-quarter and at four times the suggested exposure.

• *See also:* AVAILABLE-LIGHT PHOTOGRAPHY. FIREWORKS, PHOTOGRAPHING; MOONLIGHT PHOTOGRAPHY;

The slow shutter speeds required for many existing light subjects may be turned to special advantage for a panning effect.

Existing-Light Photography

Exploded Views

Exploded-view photographs provide the viewer with positive identification of the many parts and pieces that make up a given machine, instrument, or manufactured assembly. The various parts, shown in their order of assembly, appear to float in air in correct alignment and perspective. In parts lists, it is a simple matter to key each part with a part number or index number and to indicate which pieces are available only as complete assemblies. Instruction manuals that include exploded views are useful in original assembly operations as well as in maintenance and repair work.

This article explains one method for producing a quality exploded view.

Equipment and Materials

The following equipment and materials are needed to make an exploded view:

1. Light box (or the equivalent).
2. View camera and lens.
3. Boom spot (work light).
4. 1500-watt floodlights.
5. Mini-spots (only if necessary).
6. White cards and blotters (background and bounce fill light).
7. Ruled overlay sheets.
8. "Make-up" supplies.
9. Camel's-hair brushes.
10. Acetate sheeting (12 or 15 mil).
11. Scissors.
12. Beeswax.
13. Assorted wood blocks.
14. Glass (shelves, strips, and squares).
15. Small tools (for disassembling parts).
16. Kodak Tri-X pan professional film 4164 (Estar thick base) or Kodak Royal pan film 4141 (Estar thick base).

Light Box. A light-box background, constructed of ¾-inch plywood and measuring 38 inches square and 18 inches high, is an ideal size for most small parts. Four 30-inch fluorescent-tube fixtures are mounted in the flat-white interior and the bottom is left open. White seamless paper is slipped under the unit for additional reflection; this can be replaced readily as it becomes soiled. The top surface is ¼-inch *safety* plate glass that is capable of supporting parts weighing 25 to 30 pounds. Under the plate glass, and separated from it by a small air space, is a sheet of opalescent glass for even light diffusion. Small, 12-inch-high benches with swivel castors can be easily built and are useful when aligning parts on the glass surface. A small shelf at the bottom of these benches is a handy place for work materials.

A substitute for the light-box background is a sheet of safety plate glass firmly supported approximately 20 or 24 inches from the floor. Two floods, directed from either side of the glass, bounce light evenly from the white seamless paper on the floor up through the glass.

A light box of convenient size for photographing exploded views can be constructed with four fluorescent-tube fixtures mounted in a flat-white interior.

Applying Makeup to Parts

The first thing to do is to disassemble the parts carefully so that they can be laid out in order of assembly. Then, clean each piece thoroughly, removing any lubricating medium or foreign deposits. Lay the parts out as they will be photographed and study each piece to see if it requires make-up before you proceed.

Large areas of stainless steel or bright metal should be sprayed with a dulling spray to prevent objectionable hot spots (specular highlights). Smaller areas can be treated with material such as screen or stage makeup, applied with a camel's-hair brush. Eyeliner can be purchased for light-colored objects or for a darker effect. A second, dry brush should be used to smooth out the makeup.

Where edges or screw holes do not show readily, they can be edged with a black wax pencil, or, in many cases, even a plain lead pencil. Conversely, if the part is dark, white pencil or chalk can be used to define it. For a small, important detail, such as the recess on the thrust washer in the accompanying figure of the finished reproduction of the pump as-

sembly, particular care must be taken. Often, as was done here, a footnote can be added to emphasize the point. It should be mentioned that *including too much detail* in a single photograph is a frequent mistake of beginners. Note that three separate illustrations of the pump assembly are used, with one illustration devoted entirely to the thrust washer. Also note that only representative attaching parts are shown; the total number of parts is placed in parentheses before the part number (in this case, two seals and four screws are *not shown* in the main pump assembly illustration).

Any and all retouching that can be done before the photograph is taken will save a great deal of time and, also, the expense of final artwork. If a job is well executed, the only work necessary on the final print will be the blocking out of supporting devices.

Setting Up the Parts

After retouching all parts, place them on the glass in order of assembly, carefully following the engineering drawings to check part locations. To stand small parts up, mount them on a small strip

(Left) As demonstrated by this illustration on a page from a technical manual, it is preferable to show more complex pieces in separate detail, as in the two smaller shots below the main picture. (Below) To stand parts upright, mount them on small pieces of acetate and support them with beeswax. These supports will be airbrushed out in the final photograph.

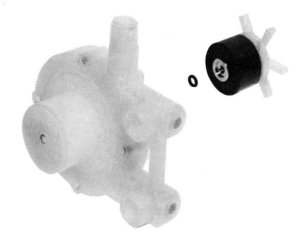

1008

The best camera angle for most exploded-view subjects is 45 degrees above and to one side of the assembly. To avoid the need for possible reshooting, light the entire set, even when only a small section is required at the present time.

or square of acetate with a little beeswax supporting the piece from behind. Even the smallest screw should be mounted on a base so that it can be slid into exact position later. The base should be cut as small as possible so that it won't interfere with other parts lined up close to it. Heavier pieces can be mounted on small squares of glass. If certain parts, such as the O-rings in the pump-assembly illustration, are standard to many different pieces of equipment and constantly reappear, it may save time to obtain a full set of the various sizes and glue them permanently to glass uprights.

To obtain an illusion of height, parts can be moved away from the camera. There is a limit to this procedure, however, and if a part becomes too small in relation to others, it will have to be elevated. This illustrates the need for various-sized blocks (painted flat white) and, in some cases, glass shelves or long, narrow strips of glass. When using glass, be careful to avoid any reflections from the edges; should this occur, the edges can be painted black and then opaqued out later.

Camera Angle

For most subjects, the most desirable camera angle is 45 degrees above and to the side of the assembly. From this vantage point, you can see the top, side, and end of most parts. In many cases, with

a 38-inch light box that is 18 inches from the floor, this places the camera (assuming a 14-inch lens on 8″ × 10″ format) at a comfortable working height. Climbing up and down a ladder each time the ground glass is checked takes its toll by the end of the day.

It is wise to fill the 8″ × 10″ format fully when composing the picture, thereby making any necessary artwork easier and more accurate. Also, light the entire set in front of the camera, even when only a small section is required. This can often eliminate reshooting the picture if the client should decide to include a larger area after seeing the finished print.

A team of two men is almost a necessity for any kind of production; one man is needed to align the parts on the ground glass while the second man moves the parts into position. Because most of the time work is done with the lens stopped down somewhat (for proper depth), the brightest ground-glass image possible is helpful. Two or three suggestions may be useful. Black paper taped to the rear bed of the camera is helpful in cutting reflections from the floor. A small bib under the camera bellows cuts the glare from the light box. (A semi-permanent bib can easily be constructed by sewing some elastic tape to the upper corners of a 12″ × 3″ or 12″ × 4″ rectangle of focusing cloth. The tape goes over the rear part of the camera bellows just ahead of the ground-glass back.) If no one else is working in the studio, it is helpful to darken the area behind the camera. Also consider setting up a separate shooting area for this type of work.

Ruled Overlay Sheets

The use of overlay masks on the ground-glass greatly simplifies the procedure of placing the parts in their exact position. These overlays are used as a guide for exploding several rows of parts and keeping these rows aligned.

The accompanying illustration (greatly reduced) shows such a mask. The actual overall size is 8″ × 10″, and spacing between lines is $\frac{3}{16}$ inch. Note the combination of alternate solid and broken lines that work out from the center; these make it easier to follow any given line from one end to the other. An additional set of overlays, with the lines ¼ inch apart, is useful for making exploded views that contain just a few parts or all-in-line parts.

When rows of parts go off in another direction, a second overlay is used on the ground glass to establish that line of direction, which is usually at a right angle to the first. A third mask, made from a 3″ × 5″ corner of solid lines from one of the 8″ × 10″ masks, is useful for moving around the ground glass and checking for even spacing between

parts on any given line of direction. To produce an exploded view that is not only neat but also easy to grasp, it is important, first, that no two parts overlap and, second, that the relative spacing between all parts be equal.

Ruled overlay sheets can be produced easily from flat copy on Kodak professional line copy film 6573 or Kodalith ortho film 4556, type 3 (Estar thick base). The artwork should be made oversized and reduced to the desired spacing between the lines when the copy is photographed.

Lighting

Lighting is a somewhat personal thing with photographers; each has his or her own lighting techniques. Here is one method that many photographers use with success. Use a 750-watt boom spot (or flood) for a work light directly over and slightly forward of the setup. Place two 1500-watt floods on either side of the camera, one slightly higher than lens level, and the other at (or slightly below) lens level. This will produce an even, well-rounded lighting that may seem somewhat flat. Flat lighting it is; its object is to retain all the detail possible without being dramatic.

If the work light does not produce flare, it can remain on to add some sparkle and highlight. Be

(Left) An overlay mask consisting of straight and broken lines, placed on the back of the camera's ground glass, is helpful in aligning rows of parts. This sample is reduced from the original 8″ × 10″ size. (Right) A view through the overlay mask shows how it is used.

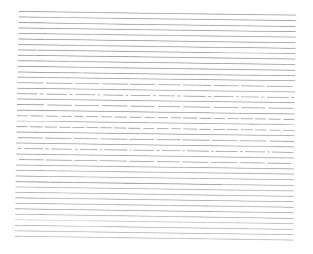

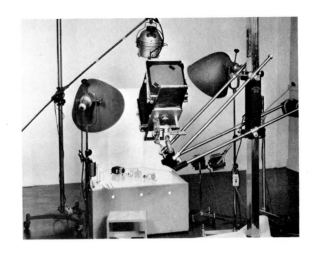

sure that it does not create any hard shadows that might confuse the outline of a part. If there are any dark holes or black sections of parts, a mini-spot or two will take care of them. Again, be careful not to create objectionable shadows. A white card or blotter supported below the lens and running from it to the front of the light box helps to fill the lower front surfaces of the subject.

Make a final check of the ground glass for accurate spacing between parts, and then expose a test sheet of film.

Exposure

Two exposures are required: one for the front-lighted subjects with the light box off; the other for the light box background with the front lights off. The negative should retain detail in both the highlight and the shadow areas. With the light box off, read the darkest area and, after calculating for any bellows factor involved, base the exposure on this reading. This basic exposure will vary somewhat with the contrast of the subject matter; this method, however, produces a fully exposed negative that can be adjusted if necessary by cutting back on the normal developing time.

The background exposure (additional light-box exposure) will also vary with the subject. Parts of stainless steel or shiny metal will burn out or lose their sharp edge if too much exposure is given. As a general rule, the light-box exposure should be 50 to 100 percent longer than the front light exposure.

Keep the shutter set on "T" rather than on the bulb-exposure setting to reduce the possibility of camera movement between the split exposures. Or better still, have the top lights plugged into a separate spider box that has its own on-off switch.

If the negative is printed with just the right amount of contrast and still holds all the detail, the exploded view will make an ideal reproduction. The light box gives a clean, shadowless edge to the parts and makes routing out the unwanted items, such as the supports and background, quite easy. By following this procedure step by step (with care), it is a simple matter to turn out a quality exploded view.

In spite of careful exposure and processing, it is sometimes difficult to get adequate density in the background so that it will print white. One technique used that produces very high background density is to make a second negative of the same setup with only the background light on, using an extremely high-contrast film like Kodalith ortho type 3 film. Exposure should be such that there is no detail in the objects being photographed, but a very high density in the background. The normal negative is registered with the high-contrast negative and taped. The two are printed as one negative. A great deal of hand opaquing can be eliminated by this method.

• *See also:* BACKGROUNDS, ELIMINATING; BLOCK OUT; RETOUCHING.

Exposure

Exposure is the action of radiant energy that produces a change in a material or substance sensitive to that energy. In conventional photographic materials, it is the action of light that reduces or breaks down silver halides sufficiently to form a latent (invisible) record of the pattern of light intensities, or—in the case of printing-out materials—a visible record.

Exposure is quantitative; it is the product of the total light intensity and the amount of time the light strikes an emulsion. Previously, the relationship was expressed by the formula

$$E = It$$

where E is the exposure, I the light intensity, and t the time in seconds. Revision of the symbols used in the International System of Measurement has changed the formula to

$$H = Et$$

where H is the exposure, E the intensity of the light, and t the time in seconds. H is expressed in meter-candle-seconds, lux seconds, or footcandle seconds, depending on the unit of measurement used for intensity.

Camera exposures are primarily controlled by lens aperture and shutter-speed settings. Filters such as neutral density filters can also be used to reduce light intensity in order to control exposure. Shutter speeds and f-stops are related in such a way that it is possible to achieve the same exposure with a variety of settings. For example, $f/4$ at 1/250 sec., $f/5.6$ at 1/125 sec., and $f/8$ at 1/60 sec. produce equivalent exposures. Photographic emulsions produce the same response to equivalent exposures over a reasonably wide range. However, long or very short exposures do not produce the same response; additional exposure or adjusted development is required to compensate. (*See:* RECIPROCITY EFFECT.)

Calculating Film Exposure

Film exposure is calculated on the basis of the emulsion speed, generally given as an ASA speed number. An exposure meter is the most accurate way of determining correct exposure. A simple rule,

however, provides universal exposure information for color and black-and-white films: *Exposure of average subjects under sun and open sky is:*

$$f/16 \text{ at } \frac{1}{\text{film speed}}$$

Exposure by flash is calculated from a guide number that relates the film speed to the shutter speed required for synchronization. Dividing the guide number by the flash-to-subject distance gives the f-number to which the aperture must be set. For example, if the guide number is 32 and the flash-to-subject distance is 8 feet, the lens must be set to $32 \div 8 = f/4$.

Generally, exposure of a black-and-white negative film is calculated so as to place the dark subject values on the toe of the characteristic curve of the film's response. Then development can be adjusted to control the contrast of middle tones and highlights. A common way to calculate such an exposure is to take a reflected-light meter reading of a dark subject area and reduce the meter-indicated exposure by the equivalent of two stops. (*See:* EXPOSURE TECHNIQUES.)

Proper exposure of reversal and color films can be calculated from an incident-light meter reading or a reflected-light reading from an 18 percent gray card held at the subject position. Alternatively, it may be based on a reflected-light reading from a key subject area such as skin tone, from a standard gray card, or by reading the entire subject area.

Exposure of Print Materials

Exposure of print materials is usually determined by exposing a variety of test strips or by making a single test exposure through a Kodak projection print scale. There are also various kinds of photometers available for on-easel exposure determination. They must be calibrated to the print material in use by practical testing. There is no uniform system of speed ratings for papers on which exposure calculations can be based.

The response of photographic material to exposure is measured by determining the density of the silver image or dye deposit produced after processing. Thus, the effect of exposure can be stated accurately only in terms of specified processing. However, some generalizations are possible. Underexposure of a film fails to register details in the darkest part of the subject, and usually produces a final image—print or slide—that is too dark and lacking in contrast. Overexposure of a film loses detail in the lightest areas of the subject, and produces images that are too light and may be excessively grainy.

Proper Exposure

Various rules of thumb for judging exposure of unusual subjects or lighting conditions are often given in phrases such as "overexpose and underexpose." The implied reference point, of course, is what would normally be done with an average subject under normal lighting conditions. When dealing with atypical situations, however, the exposure that secures the desired results is neither over- nor under-, it is the *proper* exposure. "Overexposure" and "underexposure" are correctly used only to describe misexposure of a given situation or subject. The primary method of avoiding wrong exposure is to carefully measure the luminance (brightness) range of the subject and relate it to the exposure range of the film in use. This method makes it possible to anticipate the need for other than normal processing of black-and-white films.

• *See also:* AVAILABLE-LIGHT PHOTOGRAPHY; BRACKETING EXPOSURES; BRIGHTNESS RANGE; CONTRAST; CONTRAST INDEX; EXPOSURE METERS AND CALCULATORS; EXPOSURE TECHNIQUES; FLASH PHOTOGRAPHY; *f*-NUMBER; *f*-STOP; GUIDE NUMBERS; LIGHT; MULTIPLE EXPOSURE TECHNIQUES; RECIPROCITY EFFECT; TEST STRIPS; ZONE SYSTEM.

Exposure Meters and Calculators

Photographic light meters or exposure meters measure light intensities and have computers to find camera settings that will produce good exposure of a given emulsion. Exposure calculators are mechanical devices or sets of reference tables from which exposure data can be obtained on the basis of observed subject and light conditions; they do not measure the light.

Various kinds of exposure meters may be handheld, built into a camera, or attached to or inserted in a camera as an accessory. They may measure the

To use this typical exposure meter, the ASA number is set. The large dial is then turned until the needle on the exposure indicator (bottom) becomes centered. Any matching combination of the f-stops and shutter speeds (indicated at top of dial) will give a correct exposure. This meter also indicates the equivalent exposure value or light value number at bottom of dial. Photo courtesy Berkey Marketing Companies.

light falling onto the subject, or the light reflected from the subject. And they may be for use with continuous light sources, or with flash sources.

Meter Cells

The heart of a meter is a light-sensitive cell; four types of cells have been widely used.

Selenium (Se) Cells. These cells produce a small amount of electric current when affected by light; the current is used to activate an indicator in proportion to the light intensity. Because selenium is relatively slow to respond and has low sensitivity, and because the current produced is used directly, the meter cell must be fairly large to receive a useful amount of light. For this reason, selenium cells are not used for in-camera meters where space and weight are at a premium and light intensity is reduced by the lens, even at maximum aperture. The spectral, or color sensitivity of a selenium cell is close to that of average human vision, with maximum response in the green-yellow region; however, this does not correspond to the response of film emulsions.

Cadmium Sulfide (CdS) Cells. These cells have much greater light sensitivity and respond very much faster than selenium cells. They do not generate current when affected by light, but change electrical resistance in proportion to the light intensity. They are used in circuits to regulate the flow of current from a battery to the meter indicating system. For these reasons, very small cells may be used, making them practical for in-camera use. CdS cells may be dazzled or "overwhelmed" by intense light and require as much as two minutes recovery time before they will give stable response in low light conditions. Their spectral sensitivity is almost equal for all colors of light except blue, where they are markedly deficient.

Silicon (Si) "Blue" Cells. These cells have light sensitivity and response speed equal to or greater than CdS cells. They are coated to equalize their response through the blue region, so they come very close to matching the response of panchromatic emulsions. Like CdS cells, their resistance varies with light intensity, so they too are used in battery-powered circuits. They do not become dazzled by high-intensity light and therefore may be used in all light situations without delay or difficulty.

Gallium-Arsenic-Phosphorus Cells. These cells are said to be extremely sensitive to light so that meters made with them can be used in very low light level photography. They draw very little current, so that they help maintain long battery life. They do not become overwhelmed by bright light, and can be used for low light levels immediately after being used in high light levels. They are used in meters built into cameras that have light-emitting diode (LED) displays.

Meter Indications

Whether the cell generates current or controls the flow from a battery, the power is used to provide an indication of light intensity. In the most common kind of meter, the indicator is a needle that is moved to point to a number on a reference scale. In dual-range meters, the scale numbers may change as the meter is switched from low (dim light) to high (bright light) operation. In some meters, the needle simply moves to an unmarked position where it becomes a reference mark for the dial exposure calculator. The other most common indicating system is a set of symbols or numbers that light up to signal relative light intensity, called an LED system.

In most hand-held meters, a dial is set to match the indicated reference mark or scale number. The dial is a kind of circular slide rule that is set for the film speed and that shifts a shutter-speed scale in relation to an *f*-number scale as the dial is set to the light level indicated by the meter. In at least one model, the dial is motor driven and turns automatically as the cell responds to the light.

In lighted-indicator systems as the dial is turned, an "over" or "under" (exposure) indicator lights until the dial reaches the proper setting; then both indicators come on, or a "correct" indicator lights up.

Once the dial has been correctly set, any of the indicated *f*-stop and shutter-speed combinations will give equivalent exposures. With very short or very long exposures, reciprocity effect may have to be as a corrective to the meter-indicated exposure. Whether all combinations are equally useful depends on a number of factors, most importantly unequal emulsion response. (*See:* RECIPROCITY EFFECT.) Some dials also produce a single EV or LV number as an exposure guide. (*See:* EXPOSURE VALUE SYSTEM.)

Most in-camera meters provide indications in the viewfinder display. Commonly, changing the *f*-stop or shutter-speed control settings moves a follow-pointer until it coincides with the position of the indicating needle or with a reference notch. Some viewfinder displays incorporate LED indicators in place of moving pointers. The display may or may not show the actual shutter speed and *f*-stop settings; most do not. In some cameras, the meter is coupled to automatic or semi-automatic controls of the shutter speed and/or the lens aperture. (*See:* AUTOMATIC EXPOSURE SYSTEMS.)

Meter Settings

The exposure data produced by a meter relate the light intensity to the film speed. To indicate correct exposure, the meter must be set for the speed of the film in use. Virtually all meters are marked for settings in ASA and DIN film speeds. BSI (British Standard Institute) and JSA (Japan Standards Association) speeds are the same as American ASA speeds; German DIN speeds are in logarithmic rather than arithmetic numbers.

When practical experience shows that the true speed of a film is different from the rating given by the manufacturer, the meter should be set to the ASA/DIN equivalent of the true speed. Such variations often result from shutters operating at other than their marked speeds, and for variations in the true speed of a film as affected by the amount of development. Changing the setting to twice the ASA number will produce data for exposures that are half those previously calculated; setting to half the ASA number will produce doubled exposures. In the DIN system, adding three to the setting (for example, from 11 to 14) will halve the exposure indications; subtracting three will double them.

Some in-camera meter systems, such as this Nikon F2S Meter/Finder, have exposure signal lights both inside the viewfinder and on top of the housing. The f-stop is displayed in the small window at the front of the housing. Photo courtesy Ehrenreich Photo-Optical Industries, Inc.

The most common range of ASA/DIN settings is given in the accompanying table; many meters are marked for higher and lower settings than these to increase their usefulness in highly unusual conditions. For other speed numbers, see the article SPEED SYSTEMS.

Incident-Light Meters

Incident light is the illumination falling from a source (or sources) onto a scene or subject. Incident light is much brighter than the light that actually reaches the camera because the subject absorbs some light and reflects only a portion of the total. Meters that measure incident light take this fact into account in their design and calibration. The cell of an incident-light meter is usually covered with a translucent white dome, cone, or ridged plate called the collector, which collects light from all frontal directions. Only frontal light can be reflected from the subject to the camera lens. A flat collector may be used to read light from only one direction, for example, to measure lighting ratios.

An incident-light reading is taken by holding the meter at the subject position with the white collector pointed toward the camera, or toward the light source in the case of light-ratio readings. Outdoors it may often be impossible to get to the actual subject with the meter. In that case, an accurate reading can be obtained by holding the meter in the same light as that falling on the subject, with the collector oriented to point in the same direction as the subject-to-camera axis.

Incident-light readings are especially useful with color and transparency films, because they calculate exposures that will fall in the middle of a film's exposure range, and they are more generally used in studio than in outdoor photography.

Reflected-Light Meters

The light reflected from the subject (or emitted by a self-luminous subject) is called luminance; more commonly it is called brightness, which is the perceived lightness or darkness of an illuminated object. Reflected-light meters measure brightness. The most common types have an acceptance angle of about 30 degrees, so they receive brightnesses from many parts of the subject and average them together. Narrow-angle and spot meters incorporate a small telescope-like optical system to take in only a very small

EQUIVALENT EXPOSURE METER SETTINGS	
ASA BSI	DIN
2.5	5
3	6
4	7
5	8
6	9
8	10
10	11
12	12
16	13
20	14
25	15
32	16
40	17
50	18
64	19
80	20
100	21
125	22
160	23
200	24
250	25
320	26
400	27
500	28
650	29
800	30
1000	31

area of the subject. Typical spot meter acceptance angles range from 1 to 7 degrees.

All in-camera meters are reflected-light meters. They may read the entire area taken in by a given lens, or only a small spot in the center; often it is possible to choose either method of reading. Some camera meters are weighted to give more importance to brightness in the center of the frame than around the edges, on the theory that the most important subject is centered in most pictures.

A reflected-light reading is taken by pointing the meter toward the subject from the direction of the camera. This is an *average* reading; the meter indicates the average light level of the subject. Specific readings from the camera position of individual subject areas can be obtained with a spot meter. A meter with a wide acceptance angle (averaging meter) must be moved close to the subject being read if it is to be used for a small-area reading, and care must be taken that the area is not shadowed by the meter during the reading.

Reflected-light readings are especially useful with black-and-white negative films, because it is possible to measure the actual subject brightness range by taking separate readings from light and dark areas. This information can be used to provide adequate exposure of dark-area detail, to determine the development required to achieve proper highlight densities, and to control the density range of the negative. (*See:* BRIGHTNESS RANGE; CONTRAST; CONTRAST INDEX.)

Many reflected-light meters can be used for incident-light measurement by placing a white diffusing collector over the meter cell. Alternatively, a reflected-light reading from an 18 percent reflectance neutral gray card (such as the Kodak neutral test card) held at the subject position, will be the same type of reading as an incident-light reading.

Metering Specific Subjects

The methods for taking meter readings of various subjects and determining appropriate exposures are covered in the article EXPOSURE TECHNIQUES, and in more specific entries such as AVAILABLE-LIGHT PHOTOGRAPHY and PORTRAITURE.

Specialized Meters

Spot Photometer. A spot photometer is a reflected-light spot meter that shows a small circle of subject brightness inside a larger circle of reference brightness from a battery-powered source in the meter. Turning a control ring until the two brightnesses match also turns *f*-stop/shutter-speed scales from which exposure combinations may be read.

Flash Meters. Flash meters can be either incident- or reflected-light meters that respond only to sudden great increases in illumination. Flash meters are generally intended for use with electronic flash sources. Since the camera or lens shutter setting is determined by the requirements of X synchronization, the meter is calibrated directly in *f*-stops. The incident-type meter is held at the subject position and pointed toward the camera, while the reflected type is held at camera position and pointed toward the subject. When the flash is fired, a needle moves across the scale and holds a position that indicates the *f*-stop required for proper exposure.

Focal-Plane Meters. Focal-plane meters for view cameras are reflected-light meters that may be inserted in the film holder position. Some meters take an average reading of all or a large portion of the image area; others have a small cell on a movable arm (visible from behind; through the focusing screen) that may be moved to take readings from specific areas.

Enlarging or Printing Meters. These meters for on-easel use are of two basic types. A reflected-light model is used from outside the image area to take spot readings. An incident-light model is placed on the easel to read the intensity of various areas, or the average intensity of the light passed through a diffuser.

Exposure Calculators

Reference tables, protractors calibrated for various sun positions, and other calculators are expedients; they can be useful in many outdoor situations, but they cannot produce the specific and accurate exposure data supplied by meters. The little chart of recommended exposures of average subjects under typical conditions that is incorporated in many film instruction sheets is a simple type of calculator. One of the most comprehensive and useful calculators is the *American National Standard Photographic Exposure Guide,* ANSI PH2.7–1973. It provides methods and data for computing exposures by sunlight and moonlight in a wide variety of situations and locations. It is available from the American National Standards Institute. Some exposure calculators are in dial form. Rotating the dial helps calculate exposures by daylight, photolamps, existing light, and flash (bulb and electronic).

• *See also:* AUTOMATIC EXPOSURE SYSTEMS; AVAILABLE-LIGHT PHOTOGRAPHY; BRIGHTNESS RANGE; CONTRAST; CONTRAST INDEX; EXPOSURE TECHNIQUES; EXPOSURE VALUE SYSTEM; FLASH PHOTOGRAPHY; PHOTOMETER; PORTRAITURE; RECIPROCITY EFFECT; SPEED SYSTEMS.

Further Reading: Berg, W.F. *Exposure,* 4th ed. Garden City, NY: Amphoto; Carroll, John S. *Amphoto Black and White Film Data Book.* Garden City, NY: Amphoto, 1975; Dunn, J.F. and G.L. Wakefield. *Exposure Manual.* (Published by Fountain) Dobbs Ferry, NY: Morgan & Morgan, Inc., 1975; Life Library of Photography. *Light and Film.* New York, NY: Time-Life Books, Division of Time, Inc. 1970.

Exposure Techniques

Good exposure is the result of relating accurate and meaningful meter readings to subject characteristics and intended or necessary processing.

General Exposure Rule

During a large percentage of sunlit days over a large geographic area, the illuminance of terrestrial objects from the sun plus sky is relatively constant. For average frontlit subjects this lighting condition results in a standard exposure of f/16 at a shutter speed of 1/film speed. Exposures for certain other relatively standard conditions are based on variations from this formula.

Such a general rule is limited to the conditions that it covers, even though it may cover a large percentage of actual pictures taken. For unusual situations not covered by the rule, the use of an exposure meter is a great help in finding the correct exposure.

EXPOSURES FOR OTHER CONDITIONS

Light Conditions	Subject Condition	Exposure
Bright or hazy sun	On light sand or snow	1 stop less
	Average subjects	1/film speed @ f/16
	Sidelighted subjects	1 stop more
Cloudy bright (no shadows)	Average subjects	2 stops more
Heavy overcast Open shade	Average subjects	3 stops more

Using Exposure Meters

The following suggestions should help you use an exposure meter correctly, and, as a result, get properly exposed negatives or transparencies under most conditions. Note, however, that light measurements do not take account of other variables in the photographic process that affect exposure, such as:

Variations in the accuracy of f-number and shutter-speed markings on cameras.

Changes from recommended development times to control negative contrast or to "push" film speeds.
Reciprocity effects for extremely long or extremely short exposure times.
Change in blade shutter-speed exposure at fast shutter speeds and small apertures.

Therefore, you should run tests with your own equipment, films, and processing to find the exact procedures that work best for you.

Meter Procedure. There are three types of exposure meters commonly used: averaging reflection meters with acceptance angles of about 30 degrees, spot reflection meters with acceptance angles of about 1 degree, and incident light meters. Many averaging reflection meters have diffusion adapters that convert them to incident meters. While the method of light measurement is different with each type of meter, the basic procedure is the same:

1. Set the dial for the speed of the film being used.
2. Measure the light.
3. Set the computer dial for the amount of light.
4. Select an exposure time/f-number combination from the computer dial.

See the instructions that come with your meter for steps 1 and 3.

The methods of measuring light for the purpose of exposure calculation in daylight and in artificial light are similar, but have some differences. For this reason the main emphasis is on daylight use of exposure meters, with the differences being given for artificial light use following the daylight usage table.

Metering for Daylight Exposures

The Daylight Exposure Meter Usage Table shows the methods of metering and the adjustments to make for various conditions to the exposure readings given by the meter. The reading given by the meter is labeled *Ind* in the table, standing for *indicated*. Adjustments for the brightness (reflectance) of the subject are given in changes to the indicated exposure in stops change or in fractions of stops change.

DAYLIGHT EXPOSURE METER USAGE

Meter Type	Light Condition	Light Direction[1]	Subject Type	Meter Location	Meter Aim	Special Meter Handling	Correction for Subject Brightness in Stops[5]: Very Light	Light	Normal	Dark	Very Dark	Meter Calculator Arrow
Reflection Averaging — Direct Measurement	Sun	Front	Scenes	At camera	At subject[2]	Sky to occupy ¼ meter coverage.	+1	+½	Ind	−½	−1	Regular
	Sun	Front	Close-ups	At camera	At subject	Cover subject.	+1	+½	Ind	−½	−1	Regular
	Sun	Front	Small subject against light or dark background	Close to subject	At subject	Cover *only* subject. Avoid reading background.	+1	+½	Ind	−½	−1	Regular
	Sun	Side	All	At camera	At subject	If scene, sky to occupy ¼ meter coverage.	+½	Ind	−½	−1	−1½	Regular
	Sun	Back	Scenes	At camera	At subject[2]	Shade meter from sun.	+2	+1½	+1	+½	Ind	Regular
	Sun	Back	Close-ups	Near subject	At subject	Shade meter, measure shadows.	−1	−1½	−2	−2½	−3	Regular
	Overcast and shade		All	At camera	At subject	If scene, sky to occupy ¼ meter coverage.	+1	+½	Ind	−½	−1	Regular
Spot Meter — Direct Measurement	Sun	Front	All	At camera	At subject Diffuse highlight	Highlight method. Measure subject area with step 1 and 2 values.	+1½ −1	+2 −½	+2½ Ind	— —	— —	Regular Highlight
	Sun	Front	All	At camera	At subject Open shadow	Shadow method. Measure open shadow area with step 5 to 6 values.	— —	— —	−2½ Ind	−2 +½	−1½ +1	Regular Shadow
	Sun	Front	All	At camera	At subject	Highlight-shadow method. Measure subjects with both step 1 to 2 and 5 to 6 values.[4]	Calc[6]	Calc	Calc	Calc	Calc	Regular
	Sun	Back[3]	All	At camera	At subject Open shadow	Measure shadow area, step 5 to 6 values.	−1 −3	−½ −2½	Ind −2	+½ −1½	+1 −1	Shadow Regular
	Sun	Side	All	At camera	At subject	Highlight-shadow method. Measure subjects with both step 1 to 2 and 5 to 6 values.[4]	Calc[6]	Calc	Calc	Calc	Calc	Regular
Incident Meter	Sun	Front	All	At subject	Halfway between sun and camera	Hold meter with integrator axis horizontal. If toplit, aim with axis 45 degrees up.	−1	−½	Ind	+½	+1	Regular
	Sun	Side	All	At subject			−1	−½	Ind	+½	+1	Regular
	Sun	Back	Scenes	At subject	At camera	Hold meter horizontally. Shade integrator if necessary, measuring fill light only.	−2½	−2	−1½	−1	−½	Regular
	Sun	Back	Close-ups	At subject	At camera		−1½	−1	−½	Ind	+½	Regular
	Overcast and shade		All	At subject	At camera	Hold meter horizontally.	−1	−½	Ind	+½	+1	Regular
Reflection Averaging and Spot Meters with *Kodak* Neutral Test Card	Sun	Front	All	Near subject or camera	Aim meter at neutral card. Hold averaging meter about 6" from card. Do not cast shadow on card.	Hold card vertically with gray side angled to face halfway between camera and sun. Aim meter squarely at card face.	−½	Ind	+½	+1	+1½	Regular
	Sun	Side	All	Near subject or camera			+½	+1	+1½	+2	+2½	Regular
	Sun	Back	Scenes	At camera		Hold card vertically with gray side facing toward camera. Shadow meter if sunlight falls on it. You are measuring shadow brightness.	−2½	−2	−1½	−1	−½	Regular
	Sun	Back	Close-ups	Near subject			−1½	−1	−½	Ind	+½	Regular
	Overcast and shade		All	Near subject or camera	At card	Hold card vertically, gray side facing directly toward camera.	−1	−½	Ind	+½	+1	Regular

[1]In relation to the subject.

[2]When the sky is part of the scene, aim meter 20–30 degrees downward so that the sky occupies about ¼ of meter coverage.

[3]With sunsets, aim the reflecting meter toward the sky, shading cell from direct sun, and give bracketing exposures around this reading. Ground subjects will be silhouetted.

[4]Follow meter instructions for averaging readings, or calculate the exposure based on the highlight reading and the exposure based on the shadow reading and give exposure halfway between.

[5]Ind = indicated exposure. This means to give the exposure found by using the meter without correction. The − and + figures direct whether to give less or more exposure than the dial indicates. If the correction is −½, give ½ stop less than the indicated exposure; if the correction is +½, give ½ stop more than the indicated exposure.

[6]Calc = calculated. This is an exposure calculated from two indicated exposures. It is usually halfway between the highlight and shadow calculated exposures.

NOTE: In general the diffuse highlight method works well with color transparency films, while the shadow method works well with negative films, both black-and-white and color. The highlight-shadow method is most precise. It gives added information when the luminance range is beyond the film's capability and needs lowering with reflectors or fill-in flash. It may also be used in black-and-white work when developing times are adjusted to fit the subject luminance ratio to the printing conditions. The highlight, shadow, and highlight-shadow methods can sometimes be used with reflecting averaging meters when the subject areas are large enough or close enough to obtain definitive readings.

All the exposure recommendations are given for films within their reciprocity range. When unusually long or unusually short exposures are to be given, check the film data sheet to make the corrections for the effects of reciprocity if necessary. Make these changes in the film speed, when possible, so that the calculation methods will remain consistent.

Refining Exposure Calculations for Your Equipment. The exposure measurement methods are applicable to photography with black-and-white, color negative, and transparency films. While the latitude of negative films provides an added safety factor to exposure, the best photographic quality is usually achieved with correct exposure. With transparency films, correct exposure is critical. Bracketing of exposures is recommended when possible.

While most cameras are made with a high degree of accuracy, for critical work it is advisable to run exposure series on a transparency film to check the accuracy of your shutter speeds and *f*-number markings. The most frequent error found is slow shutter speeds in blade shutters due to misuse or age. Make any corrections by changing the film speed so that the methods of measuring light and calculating exposures will remain consistent. If the speeds on a shutter are found to be slow by one-third stop, for example, increase the film speed to the next higher number as given in the following table.

ASA FILM SPEED SERIES

6	20	64	200	650	2000
8	25	80	250	800	2500
10	32	100	320	1000	3200
12	40	125	400	1250	4000
16	50	160	500	1600	5000

(Each number is ⅓ stop faster than the preceding ASA).

Corrections for Faster Blade Shutter Speeds and Small Apertures. Blade shutters at their faster shutter speeds and small lens apertures tend to give more exposure than is indicated by the shutter-speed / *f*-number combination. This is not a manufacturing defect but is due to the inertia of moving parts combined with the geometry of the lens-shutter-dia-

phragm structure. It will usually occur in daylight photography with fast films and will cause overexposure of up to one stop. You can find the correction factor to apply in these situations by running an exposure series on a fast transparency film such as Kodak Extachrome 200 film. This effect does not occur with focal-plane shutters. The accompanying table gives an example of the type of correction you may find necessary.

APPROXIMATE EXPOSURE CORRECTION FOR FASTER BLADE SHUTTER SPEEDS AND SMALL LENS APERTURES

Lens Aperture	1/125 sec.	1/250 sec.	1/500 sec.
f/1.4–5.6	None	None	None
f/8	None	None	⅓ stop
f/11	None	⅓ stop	⅔ stop
f/16 and smaller	⅓ stop	⅔ stop	1 stop

Lighting Ratio Measurement. Measure the *main plus fill-in* illuminance by holding a Kodak neutral test card vertically at the subject position and aiming the surface of the card halfway between the camera and the sun position, and by measuring it with the meter. Then aim the card at the camera, shading it from the sun but not the skylight (fill-light) and measure again. Compute the exposure for each reading and determine the number of stops difference between the two computed exposures. The lighting ratio can be found in the following table.

LIGHTING RATIO TABLE

Stops Difference	Lighting Ratio	Stops Difference	Lighting Ratio	Stops Difference	Lighting Ratio
⅔	1.5:1	2	4:1	3⅓	10:1
1	2:1	2⅓	5:1	3⅔	13:1
1⅓	2.5:1	2⅔	6:1	4	16:1
1⅔	3:1	3	8:1	5	32:1

Exposure Techniques

A 3:1 ratio is generally considered appropriate for color photography, while for black-and-white photography the ratio may vary from 3:1 to as high as 8:1, depending on circumstances. Reflectors can be used to lower the ratio. Diffuse white reflectors such as cloth or paper must be relatively close to the subject to have an appreciable effect, whereas aluminum foil reflectors can be used at a greater distance. Fill-in flash can also be used to lower the ratio. (*See:* FLASH PHOTOGRAPHY.)

Ratio Measurement with a Spot Meter. A spot meter can be used in the same manner as the averaging meter in the method described above. When a sunlit plus skylit (main plus fill-in) area has the same reflectance as a skylit area, as in the two sides of a face, direct readings can be made of the two areas and compared as in the above method to find the lighting ratio.

Ratio Measuring with an Incident Meter. At subject position, aim the meter at the sun and compute exposure. Then aim at the camera and shade the integrating diffuser from the direct sun but do not block the skylight. Compute this exposure, and compare it with the first as above to determine the ratio.

Artificial Light Exposure Measurement

In general, for artificial light measurement, meters are used in much the same way as for measurement in daylight. One factor is greatly different: While outdoors the light is constant over great areas due to the distance of the sun, in the studio the light intensity changes greatly with the distance from the light. All reflection measurements, both with averaging meters and spot meters, must be made with lights, subjects, and backgrounds in the positions they will be in for the exposure. Changing the position of the subject or a light only a small distance may make a relatively great change in the exposure required. The incident meter must be exactly in the subject position. No other location will do.

Behind-the-Lens Meters. Most current 35 mm single-lens reflex cameras have built-in averaging meters whose angle of coverage approximately covers the entire field. Follow the directions for averaging reflection meters in using these. In many cases this will mean taking the reading at a different location from that at which the picture will be taken or with a different camera aim. With most cameras you can take the reading, adjust for light and subject type, set the *f*-number and shutter speed, and then aim the camera for taking the picture.

A few 35 mm cameras have spot-type meters incorporated. The spot is usually larger (covers a wider angle) than hand spot meters, and the area covered is indicated in the ground-glass finder.

Other cameras have center-weighted meters, which are partly spot-meter and partly averaging-meter construction. Generally these are used like averaging meters; follow the instructions in the camera manual.

There are some meters that measure directly on the optical image in view cameras. These are used like spot meters; the ground-glass image helps locate the measurement locations. While the measurement methods and condition and subject adjustments will be the same as for spot metering, the readings already have the effect of the *f*-number in them. See the instruction book that comes with the meter for directions on finding the exposure from this type of reading.

Behind-the-Lens Meters with Filters. There are two ways generally used to compute exposures:

1. Measure the light with the filter off the camera and calculate the exposure without the filter. Apply the filter factor and find the exposure with the filter. Set the *f*-number and the shutter speed, place the filter on the camera, and take the picture. This is the most accurate method, and is efficient when a variety of film-filter combinations are commonly used.

2. Set the camera for the speed of your film. Use the uncorrected speed for color films being exposed with correction filters. Place the filter on the camera and measure the light with the filter in place. Do not use a filter factor in calculating the exposure; measuring the light through the filter eliminates the need for using the factor.

The second method may lead to errors because the color sensitivity of the meter may not match that of the film when filtered. Run tests to verify that the calculated speed with filter is correct or to find a speed that is correct for each combination. This method is worth the effort when many pictures are to be taken with the same film-filter combination. Check your camera if you want to use a polarizing filter this way; some cameras will not measure accurately with polarizing filters.

Averaging Meter Direct Measurement. Turn off any backlights (lights aimed toward the camera). If the background and subject have approximately the same tonal range, take an average reading of the picture area. If the background is very light or very dark, measure the subject only.

Averaging Meter and Spot Meter with Gray Card. Hold the card parallel to the main subject plane (vertical with most subjects) and at the subject position. Turn out any backlights. Angle the card halfway between the camera and the main light. Hold the meter about 15 centimetres (6 inches) from the card, being careful not to cast a shadow from either the main or the fill-in lights. Read and calculate the exposure. Use the indicated exposure. Do not add ½ stop as you do for daylight-exposure for average subjects. Decrease the exposure by ½ to 1 stop for light subjects; increase by ½ to 1 stop for dark subjects.

Incident Light Meter. Turn off backlights and hair light, if any. Hold the meter in subject position, aim it toward the camera, and take a reading. Use indicated exposure for average subjects. Decrease exposure by ½ to 1 stop for light subjects, increase by ½ to 1 stop for dark subjects. If using a single main light with no fill-in, aim the meter at the light instead of the camera.

Electronic Flash Modeling Light Measurement. Most studio electronic flash units are equipped with modeling lights to aid in judging the lighting arrangement. These lights can also be used as an aid in computing the exposure. The key to this method is an equivalent exposure time used in calculating the *f*-number from meter readings made with the modeling light on. To find the equivalent exposure time:

1. Determine the *f*-number for flash at a given distance. (*See:* FLASH PHOTOGRAPHY; GUIDE NUMBERS.) Verify this by tests.
2. With the unit placed at that distance from a subject, and with only the modeling light on, measure the light by the appropriate method with your meter.
3. With the meter dial, find exposure time at the same *f*-number as flash exposure.

(Near right) Incident-light readings are taken by holding the meter with the collector pointed toward the camera or toward the light source. (Center) Reflected-light readings, which indicate the average light level of the subject, are taken by pointing the meter at the subject and away from the camera. (Far right) A reflected-light meter can give incident-light measurements by taking a reading from an 18% reflectance neutral gray card held at the subject position. Photos by Norm Kerr.

Exposure Techniques

This equivalent exposure time can then be used to calculate the correct *f*-number for exposing future subjects lit at different distances. If the flash unit provides different power levels, find the equivalent time for each level. Because incandescent bulbs dim gradually with usage, recheck at regular intervals the exposure time used to calculate exposures.

For transparency materials, the main light is the most important one for calculating exposure. If the exposure times used for calculating the *f*-numbers are different for different lights, use the main light only for calculating exposures on transparency films, and place the other lights at the proper distances to give the proper lighting ratios.

With negative materials, it is the fill-in light that is most useful in calculating exposure. Use it to calculate the *f*-number for the exposure, and place the main and other lights by distance to get the desired lighting ratios.

Existing-Light Photography

When light conditions are outside the range of those described with the *f*/16 at 1/film speed rule, there is no general way to estimate exposure. Suggested exposures for a wide variety of low-light-level

subjects are given in the article AVAILABLE-LIGHT PHOTOGRAPHY. The Existing-Light Exposure Dial in the *KODAK Professional Photoguide,* publication No. R-28, provides a convenient method of calculating exposures for such subjects.

Where it is possible to use a light meter to calculate exposures, that method is generally more accurate than the dial. Some existing-light subjects cannot be metered, while others may be too dim to get an accurate meter reading. In these cases, the existing-light exposure dial can be used to find starting exposures.

In many cases, existing-light pictures give a more natural rendition that you can get by using flash. Most low-light-level subjects can be photographed using fast lenses and film.

In general it is best to match the balance of a color film to the illumination; i.e., use Type B film or tungsten-type film with tungsten lights. In some cases, however, photographers prefer the warmer rendition that a daylight-balanced film gives of a tungsten-lighted scene, especially an outdoor street scene. The matching of color temperatures is covered in COLOR PHOTOGRAPHY and FILTERS.

Because light levels for existing-light subjects may vary considerably, the dial must be considered a guide for starting exposures, useful when other methods of finding exposure are not practical. For this reason, bracketing exposures is recommended. Many existing-light subjects are high in contrast, so that usable pictures will result over a wide range of exposures. Bracketing gives a choice of mood renditions. Bracket at one- to two-stop intervals.

The choice between various *f*-number and exposure-time combinations is usually determined by these factors: availability of a camera support, need for depth of field, need to stop subject movement, and whether trails of light caused by moving-light sources are desired. In the special case where the moving-light source creates its own image (lightning, moving car lights, fireworks), the *f*-number alone determines the exposure for a given film speed.

Other Techniques

Neutral Density Filters. When the light is too bright to allow use of a desired *f*-stop or shutter speed with a particular film, use neutral density (ND) filters to reduce exposure. A 0.3ND filter reduces light intensity by the equivalent of 1 stop, a 0.6ND filter by 2 stops, and a 0.9ND filter by 3 stops. A neutral density filter does not affect the color balance of the light.

Time Exposures. Time exposures may require reciprocity compensation. (*See:* RECIPROCITY EFFECT.) To eliminate moving elements in a scene—such as traffic and pedestrians moving in front of a building—divide a time exposure into several brief exposures. For example, a two-minute exposure can be achieved in 60 two-second exposures. Make sure that no unwanted element is in the same location in any two exposures. The brief exposures may be spaced over a half-hour or more if the camera can be kept absolutely immobile and the light conditions do not change.

High-Contrast Subject. To reduce contrast and improve dark-area detail in a color transparency of a high-contrast subject, give a flashing exposure after the main exposure. Place a white card in the same light as the subject and give about $\frac{1}{200}$ the original exposure with the card filling the frame, but out of focus. This can be done by giving the same exposure with a 2.3ND filter. (*See:* FLASHING.)

Bracketing. Color transparency films have a very narrow latitude. Exposure calculation is sometimes not quite exact enough to result in the best exposure. Where possible, giving several exposures less than and more than the calculated exposure in half-stop increments will help achieve the best possible exposure. Since overall density is often the key to the mood a picture conveys, this method gives a choice of moods.

Color negative and black-and-white films have more latitude than transparency films, so that bracketing is less necessary. It is useful where the correct exposure is difficult to ascertain, as in available-light photography. One-stop increments are usually all that are necessary.

With more normal subjects, if there is any uncertainty as to the exposure, giving a single exposure one stop more than the uncertain indicated exposure will be all that is necessary. With black-and-white films, this will provide adequate shadow detail but can result in a slight increase in graininess in the medium-light tones. In the Kodak color negative films, giving one stop overexposure actually results in finer-grained negatives and provides adequate shadow detail.

Push Processing. Where the speed of the film in the camera is inadequate for low light levels, the pictures can be exposed one stop less than normal and the film can be given additional development. (*See:* PUSH PROCESSING.) The quality of the pictures is hardly ever as good as when a faster film is exposed and processed normally, but when quality is secondary to getting any pictures at all, push processing is useful.

Divided Exposures. Neutral density filters can be used to "dodge" the picture during the exposures on all types of films. This is an especially useful technique with transparency films that do not get printed. A low-value, gelatin, neutral density filter can be cut and held in front of the camera lens to lessen the exposure of bright areas that are likely to be overexposed. Medium to large apertures should be used to soften the image of the filter edges. This is especially useful to darken light skies while still getting enough exposure on relatively dark foreground subjects. The filter should be close to the camera lens; it can be taped to the front lens mount. Another use is to darken the corners of a picture to concentrate the interest in one central area. A few filters are manufactured with part of the filter clear glass while another part is neutral density.

The following table shows the lessening of exposure in stops of several densities.

EXPOSURE DECREASE WITH NEUTRAL DENSITY FILTERS

ND Filter	Decrease in Stops
0.10	$-\frac{1}{3}$
0.20	$-\frac{2}{3}$
0.30	-1
0.40	$-1\frac{1}{3}$
0.50	$-1\frac{2}{3}$
0.60	-2

This technique is most easily controlled on cameras with ground-glass viewing. Be sure to use the aperture setting at which the picture will be taken. With single-lens reflex cameras, this means using the preview control.

• *See also:* AVAILABLE-LIGHT PHOTOGRAPHY; BRACKETING EXPOSURES; BRIGHTNESS RANGE; CLOSE-UP PHOTOGRAPHY; COLOR PHOTOGRAPHY; CONTRAST; CONTRAST INDEX; EXPOSURE; EXPOSURE METERS AND CALCULATORS; FILTERS; FLASHING; FLASH PHOTOGRAPHY; LIGHTING; MOONLIGHT PHOTOGRAPHY; NEUTRAL DENSITY; PORTRAITURE; ZONE SYSTEM.

Exposure Value System

Prior to the growing use of built-in meters and automatic exposure control systems in hand cameras, many manufacturers attempted to simplify the task of making camera settings by use of the exposure value system.

This system centers on a series of exposure value (EV) or light value (LV) numbers. Each EV number represents a series of equivalent *f*-stop/shutter-speed combinations. The EV number for a given situation is determined by taking a reading with a meter that has an EV/LV scale or window on its calculator dial. A wide variety of meters indicate EV settings along with *f*-stops and shutter speeds. EV settings for typical subjects and light conditions are given in film data sheets and reference tables.

Once the required exposure value is known, the separate EV control of the shutter is set to that number. The lens diaphragm is coupled to the shutter so that as the EV number is set, the aperture is automatically adjusted to the *f*-stop required for proper exposure with whatever the actual shutter-speed setting happens to be. Thereafter, changing either the *f*-stop or the shutter speed causes a compensating change in the other control so that the total exposure received by the film remains unchanged. The system has been used primarily in cameras equipped with between-the-lens shutters, which can easily be coupled directly with the lens diaphragm.

An increase of one in the EV scale produces a range of settings that double a given exposure; a decrease of one produces settings that give half the exposure.

• *See also:* EXPOSURE METERS AND CALCULATORS.

Fabric Sensitizer

You can print black-and-white photographs on cloth when you coat the surfaces with the sensitizer described in this article. T-shirts, towels, and a wide variety of other cloth items can be used to produce personalized gifts or novelty items. Of course, the sensitizer described here can also be used to coat the surfaces of various kinds of paper and other porous materials such as wood. Colored paper or paper with rich texture can yield interesting results. The images you can obtain should range from recognizable to good, but they will not have the high quality you can produce with the photographic printing papers sold commercially.

Since fabrics and papers vary considerably in the basic materials and additives they contain, it is impractical to predict how good or how permanent the images produced by the sensitizer will be. You should consider the technique described here as an experiment for photo hobbyists and not as a procedure for producing long-lasting, high-quality results, or as one that should be used for commercial purposes.

Preparing the Sensitizer

You can obtain the chemicals needed to make the various solutions from chemical supply houses.

Vandyke Sensitizer Formula

Ferric ammonium citrate	90 g
Tartaric acid	15 g
Silver nitrate (See following caution)	37.5 g
Distilled water to make	1 litre

CAUTION: Silver nitrate in either the dry-chemical or solution form can cause burns of both the skin and the eyes. In handling dry silver nitrate, be careful not to inhale the dust. In case of contact with the skin or eyes, both the dry chemicals and solutions described above should be immediately flushed from the area of contact with water. If the eyes are involved, flush for at least 15 minutes and get medical attention.

Silver nitrate will produce brown stains on your hands or clothing, and these stains are very difficult to remove. You can avoid staining your hands by wearing rubber gloves. A plastic darkroom apron such as the Kodak darkroom apron, sold by photo dealers, will help keep stains off your clothing.

Mixing. Dissolve each of the chemicals in a separate container, using about 237 millilitres (8 fluidounces) of distilled water at 18.5 to 24 C (65 to 75 F). You can use stainless-steel, glass, or plastic containers and a stainless-steel spoon for stirring. The container for the ferric ammonium citrate should be large enough to hold about 1 litre (32 fluidounces).

Mix the ferric ammonium citrate and the tartaric acid solutions, and then add the silver nitrate solution slowly while stirring. Add distilled water to make about 1 litre (32 fluidounces). If you keep the resulting solution in a brown glass bottle away from direct light, it should remain in good condition for several months.

Applying the Sensitizer. You can apply the sensitizer at 18.5 to 24 C (65 to 75 F) to the fabric or paper in artificial room light, but it is best to work under a yellow safelight. Equip the safelight with a Kodak safelight filter OO (light yellow), a Kodak safelight filter OA (greenish yellow), or an equiva-

Black-and-white photographs are easy to print on sensitized fabrics. For large images, the original negative may be enlarged on direct duplicating film and contact printed from the duplicate.

of glass between the layers while you apply the sensitizer. After you have applied the sensitizer, put a piece of blotter between the layers of fabric until the sensitized area dries. The unexposed parts of the sensitized area may possibly show some coloration after a time, so when you want to confine the sensitizer to a limited part of the cloth, you should outline the area with masking tape. This will help keep the perimeter of the sensitized area from being irregular. Apply the sensitizer sparingly near the edge of the tape.

Printing

After it is dry, hold the sensitized cloth or paper in close contact with the negative you wish to print by placing a piece of clear glass over the negative. Then expose it to sunlight or very strong artificial light, such as a reflector photolamp, until details are visible in the highlight areas of the image. If you use a hinged printing frame, you can examine part of the print to determine when the exposure is adequate. Exposures require several minutes. Try an exposure of 2 to 10 minutes or longer until you determine the best time to use.

Because this sensitizing material produces a very slow contact-printing sensitive surface, negatives cannot be enlarged on it to make bigger images. However, small negatives can be enlarged easily on black-and-white direct duplicating film to make large negatives. Kodak professional direct duplicating film SO-015 (Estar thick base) is available in sizes up to 8″ × 10″. It can be handled under a red safelight and developed in Kodak Dektol developer (1:1) for 2¼ minutes in a tray.

For even larger sizes, a two-step procedure can be used to produce enlarged negatives. The original negative is employed to make a film positive, which is used to make the enlarged negative. Kodak commercial film and Kodak Super-XX pan film (both Estar thick base) are suitable and are available in sizes up to 11″ × 14″. The enlarged negative can be

lent filter, and a 15-watt bulb. Use the safelight at a distance of no less than 4 feet.

The easiest way to sensitize the material is to dip it in the solution and then hang it up to dry in a dark room. If you prefer, you can swab the sensitizing solution onto the surface with a tuft of absorbent cotton or a soft brush. To be certain of an even application, first spread the sensitizing solution with vertical strokes of the brush and then rework the surface with horizontal strokes. Then press the paper or fabric between two blotters to remove any excess sensitizer, and allow it to dry in a dark, dust-free place.

You can make a good brush or swab for spreading the sensitizer by folding several thicknesses of soft, clean cotton cloth around the end of a piece of glass that measures about 2″ × 6″. Secure the cloth to the glass by wrapping a rubber band around it. If the "handle" end is sharp, put tape around the end so that you will not cut yourself.

To sensitize only one side of a garment or other cloth item that has two layers of fabric, put a piece printed on Kodak professional copy film (Estar thick base), which is available in sizes up to 20″ × 24″.

Development

Wash the exposed print in running water at 18.5 to 21 C (65 to 70 F) for about 1 minute. The image will be yellow, but will change to brown when you immerse the print in hypo solution. Fix the print for 5 minutes at 18.5 to 21 C (65 to 70 F). To make the hypo solution, dissolve 28 grams (1 ounce) of sodium thiosulfate (hypo) in 591 millilitres (20 fluidounces) of water at room temperature. Do not use other hypo solutions recommended for film and conventional photographic paper because these solutions are too strong and may bleach the image produced by your sensitizer.

The hypo solution tends to reduce the density of the image, so make the print darker than normal to begin with by exposing longer during the printing step. You can sometimes use the hypo solution to save an overexposed print. When the print has reached the desired density in the hypo solution, wash it for 30 minutes in running water at 18.5 to 21 C (65 to 70 F) and then allow it to dry. When the print is dry, the image tone will be neutral.

The article on emulsions earlier in this volume gives directions for making a silver halide gelatin emulsion that can be applied to various surfaces for uses similar to those mentioned above. Commercially made emulsions for such purposes are advertised in the photographic magazines. The kallitype and diazotype processes can also be used.

• *See also:* DIAZOTYPE; EMULSION MAKING; KALLITYPE.

Fahrenheit

The Fahrenheit thermometer scale was named after the German scientist Gabriel Daniel Fahrenheit (1686–1736). Fahrenheit was born in Danzig, then a part of Germany, but spent most of his life in England and Holland. In Amsterdam, he manufactured meteorological instruments. He was the first to use mercury instead of alcohol as the liquid in thermometers. He was honored in 1724 by election to the Royal Society of London.

The Fahrenheit thermometer scale is based on a zero point that is the temperature of a freezing mixture of snow and salt, in equal parts. On this scale, then, the freezing point of pure water is 32 degrees, and the boiling point of pure water is 212 degrees. There are 180 degrees between freezing and boiling, as compared with the Celsius scale, which has 100 degrees between the same two points. Hence, the Fahrenheit degree is $\frac{5}{9}$ the size of a Celsius degree, and a Celsius degree is $\frac{9}{5}$ the size of a Fahrenheit degree. In translating from one system to another, however, it is necessary to take into account the "offset" of the freezing points; hence, 32 must be subtracted from the Fahrenheit temperature before multiplying by $\frac{5}{9}$. Likewise, if converting from Celsius to Fahrenheit, the Celsius temperature is *first* multiplied by $\frac{9}{5}$, and then 32 is added to the result. In short form:

$$C = \tfrac{5}{9}(F - 32)$$
$$F = (\tfrac{9}{5}\,C) + 32$$

• *See also:* CELSIUS; CENTIGRADE; KELVIN; TEMPERATURE SCALES; THERMOMETERS; WEIGHTS AND MEASURES.

False-Color Film

Normal color films are made with three layers of emulsion, sensitized to blue, green, and red light, respectively. When exposed and processed, each layer produces a dye image that is complementary in color to the emulsion sensitivity. Thus, the blue-sensitive layer produces a yellow dye, the green-sensitive layer produces a magenta dye, and the red-sensitive layer produces a cyan dye.

For certain special purposes, it is possible to make films in which either the layer sensitivity differs from normal, the dye associated with the layers differs from normal, or both. Such films, if developed as color films, produce images in which some or all of the colors are not natural in the strict sense.

One such film is Kodak Ektachrome infrared film, which has three layers, sensitized respectively to green, red, and infrared. The green-sensitive layer produces a yellow image, the red-sensitive layer produces a magenta image, and the infrared-sensitive layer produces a cyan image. While the main use of this film was intended to be in aerial surveying and reconnaissance, it has been used by creative photographers to produce a variety of pictorial effects.

• *See also:* INFRARED PHOTOGRAPHY.

Farmer, Ernest Howard

(1860–1944)
English chemist and photographic researcher

Farmer is best known for his well-known reducing bath, still called Farmer's Reducer, which he invented in 1883. In 1894, he outlined the basis of the bromoil and carbro processes, in a description of the reactions between a silver image, a bichromate salt, and the gelatin of either the original print or of a separate sheet.

• *See also:* REDUCTION.

Fashion Photography

This branch of commercial or professional photography, which has been recognized for its innovative contributions to fine photography since the 1920s, is basically divided into two fields: editorial fashion and advertising fashion. Editorial fashion covers all the photography commissioned by periodical publications—men's, women's, general consumer, and pure fashion magazines, as well as newspapers—for use in reporting on and promoting current fashions. Advertising fashion refers to photography commissioned by manufacturers of fashion and beauty products either directly or through advertising agencies. Most fashion photographers are active in both fields, which, though related, are distinct in their requirements and advantages for the photographer.

Editorial Fashion Photography

In general, magazines offer greater freedom for the photographer to initiate and carry through his or her own ideas. While the presentation of the product is important, it is usually in the context of the overall look and style of the publication, whether it be the elegant, sophisticated images of such fashion magazines as *Vogue* and *Harper's Bazaar,* or the more middle-class, everyday approach of a women's magazine such as *Good Housekeeping.* Editorial assignments sometimes involve as many as 10 or 12 pages in a single layout, which gives the photographer a broad range of possibilities. The emphasis is on a mood or story line that will create visual interest and continuity. Much of the planning is done in advance by the art director and editorial staff of the magazine, but the photographer often has a good deal of leeway in choosing models, location, and props, and in creating the mood and final look of the photographs in terms of lighting, movement, pose, and composition. In some cases, the photographer is given carte blanche to produce an editorial layout in its entirety, from initial concept to finished product.

The fees for editorial fashion photography are figured on a page rate, and range anywhere from $150 to $600 per page. While these fees are generally lower than those paid for advertising fashion, the inclusion of a credit line and the exposure in a prestigious magazine can be more than adequate compensation. The credit line has a great impact, since art directors use the editorial pages for spotting talent. It is through such work that the reputations of most fashion photographers are made.

Advertising Fashion Photography

Although there is increasing recognition of the photographer as a creative worker in advertising fashion, the emphasis is more on the product itself. The idea is to present the product clearly and prominently, to render color accurately, and to play down any effects of mood or narrative that might distract from the presentation. The client often exercises complete control over the concept and the shooting

(Left) Manufacturers of fashion and beauty products commission advertising photographs either directly or through their advertising agencies. While such photos appear in the same publications that use editorial photography, such as the photo at right, taken for Gentlemen's Quarterly, *the emphasis is somewhat different. The idea behind advertising photography is to present the product attractively and appropriately, but without allowing the setting to detract from the presentation. Photos by Robert Farber.*

itself, sometimes to the point where the photographer becomes little more than a technician carrying out detailed instructions.

Photographer's fees for advertising fashion are usually determined by the size of the budget, which may be enormous for an ad or campaign appearing in a national magazine. A common fee might be in the $1500 to $2000 range for a single ad, although it may go as high as $3000 or more for national coverage. Credit lines are seldom given unless the advertiser stands to gain by association with the name of a particular photographer.

Planning the Assignment

From the time the photographer is commissioned until the completion of a job, he or she is involved in a working relationship with a client whose attitude may amount to anything from constant surveillance to a completely hands-off approach. At advertising agencies, the key person is usually the creative director, who sometimes hires the photographer, and who has overall responsibility for the conception, planning, and execution of the work. In most cases, the photographer also deals with an art director in charge of developing a particular ad. Account executives, who represent the interests of the agency's client, and copywriters, who supply the words or sales pitch, may also be involved in the creation of an ad. On magazine or newspaper assignments, the photographer works with the art director, who plans and designs the layouts. Various fashion editors, who provide the copy and often originate story ideas, may also be involved.

Editorial planning tends to be open-ended and often encourages the participation of the photographer. The main concern is with the design of the magazine and the most appealing way, within the limits of editorial policy, to present current fashions. Advertising planning is more stringent for several reasons, the most important being that the advertising agency is responsible for producing the ad, the content, style, and general appearance of which have already been decided upon by the agency's client, the manufacturer of the product. On the other hand, most magazines and agencies realize that they have hired a photographer for the particular talent and style that he or she has to offer and that it makes sense to allow the photographer at least a measure of creative freedom to accomplish the job.

Verbal instructions are often sufficient to outline the general requirements of a job. In some cases, the art director will provide a rough sketch of a page layout, especially to show where the copy will go so that enough space will be left for it in the photograph. When the client wants to make absolutely sure of what he or she is getting, or if the layout itself is complicated and involves a number of pictures

As each publication has its own look and style, the photographer must understand the various editorial policies of each individual client. This photograph for Viva *illustrates a romantic fantasy concocted by the magazine's editorial staff; the written copy tells the story and gives information on the fashions worn by the models. Photo by Robert Farber.*

and pieces of copy, the art director will provide a comprehensive layout, or "comp." This amounts to a detailed drawing or set of drawings that represent anything from a general guide for the photographer to, in extreme cases, a precise indication of pose, setting, props, and even colors and mood, as they are expected to be captured on film.

Even with a comprehensive layout, the photographer has an obligation to use imagination and to present alternatives to the client. The shooting session is the domain of the photographer and his or her judgment has much more authority here. Still, most sessions are attended by the art director as well as assistants, copywriters, editors, account executives, and perhaps even a representative of the manufacturer. Their participation may be quite active, to the point of arranging the models and looking through the camera for each shot, so that the photographer is forced to moderate his or her own approach. But after satisfying the instructions of the client, the photographer can usually assert his or her own creative intelligence by shooting a scene in a particular way, and often it is this version that is used. While many art directors want to make sure they are getting what they planned, they also want a creative give-and-take situation and the chance to make use of the photographer's own special knowledge and inspiration.

Arranging the Shooting Session

Once a job has been assigned to a photographer, all the arrangements for the shooting itself are completely in his or her hands. This involves booking models, hiring specialists for makeup and hair styling, finding and obtaining permission for locations, renting or borrowing props, making any travel arrangements that might be necessary, and coordinating all these elements for a certain time on a certain date. The logistics can be quite simple when the

The photographer's creative and managerial abilities are called into constant play by the need to locate models, props, and settings that will interpret his client's wishes in the most advantageous manner. As illustrated here, the most successful location is not always the obvious one. Photo by Robert Farber.

The services of a stylist are at their most essential for photographs such as this, where location, props, and costumes have been used heavily to create, for Penthouse International, *an atmosphere reminiscent of a Toulouse-Lautrec painting. Photo by Robert Farber.*

photography involves a single model in the studio, or extremely complicated when the job calls for several models, elaborate props, expert assistance, and a quantity of pictures (as for an editorial layout or a catalog) in an exotic location. The photographer becomes, in effect, a producer as well as a creative talent. Additionally, in the calculations the photographer must consider how much the budget will allow for each item and what arrangements can be made to fit everything within the budget. While budget is not usually a problem in advertising fashion, it can be an important factor in the lesser-financed editorial assignments.

The Stylist. The success of any shooting depends largely on how well the people involved have been chosen both to create the intended image and to work together as a team. Perhaps the key figure in organizing a shooting is the stylist, the jack-of-all-

trades of fashion photography upon whose services the photographer relies in several areas. As a location finder, the stylist will search out the proper setting for the job and make the necessary arrangements—fees, permissions, and so forth—for its use. Some stylists keep extensive files of locations and their possible uses—for instance, places where one might be able to recreate the ambience of a Roman bath or an eighteenth-century ballroom. The acquisition of props is another of the stylist's functions. This requires knowledge and ingenuity in locating sources—costume agencies, antique shops, department stores, manufacturers, and so on—who will lend, rent, or sell whatever item is needed, from a luxury automobile to a child's toy. Stylists can also be called upon to suggest and book models, although the confirmed booking should always be made by the photographer. At the shooting, the stylist

Fashion Photography

Some models are highly specialized in certain areas. The model
used for this Revlon nail polish
commercial is known for her elegant and photogenic hands. Photo
by Robert Farber.

While all photographers' models are, by definition, photogenic, some may have individual features that put them in particular demand for
close-up work, such as this eye model in a Revlon ad. Photo by Robert Farber.

becomes a general factotum, assisting the photographer in setting up shots, making sure that clothes
and makeup remain fresh—even to the extent of
ironing out wrinkled garments—and overseeing
many of the details that determine how smoothly
and efficiently a session runs.

Hair and Makeup Specialists. A stylist might
also be able to work on hair and makeup, but usually, budget permitting, these jobs are handled by
specialists. Like photographers, hair stylists and
makeup artists have distinctive styles, and the crite-
ria for selecting them are based on the requirements

Fashion Photography

of the job. Some hair stylists, for instance, specialize in a natural, windblown look, while others create elegant, sculptured styles; certain makeup artists are adept at creating bizarre, theatrical effects, and others specialize in a healthy, all-American image. How they work with particular models is also a consideration in their selection.

Selecting Models. Numerous factors influence the selection of models. Occasionally, the client will want to use a certain model, either because the model is identified with the product or because the client thinks he or she should be. When making the selection, the most important consideration is whether the model's features fit the desired image. Some models might be appropriate for a sophisticated European look, others for an energetic all-American look. A woman might be sultry, ethereal, earthy, or animated; a man may be athletic, rugged, fatherly, or boyish. How they project these qualities determines the kinds of assignments they are chosen for. Like an actor, a model must be able to play a role. There are also those who become known for particular features. Beauty shots for eye makeup, for instance, would require someone with unusually

The choice of hair and makeup specialists is important in establishing the desired appearance of the photograph. This soft, informal look was created for Modern Bride. *Photo by Robert Farber.*

beautiful eyes, and for lipstick, a full, sensuous mouth.

The modeling agencies provide "head sheets" on all the models they represent, with pictures and pertinent information concerning height, color of hair and eyes, and clothes sizes. Individual models also provide more elaborate brochures, called "composites," showing some of the work they have done, as well as portfolios from which a photographer can gain a more complete idea of the model's look and style. But one of the overriding considerations in selecting models is how well they work with the photographer—whether they are relaxed and expressive in front of the camera, and whether there is a positive response to direction and a creative give-and-take during the shooting that results in interesting movement and posing. For this reason, established photographers continue to test models or simply to arrange "go sees" or interviews with them through the agencies.

Booking Models. For most jobs, the models are first booked tentatively. This booking reserves a model's time for a particular date and time period—two hours, a half day, a full day, or even several days. If the model has already been tentatively booked by another photographer, a secondary booking can be made in the hope that the model will become available through the cancellation of the first booking. Agencies require that confirmed bookings be made at least 48 hours before the shooting, after which the agency must be paid for the amount of time reserved, even if the entire shooting has to be postponed. For outdoor sessions, a weather permit can be obtained, which gives the photographer an option on the model's services for a rescheduled shooting in the event of bad weather. The agency is then paid only half the model's normal rate for the rained-out session.

Modeling Fees. Models' fees average from $60 to $100 per hour and from $400 to $600 per day; especially well-known models earn more. The top models often work on a negotiated fee, and in some cases, when the assignment has a low budget but offers good exposure and prestige, they may work for less than the standard rates. Where travel and a stay at some distant location are involved, a flat fee may be agreed upon. It is also possible, particularly in such active fashion centers as Paris, London, and Milan, to make use of local models. Some types of jobs, particularly for public display advertising such as billboards, posters, and product packaging, require special arrangements with the model. There are also special rates that apply to female models for photography involving nudity, escalating from the semi-nudity of lingerie and nightgowns, to complete nudity that might be required by, for example, a bath-oil advertisement. These rates are invoked only for the actual time the model spends in front of the camera. All this is detailed in the model release, which is signed by model, client, and photographer at the end of a shooting session, and which essentially provides the model's permission for the pictures to be used as intended. This release is incorporated in the model's "voucher," which also includes the amount of money the model has earned.

Choice of Location, Lighting, and Background

Whether an assignment is done in the studio or on location depends on the client's needs. The client may want to forego the atmosphere and mood of a natural setting to focus on the product—for example, a beauty aid shown in a close-up of a model's face or a suit displayed in a simple shot of a model wearing it. The studio is essential for such basic fashion shots, and it can also be used, with the correct props, to create much more elaborate settings. However, more and more, editorial and advertising fashion are photographed on location, which provides greater possibilities for visual and narrative interest, as well as an authentic quality that cannot be obtained in the studio. For instance, the idea of showing clothes as a woman might wear them in daily life has a much greater impact if real settings are used. Also, there are many effects that can be achieved only on location, from a beach for a bathing suit ad, to the romantic ambience of an old railway station for an elegant fur, as examples.

The Studio. A studio may be elaborate or simple, large or small, according to the photographer's practice. It should be no smaller than 22 feet in length, 9 feet in width, and 9 feet in height—long enough for the photographer to stand back from the model with a long lens and high enough to allow shooting from above and below. A photographer of still lifes generally needs more space to be able to arrange several shots simultaneously. If natural light is available, it should be from the north, to avoid

Location photography can be used for creating mood and ambience. The period look of these very contemporary fashions is displayed to best advantage in a setting vaguely reminiscent of a more romantic era. Photo by Robert Farber.

direct sunlight. All that is usually required is a simple, open space in which to work; walls should be white so that no color is reflected on the subject.

Basic studio equipment and accessories, aside from cameras and lenses, consist of artificial lighting, seamless paper, a slide projector and light box for viewing, a dressing area for models, and perhaps a darkroom for developing and printing black-and-white photos. Equipment that allows the photographer to shoot with projected backgrounds broadens the use of the studio.

Lighting. Lighting can be either tungsten or strobe. Tungsten produces a steady flow of light that allows the photographer to determine before shoot-

ing exactly how much light there is and the nature of the shadows it is producing. On the other hand, it requires the use of film balanced for tungsten lighting, and this reduces the options open to the photographer. Electronic flash (strobe) units produce light that approximates sunlight, so a greater variety of films can be used. Strobe does not offer the control possible with tungsten, although modeling lights in the strobe head make it possible to establish the general light quality and direction. Because of its portability, flexibility, and speed, strobe has become the most popular form of lighting among fashion photographers. The burst of light, allowing the use of slower films, makes it possible to freeze action,

Seamless paper used as a background for studio photographs is extremely versatile. Gray paper used here with simple props and carefully arranged lighting provides a featureless background against which the product is clearly and dramatically displayed. Photo by Robert Farber.

thus affording the model greater freedom of movement. Studio strobe units range in intensity from 200 to 2400 watt-seconds and above. The high-intensity units are used primarily by still-life photographers who want to close down the camera's aperture to obtain greatest depth of field.

Individual photographers develop their own approaches to lighting and the techniques to achieve them: single-source lighting from the side to create sharp, dramatic contrasts of light and shade; frontal lighting to flatten out the image; several light sources to fill in and even out the light; and various bounce devices for reducing the harshness of direct light.

Backgrounds. Seamless paper is an essential part of much studio shooting. It comes in rolls 107 inches wide and up to 50 yards in length, and in a great variety of colors, the most frequently used being black, white, and shades of gray. As a background, behind and under the model or subject, it creates a smooth, textureless setting against which the model stands out in strong contrast.

Projected Backgrounds Many fashion pictures look as though they were taken in some familiar location in a foreign country, when, in fact, they were taken in a studio furnished with front-projection equipment. A transparency of the background subject is projected onto a special, narrow-angle, ultra-high-reflectance screen through a beam splitter placed in front of the camera lens. The subject is

lighted either with electronic flash or incandescent lighting that is appropriate for the background. Care must be taken so that none of the foreground lighting spills onto the screen, because this dilutes the projected image with white light. Front-projection equipment is invaluable for the fashion photographer because it permits pictures with an infinite variety of backgrounds without the cost and time loss involved in traveling to location.

Special projectors are marketed with beam splitters for projecting the backgrounds, usually from 35 mm slides. Special front-projection screen sheeting is required, and is available in sheet form or made up into screens.

Alignment of the projector, camera, and beam splitter must be exact to avoid shadowed areas. Taking half or three-quarter figures is relatively easy, but taking full figures that involve showing the floor and screen base becomes complicated.

Cameras

During the first flourishing of fashion photography in the 1920s and 1930s, most work was done with view cameras in the studio, and as a result had a highly studied, posed, and stylized look. The view camera has survived in certain situations—for instance, in some catalog work where the poses are meant to be rather stiff and predictable. For some photographers and art directors, the large 8″ × 10″

or 4″ × 5″ images produced by the view camera also offer the advantage of being easy to retouch. The vast majority of fashion photographers working today, however, use the 35 mm camera. Its light weight, portability, and speed of operation, combined with its adaptability to a variety of lenses, make it ideal for the broad range of styles practiced in modern fashion photography. It becomes an extension of the photographer, allowing him or her to work in a much more natural and dynamic manner.

Lenses

Telephoto and wide-angle lenses for 35 mm cameras have become an integral part of fashion photography for the many effects they are capable of achieving. Among long lenses, the most popular are the 105 and the 135 mm, although the 500 mm has come into greater use as technological developments have made it possible to reduce its size and weight. With a long lens, the photographer can do tight close-ups of the face, eyes, or lips without crowding the model and without the perspective distortion of features caused by a normal 50 mm lens. Long lenses also cut down on the depth of field so that the camera focuses on the subject and cuts out both background and foreground; the out-of-focus surroundings become an effective, sometimes dramatic, abstract design, and the emphasis is placed on the product itself.

Wide-angle lenses range from 15 to 35 mm. The 28 mm wide-angle lens is used not only to create broad, panoramic views, but also to enhance visual interest by exaggerating perspective. A model, for instance, can be made to appear taller and more slender, or a certain feature, such as a shoe or a hand, can be given greater prominence in relationship to the rest of the figure. Likewise, any arrangement of forms in depth, such as a road, a running fence, or a grouping of models, becomes more pronounced and dramatic.

Films

The kind of film used can also affect the look and style of a fashion photographer's work. For color photography, many advertising clients prefer and even ask for a particular film to be used. For example, one of the Kodachrome films is sometimes requested because of the way it reproduces skin tones and other colors. Kodachrome film is also an extremely fine-grain film with high resolving power so that the image quality holds up very well in the process of enlargement for reproduction in a magazine or ad. A fast Kodak Ektachrome film, on the other hand, may be requested in order to provide various creative possibilities for editorial purposes. While most color films are close to each other in color reproduction, there are slight distinctions that appeal to different people, and this results in specific recommendations. When the speed of Ektachrome film is pushed, its graininess increases. In high-magnification enlargement, the grain pattern of the film can be used to create abstract patterns, or to make mood-evoking pictures.

Since the fashion photographer's clients call for positive color film (transparencies), all the work has to be done in the camera, with the help of different lenses, lighting setups, and filters. What appears on the developed slides or transparencies is what the client receives as a completed job, after the photographer has done some preliminary editing.

Black-and-white shooting, while not subject to the same initial controls required by color, can be more complicated and time-consuming in the final presentation. The photographer first must present contact sheets or work prints to the client and then must make final prints (usually 11″ × 14″) once the selection has been made. Many alterations can be made in the process of developing and printing black-and-white films that cannot be made with color films. How they are made may be a matter of aesthetic choice or of the client's preference for high or low contrast, a grainy, atmospheric effect, or sharp, realistic images.

Reshooting Assignments

Occasionally, the need for a reshoot occurs. If the client has had an arbitrary change of heart about the models, the props, the location, or the overall look of the photographs, the shooting is simply redone at no loss to the photographer, except in terms of time. However, if the responsibility lies with the photographer, the reshooting is done at half-fee, in most instances, although the full rates must be paid to models, stylists, and others involved. The unsatisfactory completion of an assignment can usually be avoided if rapport with the client has been maintained, the shooting has been properly organized, and precautions have been taken to prevent a breakdown in equipment. For this reason, backups for all the important and delicate equipment should always be kept on hand.

The Portfolio

A fashion photographer's career begins with the creation of a portfolio, which should reveal the full range of his or her capabilities and style. In the beginning, it is based on the work that has been done from the photographer's own imagination and resources in test shootings. Later, the results of assignments—tearsheets from actual jobs—are incorporated; however, most photographers continue to do experimental work, which remains a vital part of a

The portfolio photograph is designed to show the photographer's skill and versatility. In this mood, he creates a brittle, dramatic, low-key image that has the hardness and sparkle of a diamond. Photo by Robert Farber.

Using a different type of model, unadorned and with straightforward lighting, the same photographer displays a looser and more sensual aspect of his professional capabilities. Photo by Robert Farber.

developing portfolio, demonstrating what can be done without the restrictions imposed by a client's requirements.

Tests are arranged through the modeling agencies and contacts are made in the field with stylists, hair stylists, and makeup artists, all of whom benefit from the creation and maintenance of their own portfolios and will therefore participate at no fee. The experience that is gained by testing with models is invaluable, and the portfolio should include a wide selection of work with individual models in close-ups, full-length shots, different lighting conditions, and various moods. These should be complemented by photographs taken under conditions that might exist in an actual assignment. Gathering a team together and shooting at various locations with several models, perhaps around a theme such as beach wear or fall fashions, gives the photographer the opportunity to test his or her skill in organization and to show off his or her ability to work on a larger scale.

The building of a portfolio is the constant refinement of an individual style by experimenting and focusing on strengths and preferences that become apparent with experience. Much can be learned by studying current styles of photography as well as those of the past, and by being aware of fashions and modes of expression outside the world of fashion photography. But there is a danger in becoming too derivative or in simply following a fad that will soon pass. The essentials of an individual style are based on the photographer's own work with models, lighting, composition, and narrative content, and on how well the potential of a distinct viewpoint is realized.

Success in fashion photography is largely a product of the portfolio—what it reveals about the photographer's talent, style, and ability to organize a shooting, and how well it is presented to potential clients. Persistence, enthusiasm, and adaptability are all essential requirements of the fashion photographer, but in the end, his or her photographs must speak for themselves.

• *See also:* ADVERTISING PHOTOGRAPHY; COMMERCIAL PHOTOGRAPHY; FRONT SCREEN PROJECTION; GLAMOUR PHOTOGRAPHY; MODEL RELEASE; MODELS AND MODELING.

Further Reading: Hymers, Robert. *Professional Photography in Practice.* (Published by Fountain) Dobbs Ferry, NY: Morgan & Morgan, Inc., 1969; Gowland, Peter *Gowland's Guide to Glamour Photography.* New York, NY: Crown Publishers, Inc., 1972.

Ferric Ammonium Citrate

Ammoniocitrate of iron, iron and ammonium citrate, soluble ferric citrate

Used in sensitizing blueprint papers, kallitype process, and in iron blue toning solutions.
Formula: indefinite, composition varies
Molecular Weight: varies

Some forms of ferric ammonium citrate are green in color; others are brown. The green variety is preferable for photographic purposes, although both are light-sensitive.

Ferric Ammonium Sulfate

Ferric ammonium alum, ferric alum, iron alum, iron and ammonium sulfate

Used in certain reducers, toning solutions, and sensitizing solutions.
Formula: $(NH_4)_2Fe_2(SO_4)_4 \cdot 24H_2O$
Molecular Weight: 964.37

Violet efflorescent crystals, freely soluble in water, insoluble in alcohol.

Ferric Chloride

Iron chloride, ferric trichloride, iron perchloride, iron sesquichloride, iron trichloride, chloride of iron

Used in reducers, blue toning, and etching of copper in gravure processes.
Formula: $FeCl_3 \cdot 6H_2O$
Molecular Weight: 270.31

Orange-yellow opaque masses or lumps, deliquescent, very soluble in water and alcohol.

Ferric Oxalate

Iron oxalate, iron sesquioxalate

Used in platinotype and kallitype processes, sometimes used in blueprint sensitizers. Also used in certain iron toning solutions.
Formula: $Fe_2(C_2O_4)_3 \cdot 6H_2O$
Molecular Weight: 483.86

Greenish crystalline scales, or pearls. It is light sensitive and very soluble in water.

Ferrotype

A ferrotype is a photograph, generally known as a tintype, which was made on thin steel plates (occasionally cardboard), first painted black or brown, then coated with a collodion emulsion. After exposure, the plate was developed in an iron developer and fixed in a solution of potassium cyanide. This produced a whitish-silver negative image, which, when viewed against the black background of the plate itself, appeared as a positive. Tintypes were made cheaply by itinerant photographers who set up on any convenient street corner. They have remarkable permanence, and many of them, although they are over 100 years old, are in existence today. The ferrotype process was introduced about 1855 by an American, J. W. Griswold.

The early version of tintypes was a wet process. A later dry ferrotype process utilized a dry gelatin emulsion on a painted metal plate, which was devel-

Ferrotyping increases the apparent density range of the image, and so increases the brilliance of the print. This is because little of the light reflected by a shadow area of a glossy print reaches the eye. In the case of a textured or lustre-surface print, incident light is scattered, and regardless of the angle from which the print is viewed, some of the scattered light reaches the eye. Thus, the density of the dark area appears to be less. The difference in maximum reflection density between a ferrotyped glossy print and a matte print can be as much as 30 percent.

Papers with a smooth surface and with a special overcoat layer are necessary for good ferrotyping. Those manufactured by Eastman Kodak Company for this purpose are designated by the letter F. *Remember that water-resistant papers cannot be ferrotyped.* The surface of these papers yields a high gloss when dried as recommended.

Ferrotyping Surfaces

Since the surface of a ferrotyped print takes the form of the surface onto which it is pressed, any material used for ferrotyping must be perfectly smooth and free from blemishes or scratches. Obviously, any such imperfections will be reproduced on the surface of the print.

A number of surfaces are sufficiently glossy for ferrotyping, but the most useful are highly polished stainless steel and chromium plating. The base metal beneath the chromium plating should be stainless steel, because, due to the porous nature of the plating, other metals may react with chemicals in the prints and cause staining. Glass is sometimes used, but chipped or broken glass is a hazard, and prints are more prone to stick on glass than on most other surfaces. In the absence of a better material, prints can be ferrotyped on sheets of glossy plastic material, but it is often difficult to find such sheets with a perfect, blemish-free surface. Since the use of any sheet material for ferrotyping involves a considerable amount of time and labor in squeegeeing the prints onto the sheets, a drum-type ferrotyping machine is more suitable for large-volume use.

oped in a hydroquinone developer and fixed in hypo. A monobath, in which the fixer was mixed with the developer, was also sometimes used for processing.

• *See also:* ARCHER, FREDERICK SCOTT; CARTE-DE-VISITE COLLODION; TINTYPE.

Ferrotyping

The gelatin surface of photographs can be given a high gloss by pressing the wet prints into intimate contact with a highly polished surface. This operation is called ferrotyping or glazing and is used on conventional fiber-base papers—not water-resistant papers.

Condition of Prints for Good Ferrotyping

Difficulties in ferrotyping can usually be traced to one of several main causes outlined below.

Processing. Some ferrotyping defects are caused by improper processing. Exhausted chemical solutions are the main fault. If the stop bath is overworked, it fails to remove possible calcium scum from the surface of the prints. This scum is invisible on a wet print, but it can cause dull patches on the surface of one that has been ferrotyped. A further result of an exhausted stop bath is that the acid in the fixer becomes neutralized, and the hardening properties of the bath are reduced. As a result, soft gelatin can be transferred to the ferrotyping surface. A buildup of this material causes the prints to stick to a plate or to the drum of a machine.

When a fixing bath is exhausted, it fails to remove all of the silver complexes from the paper. Consequently, residual silver may cause yellow stains that affect the paper base as well as the emulsion. The problems mentioned above disappear when the stop bath and fixer are renewed.

Washing. Incomplete washing can cause yellow stains on prints ferrotyped by machine. Also, dried chemical residues build up on the drum or plate and mar the surface of the prints. Constant ferrotyping of incompletely washed prints may, in time, damage the plated surfaces. Also, unwashed prints leave hypo in the cloth belt of a machine. Although prints dried subsequently may be properly washed, they are contaminated by chemical residues and are therefore subject to fading and staining in the same way as they would be if not properly washed.

Cleanliness. Airborne dust, lint from cleaning cloths, and powdered cleaners are probably the worst enemies of good ferrotyping.

Airborne dust settles on ferrotyping surfaces, on the belts of drying machines, and on the surface of wash water or any liquid that may be used as a preferrotyping bath. To reduce dust to the minimum obtainable in ordinary ventilation systems, change the filters in furnaces, air conditioners, and air ducts regularly. Wash the floor; do not sweep it while dry. Clean dried chemicals from the floor, and do not mix chemicals in the finishing area. Keep ferrotyping machines, washing tanks, and trays of preferrotyping solution covered when not being used.

Temperature. When prints are ferrotyped on flat plates, they should be allowed to dry naturally. Too rapid drying causes the prints to leave the plate in steps. The result is a surface that resembles an oyster shell. The best results are obtained when drying takes a few hours.

When the plates with prints on them are put on an electric platen drier under canvas retainers, a low heat setting and relatively slow drying will help avoid the oyster-shell effect.

Temperature of Ferrotyping Drums. The maximum surface temperature of the drum should not exceed 82 C (180 F). The speed of the machine should be such that the prints dry completely before they emerge from under the cloth belt. Otherwise, the oyster-shell markings may result. Excessively high temperature may also cause the prints to stick to the drum, particularly if the gelatin is soft due to insufficient hardening in the fixer or to a very long immersion in the wash water.

Avoid a situation where a ferrotyping machine stands in a cooling draft from an open window or door. This may cause an uneven temperature over the drum surface. As a result, some prints will dry more quickly than others. These remarks apply particularly to ferrotyping machines that do not have a water jacket beneath the drum surface. The water-jacketed type is less liable to variations in surface temperature.

Residues on the Ferrotyping Surface. As water evaporates from a ferrotyping surface, it generally leaves a chalky residue. This residue can easily be wiped away with a soft, damp cloth; but if the deposit is allowed to build up and is mixed with chemicals from partly washed prints or with particles of gelatin from the edges of the prints, it may affect the polished surface in such a way that prints ferrotyped subsequently stick to the surface. The remedy for this is routine cleaning and, of course, proper processing and washing. See the section on cleaning ferrotyping surfaces in this article for further information.

Solid Particles in Wash Water. The particles of sand, rust, and other solid matter that often become embedded in the gelatin of a ferrotyped print can usually be traced to the incoming water supply. An efficient filter in the water line will trap particles that cause trouble, but remember to change the filter element at regular intervals. Also, clean the washing tanks at least once each week to remove any sediment that accumulates.

Cleaning Ferrotyping Surfaces

When a print sticks to a ferrotyping plate or drum, it can be considered a complete loss; there is no practical way to remove it without damage. Thus, a considerable investment in time, effort, and material is wasted. Sticking can generally be prevented by proper processing and washing, and by routine cleaning of ferrotyping surfaces.

General Cleaning. Clean the surface of new drums and plates with soap such as Bon Ami soap (cakes only—Bon Ami in spray or powder form must not be used). This cleaner removes most deposits from the plated surface and, at the same time, leaves a layer of fatty acid on the surface. This layer is most important, because prints tend to stick to a bare metal surface, particularly chromium plating.

The drum of a ferrotyping machine that is used daily should be cleaned every morning with Bon Ami soap; it is then sufficient to wipe away any deposits that form during normal use.

Chromium-plated ferrotyping sheets should be cleaned with Bon Ami soap before each use.

Emergency Cleaning. When ferrotyping equipment is in constant use, deposits of gelatin and other material build up on the polished surface. These deposits cannot always be seen, but their presence is indicated by prints that stick and cannot be removed. If persistent sticking occurs, follow the procedure given below; it applies to both plates and drums. *Allow drums to cool completely before using the cleaning treatment:*

1. Make a thin, watery paste from the Carborundum product called Aloxite Grade A, No. 1, Fine Buffing Powder. This powder must be used; no other known kind of Aloxite will do.
2. Apply the paste with a soft cloth to a small part of the surface at a time. Continue to rub until there is no break in a film of water applied to the surface.
3. Allow the paste to dry on the surface, and then wipe it off with a soft cloth. Remove all traces of the powder, particularly from the belt of a ferrotyping machine.
4. Polish with Bon Ami soap until the surface is repellent; that is, until a film of

water does not spread evenly over the surface. More than one application of Bon Ami soap may be necessary to achieve this condition.
5. Remove all traces of Aloxite powder and Bon Ami soap that may have settled on the cloth belt or other parts of a ferrotyping machine and from the immediate work area.

When prints stick to a ferrotyping surface, they are usually impossible to remove without soaking the paper thoroughly with warm water, and then rubbing the paper and the gelatin from the drum in small pieces. Never use a sharp instrument to scrape the paper off; this will scratch the metal surface, and these scratches will show on any prints that are ferrotyped afterwards. Do not clean ferrotyping surfaces while wearing a diamond ring or other jewelry that might scratch the plating.

Ferrotyping with Plates

Before applying the prints to the plate, clean it with Kodak ferrotype plate polish or with Bon Ami soap as described earlier in this article.

Place the prints in a tray of *clean* water. Pick the first print up by its opposite corners, and without draining the water from it, lay it on the plate, center part first; then, let the print down slowly until each corner reaches the plate surface. This method helps to prevent bubbles from being trapped beneath the print. Hold one end of the print and roll it firmly to expel most of the water. Then roll the print again twice in both directions. Place a sheet of photographic-quality blotting paper over the print and roll lightly to pick up any remaining water.

An alternative method that is preferable when several small prints are ferrotyped on one plate, is to place a sheet of rubberized cloth or a similar material over the prints immediately after they have been laid on the plate; then squeegee over the covering material. With this method, either a flat-blade or roller squeegee can be used. Again, the prints should be blotted to remove excess water.

Drying Prints on Ferrotype Plates. Natural drying over a period of several hours gives the best results. If the drying time must be shortened, place the plates in a warm, dry place, but not where the temperature exceeds 24 C (75 F). Remember, if the prints dry too quickly, oyster-shell markings and

CAUSES AND REMEDIES OF PROBLEMS IN FERROTYPING

Problem	Probable Cause	Remedy
Prints stick to plate or drum, although quite dry	1. Buildup of foreign matter on glazing surface 2. Drum too hot 3. Gelatin too soft; fixer exhausted 4. Surface not conditioned after use of Aloxite 5. Washing water too warm	1. Clean and condition surface 2. Reduce temperature to 82 C (180 F) 3. Use fresh fixer with hardener 4. Condition with Bon Ami 5. Reduce to 21–24 C (70–75 F)
Unglazed spots—regular-shaped circles or ovals	1. Air bells; imperfect contact with surface 2. Drum too hot (steam forcing print from drum)	1. Soak and reglaze; use more pressure when squeegeeing 2. Reduce temperature to 82 C (180 F)
Irregular unglazed patches	1. Scum on print surface caused by exhausted stop and fixing baths 2. Uneven pressure between drum and squeegee roller 3. Not enough pressure with manual squeegee	1. Use fresh chemicals and mix as recommended 2. Drum not resting evenly on squeegee roller. Adjust to obtain even pressure over the whole width 3. Roll with greater pressure
Oyster-shell markings—evenly spaced semicircular creases, or cracks	Prints are leaving the glazing surface in steps and are drying too rapidly	Dry in cooler place with more humidity. If a drum machine is used, reduce speed and temperature until prints are just dry as they emerge from under the canvas belt
Unglazed edges, usually with double-weight paper	Drying too rapid. Edges of print dry and lift before glazing can take place	Reduce drum speed and temperature. Where plates are used, dry in a cooler place
Markings such as small flecks and spots on the print surface	1. Dust and lint on plate or drum surface 2. Dust and lint in wash water	1. Clean plate with lintless cloth. Brush canvas belt and dust drum with lintless cloth. Cover when not in use 2. Keep tanks covered when possible. Do not place them near overhead air ducts
Flecks of uniform shape over whole area of the print	Gelatin too hard; water too cold	Use warmer water, 21–24 C (70–75 F). Also use *Kodak* hypo clearing agent before washing
Insufficient gloss	1. Gelatin too hard 2. Drum or plate surface dull 3. Drum too hot 4. Scum from exhausted stop and fixing baths 5. Prints not wet enough	1. See above remedy 2. Polish or renew 3. Adjust temperature to 82 C (180 F) 4. Renew solutions. Mix as recommended 5. Make sure a bead of water forms where print meets drum surface
Band of yellow stain on trailing edge of drum-ferrotyped print, usually on paper base	1. Processing chemicals retained in paper after washing 2. Scorched or dirty canvas belt	1. Agitate print in stop bath. Use two-bath fixing. Do not overfix; use *Kodak* hypo clearing agent. Separate prints frequently during washing 2. Renew belt
Small brown spots with dark centers	Porous plating is allowing rust to seep through and stain print	Clean drum with Bon Ami. If trouble persists, replate or replace drum

unglazed edges may result. In a humid atmosphere, a fan can be used to speed drying, but be sure that the flow of air is uniform if a number of prints are drying. One method of minimizing the risk of oyster-shelling is to place the plates, print-side-down, on stretched cheesecloth or plastic screen drying racks. For occasional drying, the plates can be placed print-side-down on clean towels laid out on a rug and allowed to dry overnight.

Machine Ferrotyping

Basically, a ferrotyping machine consists of an endless cloth belt that is held in contact with a heated drum by a spring-loaded squeegee roller. As a rule, this roller is the driven member and it, in turn, rotates both the belt and the drum. The drum may be heated either directly by electric heaters or by circulating hot water in a jacket beneath the drum surface. Although water-heated machines are more expensive than those heated directly, they are preferable for high-volume ferrotyping. The water circulating in the jacket maintains uniform drum temperature when the machine is used continuously.

In general, the surface temperature of the drum should not exceed 82 C (180 F). The speed of rotation should be adjusted so that the prints are just dry when they emerge from under the belt. A drum without a water jacket, however, will need an initial temperature greater than 82 C (180 F), because it will cool rapidly as it dissipates cold water from the prints fed onto it. Since ferrotyping machines vary in the details of construction and in the metals used for the drum and its plating, follow the manufacturer's instructions for the particular machine.

Preferrotyping Baths. From time to time, a number of different solutions have been recommended as preferrotyping baths, but generally they are unnecessary when prints are properly processed and washed, and when proper temperature and drying conditions are observed. However, when such a bath is recommended by the manufacturer of the machine, it should be used.

Straightening Curled Prints. Prints often leave a ferrotyping machine with a pronounced curl that is caused by unequal contraction of the gelatin coating and the paper base. Prints in this condition will flatten automatically if they are laid face up on a table and if the relative humidity in the room is about 40 percent or higher. A large quantity of prints can be flattened quickly by using a Kodak print straightener, model G. This machine applies steam to the prints to equalize the moisture content of the gelatin and the paper base.
• *See also:* PRINT FINISHING.

Ferrous Sulfate

Green copperas, green vitriol, protosulfate of iron, sulfate of iron

Used in ferrous oxalate developers.
Formula: $FeSO_4 \cdot 7H_2O$
Molecular Weight: 278.02

Greenish crystals, often with a reddish coating from oxidation to ferric sulfate, or with a whitish color from efflorescence. Crystals should be rinsed clean before dissolving. Freely soluble in water. Should be prepared freshly before use; stock solutions tend to oxidize to ferric sulfate. It was used as a developer in the wet collodion process.

Fiber Optics

Fiber optics is a variant optical system that utilizes glass or transparent plastic fibers as light transmitting media. When light is introduced at one end of such a fiber, it travels along inside the fiber by a series of total reflections from the surface, eventually emerging at the far end of the fiber.

If such fibers are arranged in a bundle, larger amounts of light may be transmitted, because the aperture of the system is larger. Such a bundle may be *incoherent;* that is, the fibers are arranged randomly, and the resulting device can only be used as a light-transmitting medium. For example, by the use of a random system, a beam of light may be carried around corners and into inconvenient places. In addition, the randomness of the bundle serves to even out any variations in light intensity across the beam.

In a *coherent* system, the fibers are arranged in alignment, so that a ray entering a fiber at one corner of the bundle emerges at the same corner at the output end. Such coherent fiber systems can be used to transmit images for various distances without the use of lenses. The resolution of such a system is, obviously, that of the individual fibers; no detail smaller than a single fiber can be resolved.

Early attempts at making fiber optics suffered from loss of light from the outside of the fiber into the air at sharp bends, and from transmission of light from one fiber to another at points of contact. Modern fiber optics utilize a system called "cladding" in which each fiber is coated with a material having an index of refraction much lower than the fiber material itself. This ensures total reflection at the surfaces, and it greatly increases the efficiency of the system.

Typical uses of long fiber-optics bundles include endoscopes, which take advantage of the flexibility of the fiber optics bundle to transmit images from small, inaccessible cavities. Short fiber optics are used to transmit large images over distances too short to admit a wide-angle optical system of any other type. Typically such systems include fiber-optics face-plates used on cathode-ray tubes and in devices such as image intensifiers.

Field Lens

Whenever a long optical system is used, in which a lens forms an image in space and this image, in turn, is picked up by a second lens and re-imaged, it is necessary to place a field lens at the plane of the first image. The field lens is focused so as to image the diaphragm of the first lens in the diaphragm of the second. If this is not done, the rays of light from the first lens will diverge, and only those coming from the center of the first lens will enter the second lens. The field lens bends the diverging rays around and

directs them into the succeeding lens. Obviously, this can be repeated as many times as necessary for a given system. The accompanying diagram shows a long terrestrial telescope and the position of the field lens that is required to direct the light rays through the erector and into the eyepiece. A similar system is used in the focusing magnifier of certain professional motion-picture cameras to carry the image from the film plane to the back of the camera. Without the field lens, only the central portion of the image can be seen. The light from off-axis subjects can be lost in the system and not reach the eye.

The same problem exists when focusing a camera. If you look through a camera with the ground glass removed, you will see only a small circle of light (and image) the diameter of the lens aperture. The ground glass helps to make the marginal parts of the image visible by scattering some of the light in all directions. Enough of it is directed toward the eye so that the image can be seen toward the corners of the field.

Even so, the image is always brighter at the center of the ground glass than at the corners, and this situation can also be improved by the use of a field lens. Generally, the field lens used is a thin Fresnel lens. It is placed directly under the ground glass, and serves to direct the light from the camera lens into the pupil of the photographer's eye. The use of such a field lens makes the image nearly as bright at the corners as it is in the middle of the field, and facilitates composition over the entire image area.

Actually, almost any kind of positive lens of the right focal length can be used as a field lens. When a lens is placed in the plane of a real image, or nearly so, it has practically no effect upon the correction of the main lens. The main virtue of the Fresnel lens for this purpose is its thinness. This avoids shifting the

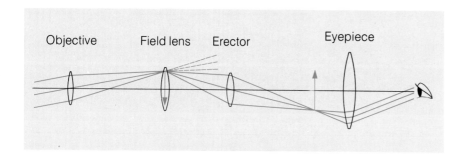

The use of a field lens in a typical long telescopic system is shown here.

position of the image and the focal point, and it reduces weight. A positive lens the size of a ground glass and of the correct focal length would be thick and heavy.

Typical examples of the use of a field lens with ground glass are the focusing screen of a reflex camera, and the projection screen of slide table viewers. The latter screen is actually not made from ground glass, but it is a beaded transmitting screen. The beads are very tiny, and are pressed into a black cement on the surface of the glass. When viewed from the glass side, the screen therefore appears to be black, but it is transparent at the millions of points where the beads are pressed through the cement into contact with the glass. A black screen can be used satisfactorily under bright ambient illumination, where ground glass would appear white and would be quite useless.

• *See also:* FOCUSING; FRESNEL LENSES; LENSES; PROJECTION SCREENS; REAR PROJECTION.

Filing and Storing Negatives, Prints, and Transparencies

A well-organized filing system for photographic negatives, prints, or transparencies provides efficiency, economy, and convenience. It can also provide protection. Professionals rely on their files to facilitate servicing repeat orders from customers, to locate previously unused images when the need arises, and to make profitable stock picture sales from their ever-growing collections of photographs of many different subjects. Nonprofessionals find that a filing system gives them increased pleasure and use from their picture and slide collections. In all cases, a good filing/storage system minimizes loss, damage, or deterioration of photographs.

A filing system does not have to be complex; in fact, the simpler it is, the easier it is to use and to keep up-to-date. A good system requires three basic characteristics:

1. Accurate identification of every image.
2. Logical organization of the filing and storage arrangement.
3. Protection of the filed photographs.

Image Identification

In the long run, a numbering system that is cross-indexed provides the most flexible identification scheme. Using subject names might seem to be a good idea for a portrait studio. Adding addresses to the names can avoid difficulties in keeping the files of, say, three different James Joneses separate, but even here a numbering system has advantages. Using category names (*Architecture, Children, Sunsets,* and so forth) might be convenient for the reference picture files of libraries or stock picture agencies, but not for the filing of negatives or original transparencies because it means that every picture in a category may have to be examined in order to find a single desired image. That may be no problem in the first year or two of a collection's growth, but as time goes by the situation can get out of hand. Such a category file also increases the likelihood of damage from repeated handling of the pictures.

A studio that routinely assigns a job number to every assignment generally uses the job number to identify the pictures as well. The same idea can be adopted for use by individuals. A convenient system uses three-part numbers composed of *Date, Roll (or Job),* and *Frame (or Shot).* For example, *78–15–5* identifies (reading backwards) the fifth frame on roll 15, taken in 1978 (or the fifth shot of job number 15 in 1978). The date information can be made more precise by adding the month after the year digits, if desired. For example, the file numbers for February, June, and November of 1979 would begin *792–, 796–,* and *7911–,* respectively. Roll or job numbering begins again from number one each month when this method is used.

Marking Photographs

An identification number must go on every negative, print, and transparency. If a roll film is cut into shorter lengths for storage, each length must carry the date and roll digits; frame numbers need be added only if the pre-exposed edge numbers common to most films are illegible after processing. Most laboratory-processed slides are returned in frame-numbered mounts. A print is identified by the number of the negative from which it is made. Here the value of the frame or shot number in the overall identification number becomes apparent. It is the only way to indicate which of several bracketed exposures, or which of a number of minor variations

A plastic album page designed to hold up to 36 exposures of 35 mm negatives facilitates storage. Contact prints may be made while negatives remain in their protective cover. Photo courtesy 20th Century Plastics.

in pose, composition, or focus, was used—things that are difficult to determine by looking at a small negative.

The unexposed areas of negative films are transparent, so numbers can be marked in the margins; the spaces between sprocket holes can be used on 35 mm films. Opaque India ink or celluloid marking ink—available in art supply stores—should be used on the base side of the film; a fine-point "crow quill" pen will deposit the ink cleanly. Waterproof ink is essential to avoid obliteration of the number or possible staining of the image in case the negative is rewashed or given chemical treatment at some later time. Some fine-point felt-tip markers with permanent, solvent-type ink are available that make it easy to mark on either side of a negative. Film cleaners should not be wiped across the markings; they may dissolve or smear some inks.

Transparency films have opaque borders. They can be marked by scratching the number into the emulsion of the film, outside the image area, with a sharp-pointed marking tool. Mounted slides can be marked in ink on the cardboard mounts, or on small self-adhesive labels stuck on the mounts.

Contact sheets will carry the numbers marked on the negatives; enlargements are usually marked on the back. The number can be penciled on conventional-base papers just before or after exposure, while the paper is not yet wet from processing. A soft pencil and light pressure will avoid show-through or pressure marks on the face of the print. The number can be gone over in ink after the print is dry, if necessary. Water-resistant or resin-coated print materials do not accept pencil or many kinds of ink. The Sanford "Sharpie" pen or the Pilot ultra-fine-point permanent pen SC-UF can be used on such materials, or self-adhesive labels with pencil or waterproof ink markings may be applied. (*See:* WRITING ON FILMS AND PAPERS.)

If enlarged proof prints are routinely made for reference, it is convenient to mark every negative in the same margin location and use a negative carrier that is cut out to let that area print through; this eliminates the need to mark each print separately.

File Organization

The function of a filing system is to keep materials identified, organized, and protected. The identification numbers provide the basis of organization; protection depends on separating reference copies from originals, and on proper storage materials, cabinets, and conditions.

It should be obvious that mounted slides cannot be intermingled with unmounted transparencies, nor can either of these be intermixed with negatives or prints in a filing arrangement. The differences in size and materials make it impractical and raise the possibility of the pictures gouging or otherwise damaging one another. Similarly, negatives should not be filed along with prints. Although negative holders are available in sheet form suitable for filing in folders or looseleaf notebooks along with contact or proof prints, this should not be done. Prints are handled, examined, studied, and used far more than negatives, and negatives should not be exposed to unnecessary handling.

Thus, it is generally best to have separate files of prints, negatives and unmounted transparencies, and mounted slides. Each file can be organized according to the sequence of identification numbers. If there is a significant number of different kinds of originals, it may be useful to use a code letter along with the roll or job number. The absence of a letter could mean a black-and-white negative, *C* a color negative, and *S* or *T* a slide or transparency, for example. Then, the identification numbers *78–10–8* and *78–10C–8* would distinguish between the eighth frame of black-and-white roll 10 in 1978, and the eighth frame of color negative roll 10 in 1978.

Storing Slides. Slides can be stored in sequence in boxes, cabinets with slotted or compartmentalized drawers, or in trays ready for projection. The disadvantage of tray storage is that it is quite bulky and makes it difficult to quickly leaf through the slides to find a desired number. Plastic sheets with individual pockets for up to twenty slides can be kept in notebooks, boxes, or file folders. They make it possible to quickly examine a number of images at the same time. Although least convenient for removing and subsequently refiling individual pictures, they do minimize the need to handle and project images repeatedly—an important point in extending the life of color slides.

Cross Indexing. A print file for individual use may consist only of contact sheets and proof prints organized for personal convenience. If cross references are required, they can be kept as written entries on file cards or notebook pages. Generally speaking, extensively organized print files are required only in libraries and stock picture agencies. The files may be organized by number, or more commonly by subject category. In the latter case, the print must be marked with the negative number to identify its original, and with its category so it may be refiled easily. Several prints of a particular image may be required if it fits into more than one category. For example, a picture of skiers on a snow-covered slope at sunset could be filed under *Skiing, Winter Scenes,* and *Sunsets.*

While cross indexing may not seem necessary as an individual photographer begins to build up a file of photographs, it becomes more useful as the file grows larger with time. When a few years have passed, it may be difficult to remember just when a certain picture was taken. If a cross-index file has been kept with the name of the location, the type of subject, the names of models, and so forth, the picture can readily be found from almost any clue remembered.

Storing Prints. Prints may generally be intermingled for file purposes without difficulty, except that stabilized black-and-white prints must not come in contact with conventionally processed materials. The stabilization process produces prints loaded with hypo, which can cause fading and staining of other materials over a period of time. This difficulty can be overcome by fixing and washing the stabilized prints in the conventional manner before they are filed. (*See:* STABILIZATION PROCESS.)

Storage Materials

At one time, negatives, and occasionally prints, were routinely filed in brown kraft paper or glassine paper envelopes. Such materials are still available, but they have a number of drawbacks. The edges of kraft paper can cause emulsion scratches as films are withdrawn or inserted. If the envelope materials are not photographically pure, they can cause staining, spotting, or fading. The adhesives used for seams

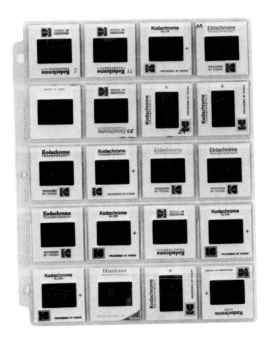

A slide protector page will hold up to twenty 2″ × 2″ mounted transparencies. Viewing is possible without removing slides from their clear vinyl pockets.

Filing and Storing Negatives, Prints, and Transparencies

may be impure or may attract atmospheric moisture. Pressure of the seams in closely packed files may cause ridging or embossing of the emulsion, even when the base of the film faces the seam. A seam running along the edge of the envelope, rather than down the middle, minimizes this problem.

Today transparent plastic sleeves, envelopes, and compartmented sheets are widely used to file and store negatives and transparencies. Such sheets have the advantage of allowing inspection over a light source or of making contact proof prints without removing the film from the enclosure. In addition, standard size sheets are made for almost all film sizes so that, for example, individual sheets holding 35 mm, 120, and 4″ × 5″ negatives can be filed together. Roll and 35 mm films are cut into strips of a few frames each to fit into the sheet pockets; storing such films rolled up in a continuous length can cause permanent curl, scratches or abrasion marks, and sticking together of layers.

Plastic storage materials should be polyethylene or polypropylene. Those made of polyvinyl chloride (PVC) or related compounds may give off hydrogen chloride, which can cause image deterioration, especially of color films.

Print Storage Materials. Materials safe for films are also safe for print storage, except that color print emulsions should not be left in contact with plastic for long periods of time because the prints may stick to the plastic. Prints may also be stored in paper file folders, envelopes, or folded sheets of paper. Unfortunately, most papers for general use are bleached with hypo, which along with other chemicals left in the paper, can cause image deterioration. For maximum protection, acid-free papers in which no hypo was employed during manufacture should be chosen. Envelopes, folders, and boxes of such material are essential for long-term storage of archivally processed prints, otherwise the care in processing will be undermined. The Hollinger Corporation offers acid-free products especially intended for safe storage of photographs.

As a practical matter, special care in storage is really only necessary for carefully made finished prints. Those used for reference and inspection can be considered expendable because of the frequent handling and careless usage they are likely to receive; consequently, ordinary file folders, envelopes, or notebooks can be used.

Storage Containers. It does little good to protect films and prints with safe envelopes or other enclosures if these are then stored in containers that may cause problems. The things to avoid are materials, adhesives, and finishes that contain or can give off substances and gases injurious to photographs, or that can attract and hold moisture. Boxes or containers of ordinary cardboard or paper are almost sure to be unsuitable, but the boxes in which photographic paper is packaged can be considered safe to use. The glues, paints, and varnishes most commonly used for wooden containers constitute a problem. Nailed or screwed construction eliminates glues as a source of trouble. Synthetic-base varnishes and epoxy-base paints seem to be acceptable; natural resin varnishes and other kinds of paints must be avoided. In no case should negatives or slides be stored in newly finished containers. A period of two weeks or more is required for a finish to give off most of its solvent vapors. Metal containers should have baked enamel finishes. There is little information about the long-term suitability of plastic boxes. Polystyrene seems to be the safest plastic material for photographic storage.

Storage Conditions

Aside from improper processing and direct contact with contaminants, the two factors most likely to damage photographic images are excessive temperature and humidity. High temperatures accelerate aging and fading. High humidity promotes condensation (especially within the storage pockets of plastic sheets), chemical reactions with airborne contaminants, and the growth of fungi that feed on gelatin. These effects are increased when the temperature is also high.

It should be fairly easy to provide temperatures below 24 C (75 F). Humidity should be kept below 40 percent. If necessary, packets of a drying agent such as silica gel can be placed in storage containers and renewed periodically.

Color images are the most likely to be affected by storage conditions and to be attacked by fungus growth. Dark, dry, low-temperature storage is essential. All photographic color dyes are subject to fading; exposure to light and especially to ultraviolet wavelengths, which are a significant component of sunlight, greatly accelerates fading. The physical stability of some water-resistant papers also changes

are discussed in the article MIXING PHOTOGRAPHIC SOLUTIONS.

Filter Materials, Sizes

Optical filters for most kinds of photography are made of gelatin film, cellulose acetate, plastic, or glass. Some filters for scientific or technical purposes may be liquid or gaseous. Filter materials contain even distributions of dyes or other substances that absorb, reflect, or disperse selected wavelengths. Glass filters may be made of colored glass, or of a gelatin layer coated on, or sandwiched between, pieces of colorless glass.

Most filters are intended to be placed in front of a camera or enlarger lens. Occasionally a filter may be placed in the image-forming beam behind a lens—for example, inside a view camera—to protect the filter or to get it out of the way of other lens accessories. There is an important exception: Acetate filters should not be used in front of a lens or in the image-forming beam. The thickness and optical characteristics of the acetate can adversely affect the optical quality of the image.

Acetate filters are used to adjust the output of light sources. Most commonly, they are placed in the lamphouse of an enlarger to control the color of the light used for printing with color or selective-contrast, black-and-white materials. Another fairly common use of acetate or plastic filters is to control the color of a light source, such as an electronic flash. In this usage the filter is placed over the light, not over the camera lens.

Plastic and glass filters are primarily available in the form of metal-rimmed, circular disks. Some filter rims are threaded and can be screwed into the front of a lens with matching threads; others are unthreaded, and are mounted by means of adapter and retaining rings (see accompanying illustration). Many unthreaded filters are supplied in standard diameters identified as "series" sizes. This is an economical scheme, because a number of lenses of different front diameters can be fitted with series adapter rings in order to accept a single filter size.

Gelatin Filters

The most complete line of Kodak filters is available in the form of colored gelatin films that are 0.1 mm thick. Because of their uniform thickness, gelatin filters have excellent optical quality and are suitable for precise work in which little effect on definition and no increase in length of the optical path can be tolerated. Clean, flat, unmounted gelatin filters are especially recommended for use with large-aperture lenses of long focal length, such as those used on view and process cameras, in map-making equipment, and on large copying cameras.

Gelatin and acetate filters are made in sheets of various standard sizes. Acetate filter sizes range up to 11″ × 14″; gelatin filters are supplied in standard sizes up to 125 mm (5 inches) square. Larger sizes are available, but they should be supported in use to prevent sagging of the thin, flexible, gelatin film.

Standard Gelatin Film Square Sizes
50 mm	(2-inch)
75 mm	(3-inch)
125 mm	(5-inch)

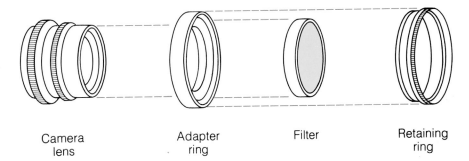

A retaining ring holds the filter in the adapter ring. If two glass-disk filters are used at the same time, or a filter and a close-up lens, a lens hood or a second retaining ring can be used to hold the second filter in place.

Camera lens　　Adapter ring　　Filter　　Retaining ring

The Kodak gelatin filter frame (for 2-, 3-, and 4-inch gelatin squares only) provides a convenient way to hold and protect gelatin filters. If the filter is to be used with a camera or enlarger lens, a Kodak gelatin filter frame holder is recommended. This holder, which is attached to the lens by an adapter ring of appropriate size (and step-up ring, if required), is available in three sizes: Series 6 for 2-inch gelatin squares, Series 8 for 3-inch squares, and Series 9 for 4-inch squares. The accompanying illustration shows how the filter frame and holder are used. Glass-square filters may also be mounted in front of a lens by means of the filter frame holder; a filter frame is not required.

Filter Designations

Filters are usually designated or identified by numbers. The most widely used system is that employed to designate Kodak Wratten filters; however, some manufacturers use other number systems, or color-number designations such as "Orange 1." Filter designations such as K2, A, G, etc., were as-

signed many years ago, when the number of filters required for photographic work was quite small and when a simple identification system was adequate.

As the need for additional filters became apparent, the present numbering system was adopted, replacing the old alphanumeric designations. Because published literature frequently contains references to the older designations only, both current and discontinued designations are shown here.

Current Designations	Discontinued Designations
No. 6	K1
No. 8	K2
No. 9	K3
No. 11	X1
No. 13	X2
No. 15	G
No. 25	A
No. 29	F
No. 47	C5
No. 49	C4
No. 58	B
No. 61	N

Some filters are usually referred to by a descriptive name rather than by number; for example: skylight, neutral density, and so-called polarizing screens. As explained in other articles, color-compensating, color-printing, and various special-pur-

Gelatin filter frame holder   Gelatin filter frame

Lens   Adapter ring   Retaining ring   Gelatin filter

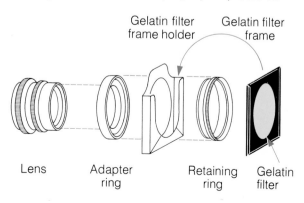

FILTER FACTORS FOR BLACK-AND-WHITE FILMS*

Filter Number	Color of Filter	Daylight		Tungsten	
		Filter Factor	Open the Lens by (*f*-stops)	Filter Factor	Open the Lens by (*f*-stops)
3	Light yellow	1.5	⅔	—	—
4	Yellow	1.5	⅔	1.5	⅔
6	Light yellow	1.5	⅔	1.5	⅔
8†	Yellow	2	1	1.5	⅔
9	Deep yellow	2	1	1.5	⅔
11†	Yellow-green	4	2	4	2
12	Deep yellow	2	1	1.5	⅔
13	Dark yellow-green	5	2⅓	4	2
15	Deep yellow	2.5	1⅓	1.5	⅔
23A	Light red	6	2⅔	3	1⅔
50	Deep blue	20	4⅓	40	5⅓
25	Red	8	3	5	2⅓
58	Green	6	2⅔	6	2⅔
47	Blue	6	2⅔	12	3⅔
29	Deep red	16	4	8	3
61	Deep green	12	3⅔	12	3⅔
47B	Deep blue	8	3	16	4
Polarizing Screen	Gray	2.5	1⅓	2.5	1⅓

*The filter factors for a specific film may vary somewhat from this listing. See the film instructions.
†For gray-tone renditions of colors in proportion to their visual brightnesses, use a No. 8 filter in daylight, and a No. 11 filter in tungsten light. See the section on Correction Filters.

pose filters have other systems of designation. Most commonly, a filter's density—its measured absorption or light-stopping power—is incorporated in the designation (see the section on neutral density filters).

Filter Factors

Because a filter prevents some portion of the exposing energy from reaching the film, exposure must be increased to obtain proper results. The amount of increase required with panchromatic films is expressed by a number called a *filter factor.* Since the wavelength composition of tungsten light and daylight is not the same, different factors may be required to obtain correct exposures. Film data and instruction sheets usually include factors for a number of different filters. The factors given in the accompanying table for Kodak films may also be used as starting recommendations for other panchromatic films. A method of determining filter factors by practical test is described in a later section of this article.

There are three ways of using a filter factor to find the required exposure:

1. Divide the normal ASA rating or exposure index of the film by the filter factor. Set the meter to this adjusted exposure index and take readings in the usual way. For example, a filter factor of 2 requires one stop more exposure for compensation. With an ASA 400 film, setting the meter to ASA 200 will produce readings calling for the equivalent of one stop additional exposure. Because meter cells do not have the same spectral (color) sensitivity as film emulsions, it is usually not possible to obtain accurate exposure indications by taking a meter reading through a filter.

2. Multiply the shutter speed called for in an unfiltered exposure by the filter factor. For example, if the normal speed is 1/30 sec. and the filter factor 2, the corrected exposure is 1/30 × 2 = *1/15 sec.* The table of corrected shutter speeds provides this information for a number of filter factor and speed combinations. Often it is preferable to make exposure adjustments by changing the lens aperture rather than the shutter speed, because films require additional compensation with long exposure times; this is especially important to consider when using color films. (*See:* RECIPROCITY EFFECT.)

3. Open the lens aperture as shown in the accompanying table.

The table of corrected aperture settings shows how to change *f*-stops to compensate for filter factors from 1× to 10×. For a given filter factor, open the aperture to the setting given in the column under the *f*-stop for an unfiltered exposure.

For a given filter factor, use the speed given in the column under the speed for a normal, unfiltered exposure in the table of corrected shutter speeds.

Filter Factor	Open Aperture (*f*-stops)	Filter Factor	Open Aperture (*f*-stops)
1.5×	½	7–9	3
2 ×	1	10–13	3½
3 ×	1½	14–18	4
4 ×	2	20–27	4½
5–6×	2½	30–35	5

CORRECTED SHUTTER SPEEDS

Filter Factor	Normal Speed (Sec.)									
	1/2	1/4	1/8	1/15	1/30	1/60	1/125	1/250	1/500	1/1000
2×	1	1/2	1/4	1/8	1/15	1/30	1/60	1/125	1/250	1/500
4×	2	1	1/2	1/4	1/8	1/15	1/30	1/60	1/125	1/250
8×	4	2	1	1/2	1/4	1/8	1/15	1/30	1/60	1/125
16×	8	4	2	1	1/2	1/4	1/8	1/15	1/30	1/60

CORRECTED APERTURE SETTINGS

Filter Factor	*f*-stop Without Filter							
	2	2.8	4	5.6	8	11	16	22
	f-stop Corrected for Filter Factor							
1.5×	1.6	2.3						
2×	1.4	2	2.8	4	5.6	8	11	16
2.5×	1.2	1.8	2.5	3.6	5	7.1	10	14.2
3×	—	1.6	2.3	3.2	4.5	6.3	9	12.7
4×	—	1.4	2	2.8	4	5.6	8	11
5×	—	1.2	1.8	2.5	3.6	5	7.1	10
6×	—	—	1.7	2.3	3.4	4.8	6.7	9.5
7×	—	—	1.6	2.2	3.2	4.5	6.3	9
8×	—	—	1.4	2.0	2.8	4	5.6	8
10×	—	—	1.2	1.6	2.4	3.4	4.8	7.1

Filter Factor Test

The filter factors given in film instruction sheets or in reference tables are starting recommendations. It may well be that a different factor will give more accurate exposure compensation, especially with tungsten illumination. There are two major reasons for this: (1) even though they have the same designations, filters of different manufacture seldom have exactly the same absorption/transmission characteristics; and (2) the wavelength composition of light from various sources can differ significantly from that used to determine the suggested factor.

The following practical test will determine the true factor of a filter under any given set of conditions, even if a starting factor is unknown.

Place a typical subject in the illumination to be used. Also place a large gray surface alongside the subject, in the same illumination. The 18 percent reflectance (gray) side of four Kodak neutral test cards taped together from behind makes an excellent test surface. The gray area must be sufficiently large in the negative to be easily evaluated.

Determining Exposure. Determine exposure by one of three methods: (1) an overall reflected-light average reading, (2) a reflected-light reading from the 18 percent gray surface, or (3) an incident-light reading from the subject position. Make one exposure at this reading without the filter. Then make a series of exposures through the filter. Increase exposure one-half stop each time, up to four stops more than the original, meter-indicated exposure. Vary exposure by changing the lens aperture—do not change shutter speed—and keep a record of the setting used for each exposure.

Comparing Filtered Exposures. Process the film normally. Compare the filtered exposures with the unfiltered exposure to find the closest match. The least accurate way to do this is to evaluate the exposures by eye over a light box or other diffused illuminator. The most accurate way is to take densitometer readings of the gray-card area in each negative. It is also possible to use an exposure meter to find an accurate match. If the meter cell is small enough, simply place the gray area in the negative against the meter cell. If the cell is too large or if the meter housing does not permit putting the negative close enough, make a tube or cone of black paper that can be fitted between the cell and the negative so that only the gray area will be read.

Using white light from a diffused source, note the meter reading through the gray area of the unfiltered negative. It may be necessary to switch the meter to its high-sensitivity (low light level) range to get a mid-scale reading. Then take readings through the same area of the filtered exposures to find the one that gives the same meter indication. The difference in stops between the unfiltered exposure and the matching filtered exposure can be translated to the exposure factor for that film-filter-light combination as follows:

Stops Difference	Equivalent Factor
½	1.5×
1	2×
1½	3×
2	4×
2½	6×
3	8×
3½	12×
4	16×

Comparison Prints. For additional information about the filter's performance, make comparison prints from the unfiltered and the matching filtered negatives; the print exposures should be the same. Observe the changes in gray-tone rendition of various subject colors and the changes in contrast.

Color Films. This same testing method may be used with color films to good advantage. Reversal films are best evaluated by viewing projected slides or comparing larger transparencies on a standard illuminator. Color negative films can be evaluated by making comparison prints.

Combining Filters

Two or more filters may be used together to obtain a combined effect. For example, a yellow filter—which reduces blue transmission—might be used with a neutral density (ND) filter to cut down the total amount of light transmitted, or with a polarizing screen to control glare. When a color filter is combined with a neutral density filter or polarizing screen, their individual factors can be multiplied to-

(Left) Photo taken without a filter shows little distinction between sky and clouds. (Right) Use of a No. 15 deep-yellow filter darkened the blue sky, emphasizing the white clouds.

gether to determine the factor of the combination: a color filter with a $2\times$ factor and an ND filter with a $4\times$ factor have a combined factor of $8\times$, which requires the equivalent of three additional stops of exposure. When two colored filters are combined, a test must be run to find the combined factor.

Another useful combination for scenic pictures with foliage is the use of a yellow-green filter with a yellow filter. The yellow-green filter lightens foliage and darkens a blue sky somewhat. Adding the yellow filter darkens the sky more without darkening the foliage. No. 13 and No. 8 filters work well together.

The greater the thickness of a filter, the more it can affect the optical quality of the image. Because gelatin filters are extremely thin, they are preferred when filters must be combined.

Handling and Storage of Filters

Filters used in the image path should be handled with care in order to avoid degraded images.

Gelatin filters are protected by a thin lacquer coating that affords very little protection against careless handling. They should be handled only by the edges or at the extreme corners. When not in use, storage in their original package, or in clean paper between the pages of a book, is safe and convenient. Gelatin filters should be kept flat and stored in a dark, dry place. Continued stress on gelatin filters can deform them permanently, and moisture tends to cloud them.

Dust particles can be removed from gelatin filters by brushing *gently* with a clean, dry, camel's hair brush; or dust can be removed by blowing clean, dry air (e.g., Freon gas in commercially available aerosol cans) across the surfaces. It is suggested that a schedule of periodic replacement be considered for gelatin filters that are used frequently or are used in critical image-forming systems.

If it is necessary to cut a gelatin filter, the filter should be placed between two pieces of clean, fairly stiff paper and cut with a pair of sharp scissors. The cutting line can be marked on the paper.

Mounting gelatin filters in the gelatin filter frames mentioned earlier, or between frames cut from stiff cardboard and taped around the four edges, provides additional protection from handling.

Glass filters or gelatin filters that have been mounted between glass should be treated with the same care accorded to coated lenses. They should be kept in protective boxes, and on no account should they be allowed to get damp or dirty. A glass-mounted filter should never be washed with water, even though the edges have been given a protective coating to resist entry of moisture. If water should come in contact with the gelatin at the edges of a glass-mounted filter, it will cause it to swell and separate the glasses so that air can enter between the gelatin and the glass. Even if the swelling does not cause air to enter in this manner, the filter might be strained and its optical surface changed.

If, for any reason, a glass or a glass-mounted filter becomes so dirty that it cannot be cleaned by simply rubbing after breathing on it, a piece of soft cloth or Kodak lens cleaning paper moistened with Kodak lens cleaner (which should not be permitted to touch the edges of the filter) can be employed for the purpose of cleaning the glass surfaces. Before attempting to clean a filter, it is advisable to make sure that the surfaces of the glass and the tissue or cloth are free from grit that might scratch the glass.

Changes in Absorption Characteristics. All filters (primarily gelatin or acetate filters) whose colorant consists of dyes will eventually fade sufficiently to change their absorption characteristics. Fading is accelerated by repeated exposure to ultraviolet energy—which is a significant component of sunlight—and by high temperatures. Temperatures in the normal range have little or no effect, but it is difficult to classify the stability of either gelatin filters or those that have been mounted between glass when subjected to high temperatures. In general, Kodak filters should not be subjected to temperatures higher than 49 to 54 C (120 to 130 F). If these temperatures are exceeded, it should only be for a short period. The factors of time, temperature, and humidity are quite closely related in their effect on filter stability. Since individual dyes respond differently when exposed under identical conditions, some Kodak filters undoubtedly will retain their absorption characteristics at temperatures above 54 C (130 F), but others will not. For this reason, precautionary measures should be taken, if possible, to avoid subjecting filters to high temperatures.

When used under tropical conditions, filters should be treated with great care. They should be protected against damage from fungus. Dry, cool storage conditions are desirable; a desiccated, hermetically sealed container is usually satisfactory.

Solid glass filters, on the other hand, are practically fade proof, and, of course, will not separate from moisture. The practical photographer will probably have a few solid glass filters that he uses regularly.

Special or Occasional Use of Filters. Because there are many more types (colors) of filters available in gelatin, a photographer is likely to use this type of filter for special purposes. Gelatin filters are less costly, especially in the larger sizes; therefore, they may be chosen for occasional use. Because of the comparative methods of manufacture, gelatin filters are likely to have more carefully controlled transmission-absorption characteristics. For this reason, where these characteristics are important—as in neutral density filters, color separation filters, color compensating filters, and color balancing and conversion filters—the photographer is likely to choose gelatin filters.

Since filters used in the studio are more easily protected than those used primarily on location, gelatin filters are often chosen.

Filter Principles

Most pictures are taken by white light falling on colored objects; very few things in nature are truly neutral. White light is the sum total of all the colors of the rainbow, while black is the absence of all the colors. For many purposes, we can consider white light as composed of three primary light colors—red, green, and blue. When one or two of these colors is subtracted or absorbed, we see the color that is left.

A piece of red paper is red because it reflects red light. The white light falling on it consists of a mixture of blue, green, and red. The red paper absorbs the blue and green light, but reflects the red light. Therefore, anything that absorbs (subtracts) both blue and green light will look red. Thus, a red filter looks red because it absorbs (subtracts) green and blue, and transmits only red.

Subtraction is the key to an understanding of photographic filters. They always subtract some of the light reflected from a scene before the light reaches the film in the camera.

Reflection

Transmission

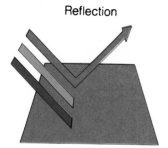
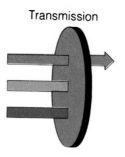

(Left) The object absorbs green and blue, and looks red. (Right) The filter absorbs green and blue, and looks red.

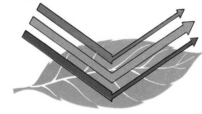

Foliage green reflects green, most of the blue, and a little of the red. The yellow of flowers and foliage reflects red, green, and a little of the blue.

The important point in selecting filters for photographic effects is not the color of a filter, but which colors it absorbs. Few objects are pure red, blue, or green; usually various proportions of two or all three of these primary colors are present in the light they reflect. For example, a lemon and an orange reflect the same colors—red and green. The lemon reflects almost equal proportions, which appear yellow when mixed by the eye; the orange reflects a greater proportion of red; both absorb blue. Green foliage actually reflects green, some blue, and a small amount of red.

FILTER ABSORPTION

Color as Seen in White Light	Colors of Light Absorbed
Red	Blue and green
Blue	Red and green
Green	Red and blue
Yellow (red-green)	Blue
Magenta (red-blue)	Green
Cyan (blue-green)	Red
Black	Red, green, and blue
White	None
Gray	Equal portions of red, green, and blue

Choosing a Filter

The basic steps in selecting a filter for black-and-white photography are:

1. Decide which object or color is to be changed in the final print.
2. Determine which primary colors are present in the light reflected from that object.
3. To make the object a lighter shade of gray, choose a filter that transmits those colors—that is, a filter that looks the same color as the object. It will absorb, and thus darken other colors with the result that the selected object will appear lighter by comparison.
4. To make the object a darker shade of gray, choose a filter that absorbs one or more of those primary colors; the more colors in an object that are absorbed, the darker it will appear.

For example, placing a yellow filter over the camera lens greatly improves black-and-white pictures of landscapes containing blue skies and white

1066

clouds. In a picture made without a filter, the blue sky may be rendered as a very light gray or white, too close to the tonal value of the clouds to provide separation between the two. A yellow filter absorbs the blue light, making the blue sky appear darker in the print. The clouds, which reflect light of all colors, are not darkened and they stand out in contrast.

However, a filter will not affect just one object in a scene; it will alter the rendition of all objects reflecting any of the colors that it absorbs. Consider a scene made up of blue sky, white clouds, and green foliage. The proportions of red, blue, and green in the light from these surfaces vary, as shown in the accompanying diagram. A yellow filter will subtract the greatest proportion of light from the sky, and the smallest proportion from the foliage. The individual brightnesses have one relationship in the scene, but the filter alters the relative brightnesses that reach the film. If the scene brightnesses have this relation-

ship: cloud, 20; sky, 16; foliage, 8; the filter changes the relationship to: cloud, 14; sky, 8; foliage, 7. (These are arbitrary examples, not real values.) In a correctly exposed negative, the filter will increase the density difference between cloud and sky, and decrease the density difference between sky and foliage. When the negative is correctly printed, the sky tone will be darker, the clouds will show up, and the foliage will be lighter than in an exposure made without a filter.

Filters for Black-and-White Pictures

The filters used in black-and-white picture-taking can be divided into three main types:

1. *Correction filters* change the response of the film so that all colors are recorded at approximately the relative brightness values seen by the eye.

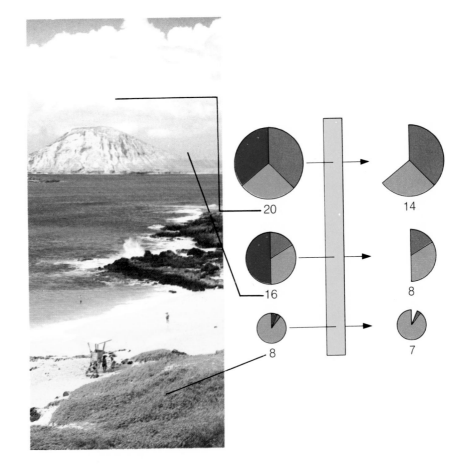

A yellow filter absorbs the blue component of the light reflected from all parts of the scene. Thus the light affecting the film has a greater brightness contrast between white clouds and blue sky, and a decreased brightness contrast between green foliage and sky and clouds. Consequently, greens are lighter, and the tone separation between sky and clouds is better.

2. *Contrast filters* change the relative brightness values so that two colors that would otherwise record as nearly the same shade of gray will have decidedly different brightnesses in the picture.

3. *Haze filters* reduce the effects of aerial haze.

Two other accessories, *polarizing screens* and *neutral density* (ND) *filters,* may be used for color as well as black-and-white photography, because they do not change the color rendition of a scene.

Correction Filters. Although panchromatic films respond to all the colors the eye can see, they do not reproduce all colors with the same relative brightness that the eye sees. For example, blue and violet normally appear darker to the eye than green does, but the film is more sensitive to these colors and they look lighter than green in a black-and-white print. Filters can reproduce the colors with the relative brightness that the eye sees.

Top row: (Left) Red geraniums look dramatic against green grass. (Right) In unfiltered black-and-white, red and green appear as similar tones of gray. Bottom row: (Left) A No. 25 filter transmits red and absorbs green. Red subjects appear light, green subjects dark. (Right) A No. 58 filter absorbs red and transmits green, producing dark flowers and light grass.

Color Filter Circle

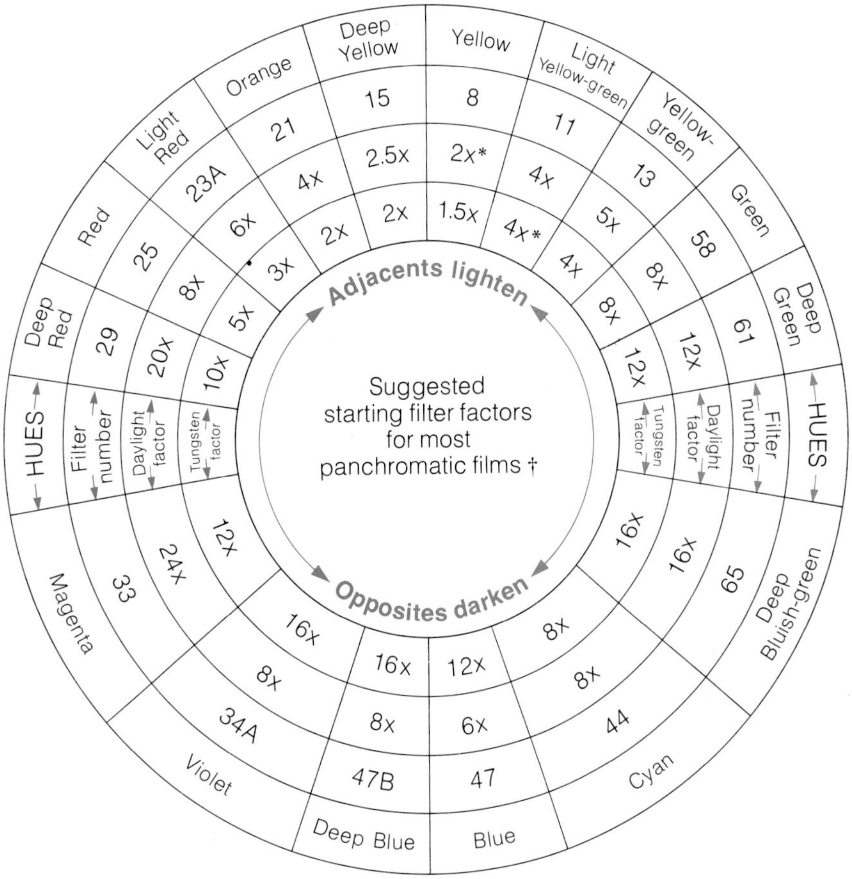

Color Filter Circle

Circular diagram — "Color Filter Circle." Reading around the circle:

Deep Yellow — 15 — 4x — 2x — 3x
Yellow — 8 — 2.5x — 2x
Orange — 21 — 4x — 2x
Light Yellow-green — 11 — 2x* — 1.5x
Light Red — 23A — 6x — 4x*
Red — 25 — 8x — 4x — 4x
Yellow-green — 13 — 4x — 5x — 8x
Deep Red — 29 — 20x — 5x — 8x
Green — 58 — 8x — 12x
Deep Green — 61 — 12x — 12x
Magenta — 33 — 24x — 10x
Deep Bluish-green — 65 — 16x — 16x
Violet — 34A — 12x — 8x
Cyan — 44 — 8x — 8x
Deep Blue — 47B — 16x — 16x — 8x
Blue — 47 — 12x — 6x

HUES — Filter number — Daylight factor — Tungsten factor

Adjacents lighten

Suggested starting filter factors for most panchromatic films †

Opposites darken

NOTE: If conditions require long time exposures, corrections for reciprocity effect in addition to the corrections for the filter factor may be necessary.

*For a gray-tone rendering of colors approximating their visual brightness.

†If negatives are thin, increase the filter factor; if negatives are dense, decrease the filter factor.

Panchromatic films are more sensitive to ultraviolet and blue light than the eyes are. To reproduce the colors in a scene in the same brightness relationship that the eye sees, use a yellow filter to absorb the ultraviolet and some of the blue light. Use a No. 8 yellow filter with panchromatic films to reproduce a *daylight* scene in the shades of gray that represent their visual brightness relationship.

Because tungsten light contains more red than daylight, a yellow-green filter is required to get the natural brightness relationship in scenes photographed by tungsten light. The yellow in the filter absorbs the ultraviolet and some of the blue light, while the green absorbs some of the red light. For a natural-looking effect, use a No. 11 yellow-green filter with panchromatic films in *tungsten* light.

Contrast Filters. Often it is desirable to increase contrast between two objects that would normally photograph as nearly the same shade of gray. Contrast filters will lighten or darken certain colors in the subject. For example, red geraniums and green grass may photograph as nearly the same tone of gray. A No. 25 red filter, will transmit the red of the geraniums and absorb the green of the grass, so that the geraniums will be light and the grass dark in the print. A No. 58 green filter, which absorbs the red of the geraniums and transmits the green of the grass, will produce the opposite result: dark flowers and light grass.

Color Filter Circle. The color filter circle is helpful in choosing contrast filters. A filter will lighten colors located near it (adjacents), and it will darken colors on the opposite side of the circle (opposites). For example, the No. 34A filter (violet) will lighten magentas, violets, and blues; and it will

Filters

darken oranges, yellows, and yellow-greens. Light color filters will not effect as much of a change as normal color filters while deep color filters will result in a dramatic change.

Darkening Blue Skies. One of the most frequent uses of filters in black-and-white photography is to darken a blue sky so that white clouds will stand out more prominently. Use a No. 8 yellow filter to reproduce the sky as the eyes see it. Darken the sky with a No. 15 deep yellow filter; or for really dramatic sky effects, use a No. 25 red or No. 29 deep red filter.

The table of filter recommendations describes the effects of using filters with a variety of common subjects.

Haze-Reducing Filters. Distant landscapes and aerial views from high altitudes often appear to be veiled by bluish haze, even on clear days. This

A No. 25 red filter is used for pictorial landscape photography to provide dramatic contrast between the clouds and the blue sky.

FILTER RECOMMENDATIONS FOR BLACK-AND-WHITE FILMS IN DAYLIGHT

Subject	Effect Desired	Suggested Filter
Blue sky	Natural Darkened Spectacular Almost black Night effect	No. 8 yellow No. 15 deep yellow No. 25 red No. 29 deep red No. 25 red, plus polarizing screen
Marine scenes when sky is blue	Natural Water dark	No. 8 yellow No. 15 deep yellow
Sunsets	Natural Increased brilliance	None or No. 8 yellow No. 15 deep yellow or No. 25 red
Distant landscapes	Addition of haze for atmospheric effects Very slight addition of haze Natural Haze reduction Greater haze reduction	No. 47 blue None No. 8 yellow No. 15 deep yellow No. 25 red or No. 29 deep red
Nearby foliage	Natural light	No. 8 yellow, or No. 11 yellow-green No. 58 green
Outdoor portraits against sky	Natural	No. 11 yellow-green, No. 8 yellow, or polarizing screen
Flowers—blossoms and foliage	Natural	No. 8 yellow, or No. 11 yellow-green
Red, "bronze," orange, and similar colors	Lighter to show detail	No. 25 red
Dark blue, purple, and similar colors	Lighter to show detail	None or No. 47 blue
Foliage plants	Lighter to show detail	No. 58 green
Architectural stone, wood, fabrics, sand, snow, etc., when sunlit and under blue sky	Natural Enhanced texture rendering	No. 8 yellow No. 15 deep yellow or No. 25 red

Filters

haze hides some of the detail when such a scene is photographed without a filter. True atmospheric haze is bluish and results from the scattering of light by very small particles of dust and water vapor, and to some extent, by the air itself. This atmospheric haze scatters a great deal of ultraviolet radiation, which the eye cannot see. Since the film is very sensitive to ultraviolet, the result may be more haze in the photograph than is visible to the eye.

To reduce the effects of haze in black-and-white pictures, filter out some of the blue light and ultraviolet radiation. The amount of recorded haze decreases with the following filters in this order: No. 8 yellow, No. 15 deep yellow, and No. 25 red. A polarizing screen may also be used.

Skylight or haze filters that are used with color films do not penetrate haze. These filters are used to reduce the bluishness in pictures made in the shade

Black-and-white film is very sensitive to the ultraviolet light scattered by atmospheric haze. More haze may be noticeable in the photograph than was apparent in the scene itself.

The No. 25 red filter absorbs ultraviolet light and reduces the effects of atmospheric haze. The filter also darkens green subjects, such as the tree foliage.

(Top) Reflections from glass, water, and other nonmetallic surfaces may destroy the quality of a photograph. (Bottom) A polarizing screen will remove or reduce reflections and increase color saturation.

and on overcast days, and in those of distant scenes.

Mist and fog are white because they are composed of water droplets. Using filters will not help to photograph a scene through mist or fog.

Some atmospheric conditions may be penetrated by use of infrared filters and infrared-sensitive films. (*See:* INFRARED PHOTOGRAPHY.)

Polarizing Screens. Polarizing screens do four things that are useful to a photographer: (1) they darken blue skies, (2) they remove or reduce reflections from nonmetallic surfaces such as water and glass, (3) they penetrate haze, and (4) they increase the saturation of colors.

How Polarizing Screens Work. Light rays travel in straight lines. Light rays also vibrate in all directions perpendicular to their direction of travel. When a light ray hits a nonmetallic surface, the vibration in only one direction, or plane, is reflected completely. (*All* vibrations are reflected by a bare metallic surface.) Depending upon the angle at which the light reflected from an object is viewed, vibrations in other planes are reduced or eliminated completely. This reflected light—vibrating in only one plane—is called "polarized light." The light from a blue sky is polarized because it is reflected off the nonmetallic particles in the atmosphere.

A polarizing screen will pass the vibration of a light ray in one plane. Some polarizing screens have handles, and these screens pass the light vibration in a plane parallel to the handle. When the polarizing screen is passing the light vibration of *polarized light,* there is no visible effect on reflections or the sky. But if it is rotated 90 degrees, the screen will not transmit the polarized light, so it removes reflections and darkens the blue sky. When a polarizing screen is rotated to its maximum darkening effect, some light reflecting from the scene is still visible. This is the nonpolarized light in the scene and the polarized light vibrating in the plane that the screen will transmit. It is the light that will expose the film.

To get the maximum effect with a polarizing screen, the angle at which the reflecting light is viewed must equal the angle of the sun (or the original light source) to the reflecting surface. For example, if the sun is shining on water at a 60-degree angle, the maximum effect with a polarizing screen is obtained by taking the picture at a 60-degree angle to the water's surface.

Exposure. A polarizing screen has a filter factor of 2.5 (increase exposure by 1⅓ stops). *This filter factor applies regardless of how much the screen is rotated.* In addition to this exposure increase for the polarizing screen, exposure increases may be required by the nature of the lighting. For example, for a dark-sky effect, the scene must be sidelighted or toplighted, which requires approximately ½-stop exposure in addition to the 1⅓-stop increase required by the polarizing screen itself.

Allow about an additional ½ stop for subjects that show reflections, because reflections often make subjects look brighter than they are.

Dark-Sky Effects. A polarizing screen provides a method of darkening a blue sky in both color and black-and-white photography. To obtain the maximum effect, take pictures at right angles to the sun (for example, when the subject is sidelighted or the sun is overhead) and with the indicator handle on the polarizing screen (if it has one) pointed toward the sun. For spectacular effects in black-and-white,

In the drawing on the right, the polarizing screen is transmitting the light vibration of polarized light, and it has no effect on reflections or the sky. In the drawing on the right, the polarizing screen has been rotated 90 degrees. In this position, the screen absorbs the polarized light so that it removes reflections or darkens the blue sky.

When a light ray from the sun hits a nonmetallic particle in the atmosphere (or any other nonmetallic surface), vibrations of the light ray in only one plane are reflected completely. This reflected light travels at a right angle to the sun and is called "polarized light." Maximum polarization occurs at an angle of about 35 degrees to the subject's surface. Partial polarization occurs from about 20 to 50 degrees to the surface.

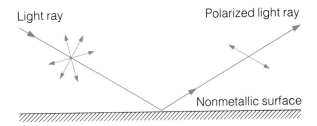

Light ray

Polarized light ray

Nonmetallic surface

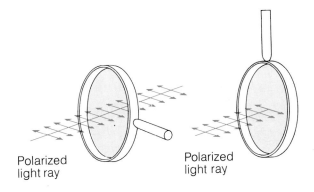

Polarized light ray

Polarized light ray

Maximum sky-darkening occurs (left) with the lens aimed at right angles to the sun, and the handle or index mark of the polarizing screen pointed toward the sun. (1) Unpolarized sunlight before it strikes particles in the atmosphere; (2) Polarized sunlight after it is scattered by particles in the atmosphere; (3) Subject area for the dark-sky effect.

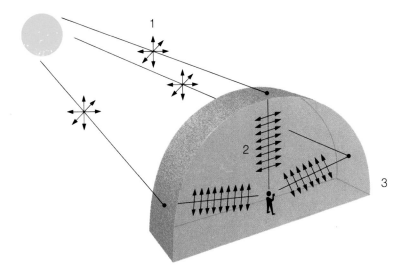

1

2

3

try a No. 8 yellow, No. 25 red, or No. 11 yellow-green filter in combination with a polarizing screen.

The only way to darken a blue sky in color photography without changing the other colors in the scene is to use a polarizing screen.

To see the range of darkening effects, look through the polarizing screen as it is rotated. To get a desired effect in a picture, mount the polarizer on the lens with the handle or index mark on the rim oriented in the same position that produced the visible effect. With a single-lens reflex camera, the range of effects can be seen in the viewfinder as the screen is rotated in front of the lens.

In some pictures the sky may appear lighter than would be expected when using a polarizing screen, for these reasons:

1. A misty sky does not photograph as dark as a clear blue sky. *A filter will not darken an overcast sky.*
2. The sky is frequently almost white at the horizon and shades to a more intense blue at the zenith. Therefore, the effect of the filter at the horizon is small, but it becomes greater as the camera is aimed upward.
3. The sky near the sun is less blue than the surrounding sky and therefore is less affected by a filter.

Increasing Saturation. There are two types of light reflection from most object surfaces: specular and diffuse. The specular reflections are achromatic, that is, neutral. The diffuse reflection from colored objects is the chromatic or colored reflection. Unless a surface is very matte, the diffuse colored reflection is diluted somewhat by the neutral specular reflection. Removing or minimizing the specular reflection increases the saturation of the color.

The specular reflections from all surfaces except metallic surfaces are partially polarized. A polarizing screen placed in front of the camera lens can absorb the polarized part of the specular reflection, allowing the diffuse, colored light through because

the diffuse light is not polarized. Rotation of the filter lets the photographer see which angle provides the greatest degree of saturation.

Polarizing screens can be used to increase color saturation in all types of lighting—sun, shade, interior floods, and even flash. With flash it is difficult to predetermine exactly what the effect will be.

Controlling Reflections. A polarizing screen can improve contrast in pictures because it reduces reflections that can degrade contrast. It can also reduce reflections in scenes that include water, glass, or other shiny surfaces. It will not control reflections from bare metal surfaces because these reflections are not composed of polarized light. Where reflections can be reduced, the degree of control depends on the angle to the subject and the amount of rotation of the screen. Often the camera-to-subject angle must be changed in order to completely eliminate reflections. Maximum polarization occurs at an angle of about 35 degrees to the surface, with partial polarization occurring between 20 and 50 degrees to the surface.

Further information about using polarizing screens is included in the article POLARIZED-LIGHT PHOTOGRAPHY.

Neutral Density Filters. Neutral density (ND) filters reduce the amount of light passing through the camera lens without changing the rendition of the colors in the scene. A neutral density filter is

helpful in taking pictures of a brilliant subject in sunlight with a high-speed film. If the fastest shutter speed and the smallest lens opening on the camera still overexpose a bright scene, reduce the exposure further by using ND filters.

Neutral density filters are also useful in reducing the exposure in order to use large lens openings under bright lighting conditions. With large lens openings, depth of field is very shallow; the resulting blurred, out-of-focus background looks especially pleasing for pictures of people or close-ups of flowers.

When fast action is photographed, using a slow shutter speed and panning with the action produces a blurred background with the moving subject in sharp focus. If the smallest lens opening on the camera still gives too much exposure, reduce the exposure with ND filters.

Neutral density filters are supplied in various densities; if necessary, two filters can be combined to create a desired density. The accompanying table shows the density values of ND filters and tells how much each filter reduces exposure. The .30, .60, and .90 densities are especially useful, because they reduce the exposure by 1 stop, 2 stops, and 3 stops, respectively.

• *See also:* ATMOSPHERIC HAZE; COLOR PHOTOGRAPHY; COLOR PRINTING FROM NEGATIVES; COLOR PRINTING FROM TRANSPARENCIES; COLOR SEPARATION PHOTOGRAPHY; COLOR TEMPERATURE; COLOR THEORY; CONTRAST; DICHROIC FILTERS; GLARE AND REFLECTION CONTROL; INFRARED PHOTOGRAPHY; MIXING PHOTOGRAPHIC SOLUTIONS; NEUTRAL DENSITY; POLARIZED-LIGHT PHOTOGRAPHY; RECIPROCITY EFFECT; SAFELIGHTS; SPECTROGRAPHY.

Further Reading: Eastman Kodak Editorial Board. *Filters and Lens Attachments for Black-and-White and Color Pictures.* Garden City, NY: Amphoto, 1976; Rothschild, Norman and Cora Wright Kennedy. *Filter Guide.* 3rd ed. Garden City, NY: Amphoto, 1971; Smith, R. *Tiffen Practical Filter Manual.* Garden City, NY: Amphoto, 1975.

NEUTRAL DENSITY FILTERS

Density	Reduces Exposure by (*f*-stops)	Increases Exposure Time by (Factor)
.10	⅓	1¼×
.20	⅔	1½×
.30	1	2×
.40	1⅓	2½×
.50	1⅔	3×
.60	2	4×
.70	2⅓	5×
.80	2⅔	6×
.90	3	8×
1.00	3⅓	10×

Filters

Fingerprint Photography

A latent fingerprint is often the most convincing evidence that a suspect was present at a crime scene. Without photography, such evidence would lose much of its effectiveness.

Since a latent fingerprint is destroyed easily by handling and by exposure to weather, fingerprints at a crime scene should be photographed promptly. Often fingerprints are found on objects that can be taken to a police laboratory. The procedures used in fingerprint photography may also be applicable in photographing palm prints, glove impressions, heel prints, and similar evidence.

Although the self-contained fingerprint camera is still in use, all-purpose cameras are now also widely used. Macro-lens-equipped 35 mm cameras and compact electronic flash units are frequently used in the field.

Well-defined fingerprints can be photographed with any fast pan film. However, weak prints that may be destroyed by dusting require the use of high-contrast or lith films.

Color filters provide some contrast control when fingerprints appear on colored surfaces. However, filters should be used only when they reveal information or help to clarify detail. To select the most suitable filter, one should view the subject through various filters.

Flash should be used wherever practical. Standard flash positioning, which can be used for most subjects, minimizes failures. Conventional tungsten lights may melt some materials and destroy the fingerprints. Portable ultraviolet lights, or "black lights," which are made for studying fluorescing minerals, are quite satisfactory for field use. The high-intensity desk lamp has proven most useful in the laboratory.

Since dusting with special powders is by far the most common method of developing fingerprints for photography, the chemical methods will not be described here. For most surfaces, one of the following powders will usually be found satisfactory: black, white, gray, or fluorescent. Select the powder that provides the best contrast against the background. With fluorescent powders, there is no need to worry about the background if it does not fluoresce.

The identification technician compares a fingerprint photograph with a suspect's fingerprints as recorded with black ink on white cards. Whatever equipment and materials are used in making the reproduction of evidence fingerprints, the final result must be the original size with black ridges showing on a light background. It must be laterally correct; that is, not reversed left to right. To satisfy these requirements, it may be necessary to use special photographic techniques. In all fingerprint photographs, the goal is to achieve the best possible definition and contrast.

• *See also:* CRIME PHOTOGRAPHY; EVIDENCE PHOTOGRAPHY.

 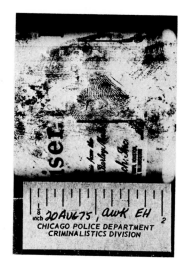

(Left) When the fingerprint on the red and white surface of this beer bottle was developed with black powder and photographed on panchromatic film without a filter, the fingerprint failed to show up completely. (Right) With a dark red filter (such as a Kodak Wratten filter, No. 25) over the camera lens, the red of the label is subdued so that the fingerprint can be seen. Photo courtesy of Chicago Police Department.

Fire and Arson Photography

Professionals who photograph fires and their aftermath use all of their wits and technical knowledge to obtain results that range from the spectacular to the mundane. Press photographers are interested in dramatic photographs or ones with human interest. A fire fighter or arson investigator is more concerned with technical details—smoke, flame, equipment and personnel use, extent of destruction, and charred remains. Amateurs may simply want to capture the color and action that are part of the fire scene. All find that their results improve with knowledge, experiment, and practice.

Equipment

Photographic equipment for fire photography must stand up to severe environments and rough handling. Under many conditions of service it may be best to have a relatively simple and inexpensive camera for field work simply because it will be easy to replace if it is damaged or lost.

Adjustable Cameras. Adjustable cameras provide much more versatility for making pictures in extremes of lighting and with flash equipment.

Press photographers, police photographers, and others who work in all kinds of weather have found many ways of protecting their equipment. One camera actually is built with a protective body that allows the camera to be used underwater, in bad weather, and in smoky or dusty environments.

Lenses. Fire photographers will find, at times, a use for wide-angle, normal, and telephoto lenses. The wide-angle lens is handy for making a record of the overall scene. It is also very useful for the cramped quarters frequently found in a burned-out building. A moderate wide-angle lens (such as a 35 mm lens for the 35 mm camera) is frequently the choice for much of the routine fire work. The slightly wider field of view of this lens is very useful. A fast normal lens may be necessary to the fire photographer for making difficult night shots or those where flash must be used to illuminate charred remains. Finally, a telephoto lens will allow the photographer to record fire details when it is extremely dangerous or physically impossible to approach the fire. A zoom lens combines many of these features.

Protecting Cameras. Protect cameras and lenses from smoke, dust, flying debris, and water. A skylight or clear glass filter placed in front of the lens will not affect exposure and will protect the front element of the lens. With such a filter in place, the photographer can wipe away moisture or dust without taking extraordinary care. If the filter should be scratched, it is easily and inexpensively replaced. A lens hood further protects the lens from collision damage and moisture, as well as serving its primary function of reducing flare from strong sidelight.

To protect the camera itself from the elements, place the camera in a loose-fitting plastic bag and secure the opening of the bag around the lens with rubber bands. The plastic bag should *not* cover the lens. Operate the controls and film advance through the flexible bag or, where this is not satisfactory, insert a hand through a hole in one corner. Plastic bags also come in handy for protecting film, spare lenses, and flash equipment. Bags with plastic ziplock closures are especially useful. Retain the plastic container in which 35 mm film is sold so that the film cassette can be returned to it after camera exposure.

Accessories for Adverse Conditions. Operating cameras under adverse conditions can be difficult when protective clothing and gloves are worn. Cameras with small knobs or levers may have to be modified with larger knobs or extension levers to allow proper operation. Again, cameras designed for use in extreme conditions or underwater are already equipped with such easily used extensions.

Low temperatures will interfere with the normal operation of motor-driven still and motion-picture cameras. With temperatures at the freezing point, battery power may be only 50 percent of normal; at −18 C (0 F), only 20–30 percent of normal. Electronic flash units are similarly affected. Light output of electronic flash units will be reduced, but the extent of the reduction is hard to predict since batteries and capacitors react differently to cold weather conditions. When the use of electronic flash is necessary, it is best to supply power for the unit directly to the capacitor of the flash from a separate heavy duty dry battery that is kept warm under the photographer's protective clothing.

A photographer's vest may be useful for the fire photographer. Worn under the turnout coat (a size or two larger than normal), the vest provides safe, convenient storage for film, batteries, filters, extra lenses, and an exposure meter in its many pockets. Items in the vest are protected from the weather and kept warm by body heat. The use of a vest also eliminates the need for carrying film and accessories in a separate bag or case.

Avoid Reloading. Try to avoid the necessity of reloading roll film or 35 mm cameras at a working fire. If you have extra roll film camera backs or an extra 35 mm camera body, these are a great advantage. Use long rolls of film whenever possible. Choose 36-exposure 135 film magazines or 220-size rolls. Have your camera loaded with a new roll of film at the start of each assignment; at the end of an assignment, do not leave a partially exposed roll in the camera. The loss of a few frames at the end of a roll cannot be compared with the loss of time and images encountered when you find you are at the end of a roll while in the midst of recording a fire.

If you find that you must change films in the field, be careful to protect the inside of the camera from moisture and flying debris. Do the loading under a spare coat or in a truck cab.

Exposure

A fire photographer encounters as wide extremes of exposure as any practicing photographer.

Subjects range from self-luminous flames to black-charred remains. Getting meaningful detail in such diverse subjects is a challenge. Conventional methods of exposure determination will not always be adequate to get correct exposures under these extreme conditions.

Bracketing Exposures. Basically, the luminous flames tend to distort the readings of scene-averaging exposure-metering systems. Spot metering is not usually practical under these conditions and, unless carefully interpreted, may be even more misleading. One of the problems that cannot be overcome with conventional photographic films is the recording of detail in flame and shadow in the same exposure. Usually the extremes of illumination must be recorded by bracketing the basic exposure.

During normal daylight hours, the extremes of illumination will not be as great for the average fire scene, and a two-stop bracket over and under the normal daylight exposure will be sufficient. At night, however, the extremes of lighting are much greater. You cannot expect to record any detail in flames and in the structure itself with the same exposure unless floodlighting provides supplementary illumination.

Recording Flame. An exposure of $f/8$ at 1/125 sec. will provide adequate detail in the flame with

As a general rule, bracketing is the only practical way to get correct exposures of fire scenes, because the luminous flames tend to distort scene-averaging exposure meters, and spot meters are not practical under such conditions. With medium speed color films, an exposure of f/8 at 1/125 sec. should provide adequate flame detail.

Flash on the camera was used to illuminate the men and equipment in the foreground of this night scene.

medium-speed color films (ASA 64–100). The shutter speed of at least 1/125 sec. is important to minimize blur caused by the flame movement.

Flash

Frequent hard use, the need for reliability, and a requirement for maximum light output mean that most fire photographers use professional flash units. While small, inexpensive cameras that use expendable flashbulbs or flashcubes are useful for some fire photography, they cannot provide the flexibility needed when flash must be used at night, out-of-doors, or in fire-blackened, dimly lit interiors.

Equipment. Whatever flash equipment is used, batteries, connecting cords, plugs, and contacts must be maintained constantly. In addition to the basic unit, one or more extension or "slave" units will provide the additional light that may be needed for night scenes, arson investigation, or other dark or extended scenes or objects.

Explosive Atmospheres. Be careful in any area where gas, explosive vapors, or volatile liquids are present or suspected. An electric spark or the heat of a flashbulb could trigger an explosion. Sparks are most likely to be created by a poorly maintained flash unit or frayed connecting cords between power pack and flash head.

Under such conditions, available-light photography must be used for safety's sake. Fast lenses (f/1.2 to f/1.4) on 35 mm cameras used with color films, with speeds up to 400 and black-and-white films up to 2000, make such pictures possible under almost any conditions.

Guide Number for Flash. Manufacturers of flashbulbs and electronic flash equipment usually publish guide numbers or light output ratings that make computation of guide numbers possible. Guide numbers are normally computed to take into account average reflectance from surrounding surfaces. Since the fire photographer frequently works out-of-doors or in smoke and fire-blackened interiors where there are no reflecting surfaces, the exposure computed from the usual guide number may be

inadequate. The photographer should open the camera aperture two or three stops to provide adequate exposure. Halving the usual guide number yields the result of a two-stop increase in exposure.

Scene Reflectance. An average scene reflects about 18 percent of the light that falls on it. Smoke-stained and charred remains left from a fire reflect as little as 2 percent of the light. This means that an approximate $8 \times$ exposure increase (3 stops) will be needed to give adequate rendition of detail.

New Guide Number. To compute a new guide number: (1) use the computer dial or table found on most flash units, simply taking the guide number for a film having a lower exposure index (dividing the EI by two is the same as increasing exposure one stop); or (2) use the accompanying computation guide.

To increase exposure	1	2	3	4	stops
Divide guide number by	1.4	2	2.8	4	

Selecting Films

For many of the purposes to which fire photographs will be put, color slide films may be best suited. For much of the work done by the fire photographer and arson investigator with an adjustable camera, a high-speed film is desirable. High-speed films allow pictures to be made under low-light conditions. Flash is more effective over longer distances with high-speed films.

Store films with care. Film should be kept cool and in the original moistureproof package until it is

Fire and Arson Photography

Events and conditions surrounding the fire-fighting attempts should be recorded by the photographer. This photo demonstrates the difficulty encountered in getting equipment close to the fire.

to be used. Do *not* leave film supplies in an uninsulated metal container, on a truck, or anywhere subject to high heat or humidity.

Fire in Progress

Eye-witness accounts of rapidly developing events are notoriously inaccurate. This is true even when the observers are well trained. By commissioning one fire fighter to make photographs upon arrival at the fire scene and at intervals thereafter, the chief and investigators can have photographs to examine for clues of the fire cause and as part of a postmortem on fire-fighting methods.

Initial Survey. In addition to the appearance of the scene upon arrival of fire fighters, the initial deployment of equipment is important. Photographs establish the position of each piece of equipment and the use of available water sources and other resources. As soon as possible after arrival at the fire scene, the photographer should make a complete survey of the scene from all sides. As much of the structure or scene as possible should be recorded— even adjacent buildings—since these may be consumed in the course of the fire.

Recording Events. As the fire fighting progresses, a photographer can continue to record the sequence of events and the attempts at controlling and extinguishing the fire. Included in the survey of

the fire scene should be the involvement of the fire (from as many angles as necessary and accessible), the appearance of smoke and flames, condition of the structure, fire-fighting methods, and record shots of onlookers (for possible arson suspects).

The photographer should also record the evacuation of persons from the fire scene; the administration of first aid or other care; and the injuries to fire fighters, including the use, or non-use, of a protective helmet, a coat, or other equipment.

Clues to Fire Cause. While the fire is in progress, the photographer should try to document the effects of the fire. An attempt should be made to show the point of fire origin and the extent of initial involvement. It may be apparent that fires have been started in more than one area. By documenting the presence of steam, color and density of smoke, and color and size of flames, the photographer can provide information to help in the determination of the nature of the burning substances. For those purposes, color film must be used.

The successive exposures should be identified by some method of time sequencing so that the frames are reviewed in the right order and so that the total elapsed time is readily grasped. The photographer may keep a time log for complete identification. There are several 35 mm cameras with data recording backs that have provisions for a clock face to give a precise time, frame-by-frame.

Investigating the Fire Scene

After the fire, photographs should be made during successive stages of the clearing and search, with particular attention to the burned and charred areas. The building exterior should be photographed from all sides in order to identify the structure and to show damaged areas. Significant interior features must then be examined and recorded. Some of the things to look for and photograph carefully are the following: all types of incendiary devices and combustible materials, including candles, matchbooks, paper, cloth, excelsior, and containers of liquids such as paint thinners and kerosene. Note that a fuse may have left a visible trail or burn pattern, even though the fuse itself burned completely, and the combustible material may have burned out before igniting the building.

Working with Investigators. Every effort should be made to photograph important evidence in the interior before the debris is sifted by the investigating officers. Pictures should also be made during the sifting operation to record any evidence that might be uncovered. All items should be photographed carefully as you go, since they relate to the most difficult element of proof—intent.

Arson. Arson for profit is planned to burn special objects or areas, in addition to general destruc-tion. It is of great importance to photograph any special arrangements that indicate the plan of the arsonist, such as flammable trailers leading from one room to another.

Pictures should be made of any evidence such as exposed business records, closet doors left open to aid burning of contents, firedoors left open to promote drafts, and alterations in protective devices, such as sprinkler systems. When included with the fire investigator's report, these pictures will furnish substantial proof of arson.

Photographic Problems. Since the areas of interest are usually blackened and therefore reflect less light, careful technique must be used to avoid underexposure. Such scenes consisting of black, charred wood usually require two to three f-stops more exposure (an increase from four to eight times) than normal scenes. If the flash guide number for normal scenes is 110, use a guide number of 55 for charred wood.

• *See also:* CRIME PHOTOGRAPHY; EVIDENCE PHOTOGRAPHY.

Further Reading: Eastman Kodak Co. *Using Photography to Preserve Edidence.* Rochester, NY: Eastman Kodak Co., 1976; Sansone, Sam. *Modern Photography for Police.* Cincinnati, OH: Anderson Publishing Co., 1977; Siljander, Raymond P. *Applied Police and Fire Photography.* Springfield, IL: Charles C. Thomas, 1976.

Photographs are essential in establishing suspected cases of arson. (Left) A fuse device was used to spread fire from one room to another. (Right) The deep charring pattern is evidence of the use of an accelerant. Photo courtesy of Chicago Police Department.

Fireworks, Photographing

Taking pictures of fireworks is much easier than most people imagine. To get good pictures, you need an adjustable camera, a tripod or other firm support for the camera, a cable release, and either black-and-white or color film. Fireworks are especially exciting because of their vivid colors, so the best results will probably be in color.

Exposure

Since the pictures taken of most fireworks will be time exposures, the main concern is the lens opening to use. Almost any lens opening will produce interesting fireworks pictures. An overexposed picture will show the aerial traces thick and light in color; an underexposed picture will show thin lines and dark, more intense colors.

Use the table below as a *guide* for setting your camera.

SUGGESTED EXPOSURES FOR FIREWORKS

Type of Display	Film Speed			
	ASA 25–40	ASA 50–80	ASA 100–160	ASA 200–400
Aerial bursts—keep shutter open for time exposure	f/5.6	f/8	f/11	f16—22
Ground displays	1/30 sec. f/1.9	1/30 sec. f/2.8	1/30 sec. f/4	1/60 sec. f/4—5.6

Taking the Picture

For best results follow these steps:

1. Place the camera on a tripod or other firm support.
2. Set the focusing scale on infinity and set the lens opening according to the suggestions in the accompanying table.
3. Aim the camera in the direction of the bursts.
4. Set the camera shutter on "T" (Time) or "B" (Bulb). Open the shutter (preferably with a cable release). Keep it open for several bursts or for only one. If the shutter is kept open for several bursts and there are bright lights or moving cars nearby, put a hat or a piece of dark paper in front of the lens between bursts to keep stray light out while the shutter is open.
5. Close the shutter.

Additional Tips. Photos can be improved if these suggestions are followed:

Add interest and a feeling of depth by including silhouettes of objects or people in the foreground of pictures.

If a telephoto lens is used, get "close-ups" of the fireworks displays.

Time exposures cannot be made without a tripod. However, successful results can be obtained with a hand-held camera at 1/30 sec. with an *f*/2 lens, timing the exposures with the fireworks bursts.

(Left) Ground displays, which do not move within the scene, require shorter exposure times than aerial displays, and may be photographed with hand-held cameras. (Right) For aerial displays, which are composed of a number of bursts, a tripod and an open shutter are required.

A city skyline and harbor add interest and depth to a wide-angle time exposure.

Ground Displays. Since displays on the ground are fairly bright and do not move across the scene as aerial displays do, shorter exposure times can be used. Also, with ground displays a tripod will not be necessary; the camera can be hand-held at 1/30 sec. Be sure to hold the camera steady and squeeze the shutter release gently.

Making Movies. To make color movies of fireworks displays, set the focusing scale on infinity and use the largest lens opening on the camera (such as $f/1.9$ or $f/2.8$). If the camera has automatic exposure control, it will set the largest lens opening automatically. Best results will be obtained if a tripod is used. Aim the camera in the direction of the bursts; then start the camera when you see the trail of the rocket going up and continue running it until the burst has disappeared.

• *See also:* AVAILABLE-LIGHT PHOTOGRAPHY; NIGHT PHOTOGRAPHY.

Fischer, Rudolf

(1881–1957)
German chemist

Rudolf Fischer, with H. Siegrist, did the original research into the properties of the so-called "chromogenic developer"—a developer that deposits a colored dye along with a silver image. This was the basis of nearly all present-day color processes, though Fischer & Siegrist did not succeed in producing a practical color film at the time (circa 1911). The entire field of couplers and coupler development started with this research. The first practical film marketed that was based on couplers was Kodachrome film in 1935.

Fisheye Lens

A fisheye lens is an extreme-wide-angle lens with a field of view approximating 180 degrees. Such a lens does not have rectilinear rendition. The fisheye lens is the outgrowth of the Hill Sky Lens (Beck, 1924) in which an image of the entire sky is produced on a small plate by the simple expedient of introducing enormous barrel distortion. The image on the plate or film takes the form of a circle, though in some cases, part of the circular edge is cropped off when 180-degree coverage is not required. It is possible to rectify the distorted image in printing, if parts of the image not too close to the edges are projected back through the same or a similar lens. There are also fisheye lens adapters that are extreme-wide-angle

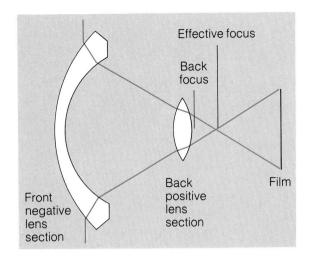

This is a simplified structure of a fisheye lens.

This image, photographed with a fisheye lens from the top of a boat's mast, takes the form of a complete circle. Note the photographer's own hand and leg at lower left segment of the picture.

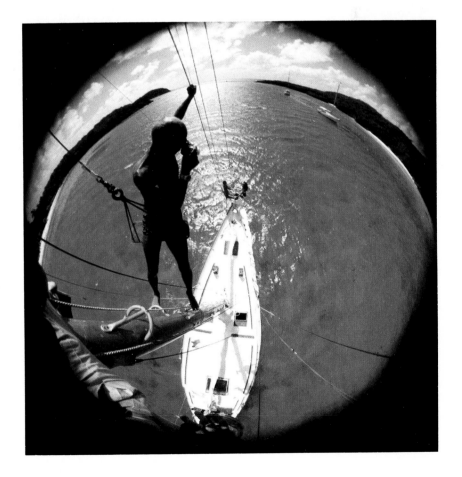

The fisheye lens creates consider-able distortion of shape and size relationships. While in reality the pencils are all straight and of equal size, this is not the impres-sion given by the photograph.

afocal converters used in front of the manual camera lenses.

The basic formula for a fisheye lens is the in-verted telephoto formula with a very strong negative element or elements that are curved into meniscus shape forming the front section, while smaller, stronger, positive elements at the rear form a real image of the virtual image created by the front sec-tion. This structure permits the extremely short focal length required to achieve maximum field an-gles, while allowing the relatively long, back focus required by the mirrors in single-lens reflex cameras.

• *See also:* LENSES.

Fixers and Fixing

The basic photographic process for both black-and-white and color films and papers is based on the development of a silver image exposed on a silver halide emulsion. In the developer, exposed silver halide crystals are reduced to black metallic silver. If the process were stopped at this point, the image would be neither permanent nor usable. The silver halide crystals left in the emulsion would darken rapidly on exposure to light if they were not

The hardener can also be mixed separately as a stock solution as follows:

Kodak Hardener F-5a

Water, about 50 C (125 F)	600.0 ml
Sodium sulfite (anhydrous)	75.0 g
Acetic acid (28%)*	235.0 ml
Boric acid, crystals**	37.5 g
Potassium alum, fine granular (dodecahydrated)	75.0 g
Cold water to make	1.0 litre

---

*To make approximately 28% acetic acid from glacial acetic acid, add 3 parts of glacial acetic acid to 8 parts of water.

**Crystalline boric acid should be used as specified. Powdered boric acid dissolves only with great difficulty, and its use should be avoided.

Slowly add 1 part of the cool stock hardener solution to 4 parts of cool 30 percent hypo solution (300 grams of sodium thiosulfate per litre of water), while rapidly stirring the hypo.

Kodak **Fixing Bath F-6.** In warm weather and in inadequately ventilated dark rooms, the odor of sulfur dioxide given off by the Kodak fixing bath F-5 may be objectionable. This can be eliminated almost entirely by omitting the boric acid and substituting twice its weight in Kodalk balanced alkali. This modification, which is known as Kodak fixing bath F-6, can also be used to advantage for fixing prints, since it washes out of photographic papers more rapidly than the baths that have a greater hardening action. It should be used in conjunction with a stop bath such as Kodak indicator stop bath or Kodak stop bath SB-1 to obtain the full useful life.

Water, about 50 C (125 F)	600.0 ml
Sodium thiosulfate (pentahydrated)	360.0 g
Ammonium chloride	50.0 g
Sodium sulfite (anhydrous)	15.0 g
Acetic acid (28%)*	48.0 ml
Boric acid, crystals**	7.5 g
Potassium alum, fine granular (dodecahydrated)	15.0 g
Cold water to make	1.0 litre

---

*To make approximately 28% acetic acid from glacial acetic acid, add 3 parts of glacial acetic acid to 8 parts of water.

**Use crystalline boric acid as specified. Powdered boric acid dissolves only with great difficulty and its use should be avoided.

Kodak **Rapid Fixing Bath F-7.** This bath fixes much more rapidly than Kodak fixing bath F-5 or F-6, and its useful fixing capacity is greater. CAUTION: With rapid fixing baths, do not prolong the fixing time for fine-grain film or plate emulsions or for *any* paper prints; with prolonged fixing, the image may have a tendency to bleach, especially at temperatures higher than 20 C (68 F). This caution applies particularly to warm-tone papers.

Kodak **Rapid Fixing Bath F-9.** If corrosion is encountered when Kodak rapid fixing bath F-7 is used in stainless steel containers, it can be minimized by substituting 60 grams of ammonium sulfate for the 50 grams of ammonium chloride in each litre of solution. When this change is made, the resultant formula is known as Kodak rapid fixing bath F-9.

Kodak **Fixing Bath F-24.** This bath can be used for films, plates, or papers when no hardening is desired. For satisfactory use, the temperature of the developer, rinse bath, and wash water should not be higher than 20 C (68 F).

Water, about 50 C (125 F)	500.0 ml
Sodium thiosulfate (pentahydrated)	240.0 g
Sodium sulfite (anhydrous)	10.0 g
Sodium bisulfite (anhydrous)	25.0 g
Cold water to make	1.0 litre

• *See also:* Acetic Acid; Alkali; Buffer; Chemistry of Photography; Developers and Developing; Development; Formulas for Black-and-White Processing; Kodalk Balanced Alkali; Storage of Sensitized Materials and Processing Solutions.

Further Reading: Eastman Kodak Co. *Basic Developing, Printing, Enlarging in Black and White.* Rochester, NY: Eastman Kodak Co., 1977; Hertzberg, Robert. *Elementary Developing and Printing.* Garden City, NY: Amphoto, 1973; Mason, L.F. *Photographic Processing Chemistry.* New York, NY: Halsted Press, Division of John Wiley & Sons, Inc., 1975; Vickers, John. *Making and Printing Colour Negatives.* (Published by Fountain) Dobbs Ferry, NY: Morgan & Morgan, Inc., 1971.

 Flare

Flare is any unwanted or stray light in an optical system. It may be a general or overall illumination, or it may be focused at one or more points in the image area.

Overall flare is usually caused by reflection or scattering of light by various things in the system, including the lens surfaces themselves, the interior of the lens barrel, diaphragm blades, and the interior of the camera body. Even a small amount of flare light, evenly scattered over the image area, can have a very destructive effect upon the contrast of the resulting image.

For example, assume a subject has a brightness range of 1:50. If there were no flare in the system, then the brightnesses of various parts of the image, as seen in the image plane of the camera, would be the same—that is, 1 unit of light in the darkest part, and 50 units in the brightest. Now, imagine that a single unit of stray light is introduced into the system, uniformly distributed in the image plane. Then, in the shadows, there are $1 + 1 = 2$ units of light; and in the highlights, there are $50 + 1 = 51$ units. So, image contrast is reduced from 50:1 to 51:2, which is about 25½:1. The addition of a single unit of flare light has reduced the contrast of the image to about half of what it should be.

By and large, clean lens surfaces may be eliminated as a source of flare light. Modern lenses are coated with an anti-reflection material that substantially eliminates this source of scatter. But this presupposes that the lens is perfectly clean; a fingerprint on one of its surfaces, a trace of grease, or some dust can seriously increase the flare level of the lens.

In a camera, one possible source of flare light that is likely to be overlooked is the film itself. The emulsion side of the film is light in color, and more or less glossy. It can reflect considerable light back toward the lens, and some of the light will reflect back to the film again. Generally, good baffling of the camera interior is required to minimize this source of stray light.

The interior of the lens barrel is usually blackened and fitted with knife-edge baffles to eliminate scattered light from this area. If, however, the black paint flakes off and exposes bright metal, a good deal of light can be reflected.

Even the ground edges of the lens elements themselves can reflect light into the image area. If any part of the lens edge can be seen from the film plane, it should be carefully blackened. This is usually done by the maker of the lens, but the black paint used can chip off and may require touching up.

Bellows-type cameras can be plagued with flare, especially when used with wide-field lenses that have coverage a good deal greater than the film area. In this case, the excess area of coverage of the lens illuminates the interior of the bellows, and from this, some light is reflected toward the film. To avoid such a problem, you should use a compendium type of lens hood that can be adjusted until it is just barely outside the field of view of the lens. Then all light outside this field is stopped before it can enter the lens, and there is none inside the camera to reflect from the bellows.

Inexpensive, plastic-bodied cameras, while black in color, may be quite shiny inside, and they, too, can have a high degree of flare. When buying this type of camera, inspect the interior to see that it has been sprayed with a matte black paint. The performance of such cameras can often be improved by the use of a lens hood.

It is a help to the careful photographer to know the flare level of his or her lenses. The highest quality black-and-white photographic reproduction can be obtained by maintaining consistent negative density ranges. Camera flare level is one of the controlling factors of negative density range. (*See:* CONTRAST.)

Color films are made and their processes controlled to provide a given degree of contrast suitable for subjects with a normal luminance range when imaged with lenses that have moderate to low flare levels. Because the contrast of color films cannot be readily controlled by changing developing times, it is very useful to the photographer to know about the flare level of the lenses being used and how it affects the contrast of the pictures.

Focused Flare

Sometimes a reflection will occur in a lens system at such a point that the lens will then image it in or near the film plane. As shown in the accompanying illustration, any doubly-reflected light beam from a lens will cross the lens axis somewhere, and at that point it will form a well-defined image of the iris diaphragm itself. If this happens to fall close to the film plane, it will cause a more or less sharply defined image of the iris, superimposed on the middle of the picture.

If several of these multiple-reflected images of the iris diaphragm fall close to the film but not in focus upon it, their intensities may nevertheless add up to a considerable amount of light, causing a "flare spot" in the middle of the picture.

A flare spot, or an in-focus central diaphragm image, is visible only at the smallest diaphragm openings, because it is usually highly magnified and at the larger diaphragm openings the image falls entirely outside the picture area. Moreover, the

brightness of the diaphragm image is independent of the size of the iris, while the brightness of the background increases as does the square of the iris opening. Hence as the diaphragm is opened, the background brightens rapidly and soon drowns the faint iris image entirely. The color of a flare spot is, of course, the average of the whole scene.

A flare spot is particularly unfortunate when stray light reflected from shiny regions in the lens mount is also present, because the two sources add up and may lead to a serious situation. Indeed, many cameras have been entirely cured of their flare-spot troubles by an adequate blackening of the interior of the lens barrel.

• *See also:* CONTRAST.

  Flashing

Flashing a photographic material means giving it an exposure to non-image light. When the exposure is even and overall, it is called a fogging exposure. Flashing is used on both films and papers. On films, it is usually used to lower the image contrast and to increase the speed of the film. On papers, it is generally used to modify the print image.

Flashing Films

In cameras that permit double exposure, a single frame can be flashed by exposing the frames twice, once to the subject and once to an overall even time.

Since a flash exposure of about $\frac{1}{100}$ of the normal exposure is usually about right to lower the film

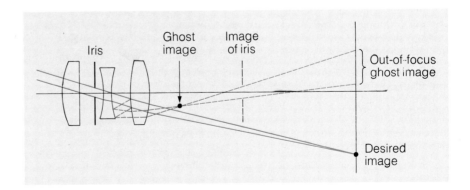

Ghost images are formed by light reflected from the internal surfaces in a lens.

Iris
Ghost image
Image of iris
Out-of-focus ghost image
Desired image

contrast slightly without introducing too much fog, a 2.0 neutral density filter can be used. A Kodak neutral test card provides a good even tone, and being out of focus is better than in focus. Just place the neutral density filter over the lens, hold the gray card so that it receives the same illumination as the subject, and so that it is evenly illuminated, and give the same flash exposure as the subject received. The flash exposure can be given before or after the main exposure.

Such flash exposures are especially useful to lower the contrast of transparency films when they are being used to copy color prints or to make duplicates of color transparencies. The film speed is likely to be increased from one-half to a full stop. Similar exposures can be used to increase the speed of color or black-and-white negative films, or to lower the contrast when the subject has an extremely long luminance range.

With black-and-white negative films, giving a flash exposure combined with push processing can result in an increase in film speed of up to two stops. Somewhat more flash exposure can be used. Experiment until you find the amount of flash exposure on the film that results in noticeable fog level when the film is push processed. Kodak HC-110 developer is a good developer to use for push processing. It increases film speed more with less increase in contrast than do most other developers. This procedure results in an increase in graininess.

Camera lengths of film can be flashed in the darkroom after being exposed in the camera just before placing in the developing tank. One way is to use a Kodak darkroom lamp or Kodak adjustable darkroom lamp placed so that the safelight filter is five feet above a level work surface, such as a table or bench. A Kodak safelight filter No. 3 (dark green) is used, and a 7½-watt bulb. In the dark, the film is opened and laid out on the flat surface emulsion-side-up, centered under the safelight. It is exposed to the safelight, and then put in the developing tank for processing. Exposure times must be found by trial; the following times can be used as starting times:

Film Speed	Flash Exposure Time
32	60 seconds
125	20 seconds
400	6 seconds
1250	2 seconds

Kodak recording film 2475 (Estar-AH base) has a relatively low grain sensitivity; it should be exposed for about 8 to 10 seconds with a Kodak safelight filter No. 10 (dark amber).

Push-processing recommendations usually indicate giving a developing time 50 percent greater than the time recommended for the film-developer combination being used. While the relatively high fog level resulting from this method of increasing film speed does not interfere with making prints, it can be reduced by the use of Kodak antifog No. 1 (benzotriazole) in the developer. Of course, increasing the film speed by such extraordinary measures is considered an emergency procedure. Better quality always results from using a faster film and normal development, when possible.

Flashing Prints

Flashing is primarily used with photographic papers as one of the three enlarging controls: holding back, burning-in, and flashing. Holding back means giving certain areas of the print (usually shadow areas) less exposure, while burning-in means giving certain areas more exposure. Both of these procedures are used with the negative in the enlarger, and are used to enhance detail. On the other hand, flashing is an exposure without an image, and is usually used to subordinate detail—to make it less important.

The primary use of flashing is to darken the edges of the print. One way of fading out the image to black in the margins is to use a vignetter in front of the camera; this will produce the desired effect of progressive darkening and lowering of contrast at the same time.

If you want to get the same effect in printing, it must be done by superimposing an exposure to white light on the image exposure. This will produce the necessary black margins and will also lower the contrast in the flashed areas.

How this comes about can be demonstrated with some simple arithmetic. Say, for example, your negative has a contrast range of 9:1 (the shadows transmit nine times as much light as the highlights). If you expose the paper through this negative, then the shadows will get nine units of light, the highlights one unit.* Suppose you give the paper a flash-

*For simplicity, we are ignoring the Callier effect in this example.

(Left) A good picture may be spoiled by unwanted details, such as the pole apparently growing from the boy's head. (Right) Flashing the area around the pole decreased the contrast enough to make the pole less obtrusive.

ing exposure of three units of light. The highlights have now received 1 + 3 units = 4 units of light; the shadows have received 9 + 3 units = 12 units of light. So your image contrast is now 12:4, or 3:1, compared with the 9:1 of the negative alone. This is a very marked reduction in contrast.

Flashing Methods for Prints. At first thought, it might seem that the easiest way to flash a print would be simply to remove the negative from the enlarger and make the added exposure with the enlarger light, using dodgers of various shapes to put the light just where it is wanted. Without a negative, though, the enlarger light is too strong and requires exceedingly short flashing exposures, which are hard to control. You could stop down the enlarger lens, and if you are making only a single print, this works; but making several prints in succession involves stopping the lens down again, opening it again, and so on, with multiplying chances for error.

Another suggestion is to use a pocket flashlight and move it around the borders of the print, thus putting the extra light just where it is wanted. A few people have mastered this technique; however, most find it too difficult, except for occasional use just to put a little spot of light in an inconvenient place. Again the problem is one of control. It is very difficult, when exposing various parts of the print in

succession, to be sure that all will get exactly the same exposure.

The most controllable way to flash is to set up a space alongside the enlarger, to which you can shift the easel after the print exposure has been given. Above this space, install a socket with a tiny incandescent bulb, suspended on a bracket that puts it just above the center of the easel at a predetermined distance. Connect this lamp to a separate foot switch.

For normal enlarging papers, only a very small bulb is needed if the light is hung at least three feet above the table. Even the little globe-shaped 7½-watt white bulbs may be too strong for the faster papers, but they can be made usable by partly covering them with black masking tape, leaving a small uncovered area for light to emerge.

For a better way to flash, and to provide some control for different papers, you need a little cardboard or wooden box with the socket glued into a hole in one side using epoxy glue. In the cover, which is removable for bulb replacement, insert a hole, to cut down the light to the desired degree. Make black cardboard masks with different-size holes in them, and place these inside the box to adjust for different paper speeds. Only a few tests, to be made as will be described here, will be needed to tell what size aperture is required.

The beauty of this setup is that for any particular enlarging paper, once the exposure has been determined, it remains constant, regardless of the exposure given to the negative.

Exposure Tests. For a first estimate, the Kodak projection print scale may be used to make a test. Put the scale and a 4″ × 5″ piece of paper (the *same* batch of paper from which you intend to make your enlargement) on the board under the exposing light and make a first test, exposing for one minute exactly, as you do when making a print test. Develop this test for your normal developing time. The result should be a series of gray steps, with full black somewhere in the middle of the scale.

If the entire scale is black, then the light is too strong. If you are using a bare bulb, cover part of it with black masking tape. If you have made an exposing lamphouse, then put a diaphragm with a smaller hole in the bottom. If, on the other hand, none of the steps is fully black, the light is not strong enough; remove tape from the bulbs if you have used it, or put a larger aperture in the lamphousing.

The ideal to work for is a 16-second step that is just barely black, the 24-, 32-, and 48-second steps that are fully black, with the rest all tones of gray. Then your flashing exposure will be 15 to 20 seconds, depending upon how much dodging you are doing, and how much of an image you are printing over. There is nothing critical about this; the only purpose of the test is to be sure you can get a good black flash with a convenient exposure time—that is, between 15 and 20 seconds.

For a first test, choose a negative in which most of the subject matter is in the middle. The aim here is to have the image fade out equally to black on all sides. You will also need an ordinary dodging tool, roughly oval in shape, on the end of a wire handle. The steps are as follows:

1. Insert the negative in the enlarger, focus, and compose. Stop the lens down to a normal printing aperture.
2. Make an exposure test using the Kodak projection print scale or your usual test-strip procedure. Set the enlarger timer to this exposure.
3. Place a full sheet of paper on the easel and make the exposure. Any routine dodging, burning-in, or holding back is done at this stage, as when making a straight print.
4. At the end of the exposure, move the easel to the working position under the flashing lamp. Take the dodging tool, hold it just under the flashing lamp, and turn on the lamp.
5. As soon as the lamp is lit, start to lower the dodger slowly, while continuing to move it in the little orbital motions necessary to avoid printing a sharp outline. Watch the way the light hits the paper: it should illuminate the outer edges evenly, and should fade inward about halfway, but no white light should reach the middle area of the paper. It will help if, before you make an actual print, you practice this shading technique until you can put the dodger at the right height almost instantly (though there is really no great hurry) to get an even ring of light around the outer areas of the paper.
6. At the end of 15 to 20 seconds, shut off the flashing lamp, develop, stop, and fix the paper.

Controlled spot flashing can be accomplished with an ordinary pen flashlight with a paper hood taped over the lens to help direct the light beam.

If everything is right, the image should be clean and bright in the middle of the paper, gradually diminishing in contrast and getting darker toward the margins, and ending up pure black at the extreme edges of the image area.

If the edges are not dark enough, then more flashing exposure is needed. If, on the other hand, the black area extends too far into the picture, then either give the print less exposure or use a larger dodger. Like everything else, practice makes the whole process easy and quick. Dry runs are useful for a preliminary trial, just to get used to the method. In any case, make a number of prints, preferably from the same negative, varying the flashing time, the distance of the dodger, and the amount it is moved around during the exposure.

Once you get the hang of this, you will find it possible to use the same technique for more subtle effects. Using a much dimmer lamp, or a shorter flash exposure, you can put just a trace of darkening around the edges of the picture. This should be far less than you would need to produce a complete black outer rim. It should just barely darken the outer parts of the image, which will enhance the picture by directing the eye to the important detail in the middle.

The method can be used for other purposes. One thing that often happens is a glaring white highlight outside the important subject area, which draws attention away from the subject. Such an area can be flashed to make it less obtrusive. Here a regular dodging tool with a hole in the middle is used to direct the light to the area and to flash in details.

You will need some way to find the spot that is to be flashed-in. The best way is to make the image exposure as usual; then before moving the easel to the flash area, put the red filter under the enlarger lens, turn the light on again, and make a few light pencil dots around the area to be flashed. Now move the easel to the flashing area, and use the dodger to put the light just inside the dots. Rub off the pencil marks with the ball of your finger as soon as you put the paper into the developer.

The same technique may be used to darken a washed-out foreground in a landscape, or to darken sky areas instead of printing in clouds. There are times when a clouded sky does not look right in a given scene, yet a blank white sky is equally wrong. In this case, careful and subtle flashing is a good

idea. Take a piece of cardboard with a straight edge, put it under the flashing lamp, then slowly move it down toward the horizon, but not quite to it, during the 15-second (or shorter) flash exposure. The thing to aim for here is a medium-gray at the extreme top edge of the image, shading down to white at the horizon. This, in fact, is exactly what a landscape looks like on a clear day, and the effect is both natural and emphatic.

Dark Borders. While the great majority of prints are made with the time-honored white margin, produced by the masking bands of the enlarger easel, there are subjects for which some other treatment is more appropriate. One such treatment is the borderless print, but this has limited value except where it is to be mounted on a larger white or light-colored background. Numerous easels and other devices are available to make borderless prints, but none of them is really necessary. All you have to do to make a borderless print is set the easel for the narrowest practical margin, and then trim this white margin off the finished print. It is seldom that an exact 8″ × 10″ print has any real necessity as compared with, say, one 7½″ × 9½″.

Another possibility is a print with a dark or even black border. These are often quite attractive, especially with high-key prints that are to be mounted on white or light-colored boards. With the flashing-lamp setup already described, making a dark border is an easy additional step in the exposure of a print.

All you need to form the width of the border desired is a piece of black cardboard, cut smaller than the paper to be used. Thus, say, for a ¼-inch margin on an 8″ × 10″ print, you need a piece of black cardboard 7½″ × 9½″ in dimensions. Place this over the paper, which has already had the image exposure, and give the additional exposure with the flashing lamp. If you have made a preliminary test with the Kodak projection print scale, it will be easy to make the outline any desired tone of gray.

If you prefer a gray rather than black border, the edges of the paper must not be exposed before the border is flashed. In this instance, use the usual enlarging easel, set to almost exactly the same dimensions, when making the image exposure. To avoid an unsightly white line on one or more sides, make sure the black masking card is somewhat smaller than the unexposed white border, because a little bit of overlapping image will not be noticeable.

Assuming you intend to make an 8″ × 10″ print with a ¼-inch gray border around it, set the enlarger easel to produce a 3/16-inch white border. The masking card will be exactly 7½″ × 9½″, but the easel opening will be 75/8″ × 95/8″ to produce the necessary overlap. The procedure is as follows:

1. Compose the image on the easel and make an exposure test.

2. On a separate piece of paper, make an exposure test under the flashing lamp to determine the exposure required for a given tone of gray. Develop both tests.

3. On a full sheet of paper in the easel, make the image exposure determined by the test. Any necessary dodging or burning-in is done at this stage.

4. Remove the paper from the easel and place it under the flashing lamp.

5. On top of the paper, place the masking card and adjust its position carefully to get an even margin all around.

6. Now give the flash exposure for the desired tone of gray.

7. Develop, stop, and fix the print.

If a subject requires black outlines, then any flashing exposure long enough to produce the maximum black of the paper may be given. It is possible to make black borders of shapes other than rectangles by using a card that is oval, round, or any other shape. If you want a black border, you do not have to mask the print during the image exposure; the mask flashing will simply burn out the image exposure in the border area.

• *See also:* BURNING-IN; COLOR PRINTING FROM TRANSPARENCIES; GRAPHIC ARTS PHOTOGRAPHY; LATENSIFICATION; PUSH PROCESSING.

Flash Photography

A brief flash of light produced by burning metal wire (flashbulb) or an electrical discharge through a gas-filled tube (electronic flash) is the most common supplemental light used for still photography. Flash offers great light output in compact, lightweight, economical form. It avoids the effects of heat and glare during setup that are common with most continuous light sources. Because flash may be battery powered, it is especially convenient for location work where ac power is not available. As with other sources of artificial light, flash allows the photographer to control the direction, quality, and intensity of lighting to achieve any desired effect.

Flash Sources

Electronic flash units produce light by means of an electrically fired gas discharge tube. Portable units usually have self-contained reflectors; studio units employ a variety of accessory reflectors. Most units may be powered by ac as well as batteries. The color temperature of the light output is in the 5500–6000 K range, essentially matching the balance of daylight color film emulsions. Electronic flash typically has a duration of 1/1000 sec. or faster, which makes it especially suitable for stopping fast action. The flash tube is good for tens of thousands of flashes, so it is not necessary to have a supply of bulbs to reload the unit after each exposure. This makes it practical to place units in inaccessible locations—such as at ceiling level in a studio—when necessary. Types of units and other details are discussed in the article ELECTRONIC FLASH.

Flashbulbs consist of a metal wire, usually aluminum or zirconium, inside a transparent glass or plastic housing; when fired, the wire burns completely in a fraction of a second. Single bulbs are used in appropriate reflector-plus-socket units that may be small enough to be hand-held or conveniently attached to the camera, or may be mounted on light stands or similar supports. The size and shape of the reflector determine which bulbs can be used and the spread or coverage of the light (see illustrations and notes in the Exposure Guide Number table) as well as the intensity of the light on a subject. Multiple-bulb units such as flashcubes and flipflash have built-in reflectors.

When a single flash unit—electronic or bulb type—is used, it is almost always connected to a synchronizing switch circuit in the camera or lens shutter. (The major exceptions to this arrangement are open flash and painting with flash, described in later sections.) When more than one flash unit is used, the remote or "slave" units must fire simultaneously with the shutter-synchronized unit. Flashbulb units usually have to be interconnected by wires to form a complete circuit; this is often an inconvenience in the studio and usually a source of some missed exposures on location where connections can easily be broken. Multiple electronic flash units can easily be synchronized by photosensitive switches that respond instantaneously to light from the main unit, eliminating the need for connecting wires between units. An electronic flash unit equipped with such a switch is often called a "slave" unit.

Flashbulbs

Flashbulbs are identified by one- or two-digit numbers and usually one or more accompanying letter. *AG* designates an all-glass miniature bulb that makes electrical contact by means of two pins that protrude from the base. Other bulbs have screw-type, bayonet or prefocus-flange metal base caps. *M*-class bulbs reach peak intensity at a medium speed and are intended primarily for use with shutters set for M synchronization, as discussed in the section on flash exposure in this article. The letter *B* following a bulb number indicates that its glass envelope is blue, which produces light with a nominal color temperature of 5500 K for use with daylight color films as well as panchromatic films. Clear flashbulbs have no final letter. They may be used without filtration with black-and-white films, but require some filter correction for use with color films; see the table on flashes and filters.

A flashcube consists of four bulbs in a blue, cube-shaped plastic housing measuring about one inch across each face. The base permits the cube to be rotated to bring an unused face into position after each exposure. Hi-Power flashcubes have twice the light output of standard flashcubes, so exposures may be made with the lens set one *f*-stop smaller. Magicubes are flashcubes that do not require electrical power to fire. Flashcubes will not fire in cameras that accept magicubes, and magicubes may not be used in flashcube-type cameras without danger of damaging the camera.

Flipflash units consist of eight miniature bulbs arranged in an array on a rectangular card-like support. The bulbs are blue and have built-in reflectors; they are integrally wired to prong contacts at the base of the card. After the four flashes on one half have been used, the card is turned upside down to bring the other four bulbs into working position. This places the bulbs to be flashed some distance from the camera lens, which minimizes the possibilities of getting red-eye in the pictures. Flipflash units are primarily used with small, amateur cameras. Like flashcubes, they eliminate the need for a separate reflector unit and provide the convenience of several flashes without having to change bulbs. Switching from one bulb to another is automatic, and is accomplished by the heat generated by the firing bulbs.

Power Supplies for Flash

Flashbulbs and flashcubes are designed to be fired by 3 volts dc power; a maximum of 45 volts dc can generally be used without damage to equipment or misfiring of the bulb. "B-C" flash units use a capacitor in conjunction with batteries to extend the useful battery life. For the most part, expendable batteries are used in small flashbulb units; rechargeable batteries are widely used in electronic flash units. Magicubes contain an internal primer tube that is fired by a mechanical striker activated by the camera shutter, not by electrical power. No batteries are needed.

Some larger, conventional flashbulbs can also be fired by 110–120 volt ac power. This makes it convenient to replace normal incandescent bulbs with screw-base flashbulbs in existing lights on location, in order to avoid transporting and erecting a large number of flash units and their accompanying battery power supplies. Certain precautions are essential. Only No. 2, 3, 22, and 50 clear and blue bulbs have a special internal fuse to protect the circuit against surge currents. The camera synchronizing contacts *must not* be connected to the ac power. The high voltage will damage or fuse the contact

FLASH AND FILTERS			
	Filter to Use with Color Films		
Kind of Flash	**Daylight**	**Type A (3400 K)**	**Tungsten (3200 K)**
Blue bulbs	None	85	85B
Clear zirconium-filament bulbs (AG-1, M3, M5)	80D	81C	81C
Other clear bulbs	80C	81C	81C
Electronic flash	None	85	85B

permanently together, and is likely to shock or injure anyone touching the camera. The safest method is the open-flash technique, in which the flash is independently fired after the shutter has been opened. This will be discussed further.

Because flash lamps have low resistance, when fired they can cause a sudden surge of current that may overload the ac circuit fuse. This is especially likely to happen when the flashbulbs are connected in parallel. The surge current can be minimized by wiring a standard incandescent lamp in series with the parallel-connected flashbulbs. The accompanying diagram shows the connection and the size of lamp needed to balance various numbers of flashbulbs. If the flashbulbs are connected in series, no standard lamp is required in the circuit. However, any loose connection, or a faulty or improperly seated bulb in a series circuit will cause all bulbs to fail to fire; in a parallel circuit only the faulty unit will fail. It should be emphasized that ac firing of flashbulbs is a special technique that should not be used for normal situations.

Flipflash bulbs are fired by a piezo generator built into the camera. As the shutter is released, a hammer strikes a piezo crystal that gives off a pulse of high-voltage (about 1000 to 2000 volts), low-amperage electric current. The very low amperage makes the high voltage harmless. The pulse of current is wired to the bulb, which is designed to fire with this type of pulse. Flipflash cannot be fired with normal batteries. One reason the voltage is made so high is to avoid accidental firing by static electricity, which can be generated by walking on a rug in a dry atmosphere.

Exposure with Flash

Both flashbulbs and electronic flash provide light at a relatively high-illumination level for a relatively short period of time. Because it is important for the camera shutter to be open for this brief period, the flash and the shutter are usually synchronized. Open flash, an acceptable alternative when there is no motion to be stopped and when the ambient illumination is very low, is accomplished by the manual opening of the shutter, and the firing of the flash when the shutter is open.

Flash Synchronization. There are various types of flash synchronization: M, X, and FP or F are in current use. M synchronization times the flashing of

most bulbs and flashcubes with the opening of blade-type shutters. Electronic flash requires the use of X synchronization when employed with both blade and focal-plane shutters. FP or M is the type of synchronization used to synchronize focal-plane shutters with FP flashbulbs (No. 6 and No. 26). The flash terminal provided on many current focal-plane-shutter cameras in addition to the X terminal is the FP terminal. It may be identified with the symbol of a flashbulb.

The X setting is a "no-delay" setting for use with electronic flash units at any blade (between-the-lens) shutter speed, and with flashcubes and all flashbulbs (except No. 6B and No. 26B) at a shutter speed of 1/30 sec. If in doubt about the synchronization setting to use with a blade shutter, use the X setting at a speed of 1/30 sec.

The M setting delays the opening of the shutter for a fraction of a second to give the flashbulb time to reach peak brightness. Use the M setting with flashcubes and all flashbulbs except No. M2B (which requires X synchronization). The M setting allows use of shutter speeds up to 1/500 sec.

Direct Flash. Flash exposure is usually computed by the use of guide numbers. A guide number depends on the film speed, shutter speed, the light output of the bulb or electronic flash unit, and in the case of flashbulbs, the type of reflector. Flashcubes and electronic flash units have built-in reflectors that provide a standard reflector condition. The guide numbers for various film-speed, flashbulb, and reflector combinations can be found in the accompanying Flash Exposure Guide Number table.

In using flashbulbs for picture-taking, the guide number should be adjusted to the type of room or other surrounding conditions. The flash guide numbers in the table are based on exposures made in a room of average size and average reflection level. Actual exposure depends both on light that reaches the subject directly from the flash and reflector and on light that reaches the subject by reflection from surfaces in the room, primarily from the ceiling and walls. When making flash exposures in rooms smaller than normal, or with lighter-than-normal surfaces, use an exposure one-half to one stop less than that given by the guide number. For larger rooms or rooms with surfaces darker than normal, use one-half to one stop more exposure than that found by the use of the guide number. This is especially important either in very large rooms, such as auditoriums, or outdoors at night. Such exposure corrections are not usually necessary with electronic flash because of the reflector design.

Electronic-flash guide numbers are based on the reflected-light output of the unit as measured in beam candlepower-seconds (BCPS), or effective candlepower-seconds (ECPS). The guide numbers for different film speeds and various output electronic flash units are given in the Electronic-Flash Guide Number table in this article.

Guide numbers are used to find the f-number at which the exposure should be made by the following formula:

$$\frac{\text{Guide number}}{\substack{\text{Flash-to-subject} \\ \text{distance (in feet)}}} = f\text{-number*}$$

For example: The guide number is 64; the flash-to-subject distance is 8 feet:

$$\frac{64}{8} = 8$$

The lens should be set to $f/8$.

Some electronic flash units are automatic. With such units, the camera lens aperture is set at a single f-number for all distances within a range, depending on the film speed, and the unit automatically controls the duration of the flash to give the correct exposure. Guide numbers are *not* used with this type of unit, unless it is set in a nonautomatic mode. (See the instructions packaged with the unit for specific information.)

A flash dial that combines all the factors for flash exposure can be found in the KODAK *Professional Photoguide*, publication number R-28. Methods of adjusting guide numbers and exposures for various subject conditions and flash placements are given in the following sections and in the article GUIDE NUMBERS.

---

*There are also metre guide numbers. When these are used, the distance in metres, rather than feet, should be used. To convert feet guide numbers to metre guide numbers, divide the feet guide number by 3.28. To convert meter guide numbers to feet guide numbers, multiply by 3.28.

On-Camera Flash

Flash on the camera or held close to the camera by a bracket provides a direct, hard light. It puts a maximum of the available light directly on the subject, but with a minimum of modeling. There will be harsh shadows behind the subject, and important detail may be obscured in deep shadow. In color work, the hard shadows and light falloff may give the erroneous impression of color changes where no changes actually exist.

Two problems resulting from on-camera flash are "red eye" and reflections of the flash.

Red eye. In some color flash pictures the pupils of the subject's eyes may look red; in black-and-white pictures the pupils may look white. This phenomenon in color pictures is a reflection from the blood-rich choroid layers of the retina, and is caused by the flash being close to the camera lens. This effect usually occurs when the subject is looking directly at the camera and the light level of the room is relatively dim so that the pupils are large.

The best way to minimize red reflections is to move the flash away from the camera lens. If the camera accepts magicubes or flashcubes, this effect can be minimized at distances up to 15 feet by use of an extender available at photo supply stores. There are two kinds of extenders—one designed for use with magicubes and another for flashcubes; they are not interchangeable.

If the camera has an integral flash unit that cannot be removed, it helps to increase the level of light in the room by turning on all the room lights. This reduces red reflections because the added light will cause the subject's pupils to contract, reducing the reflective surface that causes red reflections. (*See:* RED EYE.)

If the subject looks at a bright light (for example, a room lamp) just before the flash picture is taken, the bright light will reduce the size of the subject's pupils.

A final resort is to use existing light, not flash.

Reflections. An otherwise good picture can be spoiled by reflections of the flash. Try to avoid shiny surfaces in the background of pictures, such as mirrors, windows, and shiny walls. To reduce the reflection if a shiny surface background is unavoidable, stand at an angle to the shiny surface, or move the flash away from the camera so that it strikes the background at an angle.

FLASH EXPOSURE GUIDE NUMBER TABLE
(For Flash-Subject Distances in Feet)

Film Speed	Shutter Speed (sec.)	Flash-cube	AG-1B	AG-1B	M3B 5B 25B	11* 40	2B 22B	AG-1B	M3B 5B 25B	11* 40	2B 22B	3* 50	M2B	M2B	6B 26B	6B 26B
32	1/25–1/30	34	26	36	65	85	110	50	90	120	160	240	50	70	70	100
	1/50–1/60	34	26	36	65	85	110	50	90	120	150	—	40	60	50	75
	1/100–1/125	28	22	30	55	70	90	45	25	100	130	—	—	—	34	50
	1/200–1/250	22	18	26	42	55	70	36	60	75	100	—	—	—	24	34
	1/400–1/500	18	14	20	32	42	55	28	45	60	75	—	—	—	17	24
40	1/25–1/30	38	28	40	75	100	100	60	110	140	130	260	55	75	80	110
	1/50–1/60	38	28	40	70	90	90	55	100	130	130	—	45	65	60	80
	1/100–1/125	32	24	34	60	80	75	50	85	110	110	—	—	—	38	55
	1/200–1/250	24	20	28	45	60	55	40	65	85	80	—	—	—	28	38
	1/400–1/500	20	16	22	36	45	42	32	65	65	60	—	—	—	20	28
80	1/25–1/30	55	40	60	110	140	130	80	150	200	200	380	25	110	110	160
	1/50–1/60	55	40	55	100	130	130	80	140	180	180	—	65	90	80	120
	1/100–1/125	45	34	50	85	115	110	70	120	160	150	—	—	—	55	75
	1/200–1/250	34	28	40	65	85	80	55	90	120	110	—	—	—	38	55
	1/400–1/500	28	22	32	50	65	60	45	70	90	85	—	—	—	28	38
100	1/25–1/30	60	45	65	120	150	150	90	170	220	220	420	85	120	130	180
	1/50–1/60	60	45	65	110	140	140	90	160	200	200	—	70	100	90	130
	1/100–1/125	50	38	55	90	130	120	75	130	180	170	—	—	—	60	85
	1/200–1/250	38	32	45	75	90	90	65	110	130	130	—	—	—	42	60
	1/400–1/500	32	24	34	55	70	70	50	80	100	100	—	—	—	30	44
125	1/25–1/30	70	50	70	130	170	170	100	180	240	240	450	100	130	140	200
	1/50–1/60	65	50	70	120	160	160	100	180	220	220	—	80	110	100	140
	1/100–1/125	55	42	60	100	140	140	85	150	200	200	—	—	—	70	100
	1/200–1/250	44	36	50	85	110	100	70	120	150	140	—	—	—	50	70
	1/400–1/500	36	28	38	65	85	75	55	90	120	110	—	—	—	34	50
160	1/25–1/30	75	60	80	150	200	200	120	220	280	260	550	110	150	160	220
	1/50–1/60	75	55	80	140	180	180	110	200	260	260	—	90	130	120	160
	1/100–1/125	65	50	70	120	150	150	100	170	220	220	—	—	—	75	110
	1/200–1/250	50	40	55	90	120	110	80	130	170	160	—	—	—	55	75
	1/400–1/500	40	32	45	70	90	85	60	100	130	120	—	—	—	38	55
200	1/25–1/30	85	65	90	170	220	220	130	240	300	300	600	120	170	180	260
	1/50–1/60	85	65	90	160	200	200	130	220	280	280	—	100	140	130	180
	1/100–1/125	70	55	75	130	180	170	110	180	260	240	—	—	—	85	120
	1/200–1/250	55	45	65	110	140	130	90	150	200	180	—	—	—	60	85
	1/400–1/500	45	34	50	80	110	100	70	110	150	140	—	—	—	44	60
250	1/25–1/30	100	70	100	180	240	240	140	260	340	340	650	130	200	200	280
	1/50–1/60	100	70	100	180	230	220	140	240	320	320	—	110	160	140	200
	1/100–1/125	80	60	85	150	200	200	120	200	280	280	—	—	—	100	140
	1/200–1/250	60	50	70	120	150	140	100	170	220	200	—	—	—	70	100
	1/400–1/500	50	38	55	90	120	110	80	130	160	150	—	—	—	45	70
320	1/25–1/30	110	80	120	220	280	260	160	300	400	380	750	150	220	220	320
	1/50–1/60	110	80	110	200	260	260	160	280	360	360	—	130	180	160	240
	1/100–1/125	90	70	100	170	230	220	140	240	320	300	—	—	—	110	150
	1/200–1/250	70	55	80	130	170	160	110	180	240	220	—	—	—	75	110
	1/400–1/500	60	45	60	100	130	120	90	140	180	170	—	—	—	55	75

Column groupings:
- **Shutter Type — Blade (Between-the-Lens), M sync:** Flashcube; Magicube (Flash-cube); Shallow Cylindrical Reflector (AG-1B); Intermediate-Shaped Reflector (AG-1B, M3B 5B/25B, 11*/40, 2B/22B); Polished Bowl-Shaped Reflector (AG-1B, M3B 5B/25B, 11*/40, 2B/22B, 3*/50)
- **X sync:** M2B, M2B
- **Focal Plane, FP or M:** 6B/26B, 6B/26B

Flash Photography

FLASH EXPOSURE GUIDE NUMBER TABLE
(For Flash-Subject Distances in Feet)

Shutter Type — Type of Sync		Blade (Between-the-Lens) — M											X		Focal Plane FP or M	
		Flash-cube; Magicube	Shallow Cylindrical Reflector	Intermediate-Shaped Reflector				Polished Bowl-Shaped Reflector								
Film Speed	Shutter Speed (sec.)	Flash-cube	AG-1B	AG-1B	M3B 5B 25B	11* 40	2B 22B	AG-1B	M3B 5B 25B	11* 40	2B 22B	3* 50	M2B	M2B	6B 26B	6B 26B
400	1/25–1/30	120	90	130	240	320	300	180	340	450	420	850	170	240	260	360
	1/50–1/60	120	90	130	220	280	280	180	320	400	400	—	140	200	180	260
	1/100/1/125	100	75	110	180	260	240	150	260	360	340	—	—	—	120	170
	1/200–1/250	75	65	90	150	180	180	130	220	260	260	—	—	—	85	120
	1/400–1/500	65	50	70	110	140	140	100	160	200	200	—	—	—	60	85
500	1/25–1/30	140	100	140	260	360	340	200	380	500	500	900	200	260	280	400
	1/50–1/60	130	100	140	240	320	320	200	360	450	450	—	160	220	200	280
	1/100/1/125	110	85	120	200	280	280	170	300	400	380	—	—	—	140	200
	1/200–1/250	85	70	100	170	220	200	140	240	300	280	—	—	—	100	140
	1/400–1/500	70	55	80	130	170	150	110	180	240	220	—	—	—	70	100

*Clear Bulbs: 11, 40, 3, and 50 are clear bulbs; the others listed are blue. To find the approximate guide number of the clear version of a blue bulb listed in the table, multiply the blue bulb guide number by 1.3; and to find the blue bulb guide number version of a clear bulb listed in the table, divide the clear bulb guide number by 1.3.

CAUTION: Bulbs may shatter when flashed. Use a flashguard over the reflector. **Do not flash bulbs in an explosive atmosphere.**

ELECTRONIC FLASH GUIDE NUMBER TABLE

Film Speed	Output of Unit (BCPS or ECPS)									
	350	500	700	1000	1400	2000	2800	4000	5600	8000
32	24	28	32	40	50	55	65	80	95	110
40	26	32	35	45	55	65	75	90	110	130
50	30	35	40	50	60	70	85	100	120	140
64	32	40	45	55	65	80	95	110	130	160
80	35	45	50	60	75	90	110	140	170	200
100	40	50	55	70	85	100	120	140	170	200
125	45	55	65	80	95	110	130	160	190	220
160	55	65	75	90	110	130	150	180	210	250
200	60	70	85	100	120	140	170	200	240	280
250	65	80	95	110	130	160	190	220	260	320
320	75	90	110	130	150	180	210	250	300	360
400	85	100	120	140	170	200	240	280	340	400
500	95	110	130	160	190	220	260	320	370	450
650	110	130	150	180	210	260	300	360	430	510
800	120	140	170	200	240	280	330	400	470	560
1000	130	160	190	220	260	320	380	450	530	630
1250	150	180	210	250	300	350	420	500	600	700
1600	170	200	240	280	340	400	480	560	670	800

These guide numbers are for use with distances measured in feet. For distances measured in metres, divide the table guide number by 3.28.

Eyeglasses can also cause reflection problems in flash pictures. People who wear glasses do not look natural without them—in real life or in pictures. However, the light from the flash can be reflected by the glasses, causing a distracting glare that can obscure the subject's eyes. Avoid glare from glasses in the same way as with shiny backgrounds—turn the subject or move the flash so it is at an angle to the glasses. Or, use existing light.

Off-Camera Flash

By moving the flash unit away from the camera an arm's length or more, the photographer can often improve the effectiveness of the flash lighting. When the light is held higher than the subject and to one side, the shadow is dropped out of view behind the subject. The light coming from the side creates more modeling and increases the three-dimensional effect, a necessity for realistic appearance of objects rendered in two-dimensional photographs. In rain or snow, holding the flash well away from the lens axis reduces the direct lighting of raindrops or snowflakes that can obscure the scene when lit by on-camera flash.

When a single flash unit is used in this way, exposure is determined directly from the guide number and the flash-to-subject distance (not camera-to-subject distance). Placing the flash directly above the camera lens (far enough to avoid red-eye) provides useful, almost shadowless lighting. It can be effective in pictures of babies and some types of still-life subjects. This position for the flash is effective for the fill light in multiple-flash pictures and outdoor, back-lit, fill-flash pictures. Much more subtle and expressive lighting can be achieved in several ways:

1. By use of more than one flash unit directed at the subject (in essentially the same arrangements used with multiple continuous-light sources).
2. By using flash to fill in dark areas or supplement existing illumination, especially sunlight.
3. By open flash exposure and "painting" with light.
4. By reflecting or "bouncing" the flash illumination from suitable surfaces.

Multiple Flash

Use of more than one flash unit can create a feeling of depth and form in pictures. The addition of one or two extension or remote flash units produces a two- or three-light "studio" at any location.

The main, or key light, which creates shadows and depth on the subject, is usually one of the off-camera units. It is placed closer to the subject than the fill light. The fill-light unit is on the camera (or at the camera position); it increases the illumination in shadow areas. A third flash unit can be used to illuminate the background, or as a backlight to produce rim lighting and highlights on the subject.

Calculating Exposure. Exposure is based on the distance from the main light to the subject, with some adjustment for the fill light if necessary; the backlight will not affect subject exposure. Use the guide numbers for the main and the fill units to determine the f-stop required by the subject distance of each. If the difference between them is two or more stops, expose at the smaller (the main light) f-stop. If the difference is ½ to 1½ stops, give ½ stop less exposure than the smaller stop. If they are the same, give one stop less exposure.

Lighting Large Area Scenes. Large area scenes are sometimes lighted with multiple flash. In some cases, the light from several flash units is overlapped on the subject to permit the use of a smaller lens opening. The following two formulas show how to calculate the f-numbers when two or four flash units of the *same output* are used in this manner at the *same distance*.

$$f\text{-number for 2 superimposed flash} = 1.4 \times \left(\frac{\text{Guide number}}{\text{Distance}}\right)$$

$$f\text{-number for 4 superimposed flash} = 2.0 \times \left(\frac{\text{Guide number}}{\text{Distance}}\right)$$

Two flash units used with film that gives a guide number of 400, (distance 36 feet) results in:

$$f\text{-number} = 1.4 \times \frac{400}{36} = 1.4 \times 11$$
$$= f/15.4 \text{ or } f/16$$

Another multiple-flash method used is to light separate sections of a large scene with several flash units in such a way that there is little or no overlap of the light beams. The key to exposure when using this method is to *have the same flash-to-subject distance for each flash.* The f-number is computed by using the distance and the guide number in the same manner as if it were single, direct flash. The area near the camera is usually illuminated by one flash synchronized to the shutter, with other units being fired by electronic switches triggered by the light of the synchronized flash (slave units). The units are hidden from the camera lens by placing them behind various objects in the scene.

Fill-In Flash Outdoors

On days when the sun is shining (bright sun or hazy with distinct shadows), blue bulbs or electronic flash can be used to lower the lighting ratio in sidelit, toplit, and backlit situations. This procedure is espe-cially useful in pictures of people; not only does it provide a pleasing lighting effect, but it also results in improved expressions because the subjects do not have to squint as they would in facing the sun.

For a natural effect, fill in the shadows but do not eliminate them. The following tables are based on a 3:1 lighting ratio. To decrease the ratio to about 2:1, decrease the distances given in the table by about one-third. To increase the lighting ratio to 5:1, increase the distances given by one-third.

Flash on the camera is quick and convenient but tends to produce flat and often unflattering lighting. If the flash is directly above the lens, a shadowless lighting results.

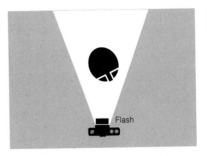 

Off-camera flash placed high and to the right of the camera produces more dramatic lighting with considerable contrast between light and shadowed areas.

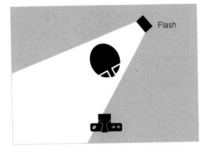 

Off-camera flash placed low and to the left of the camera, with a reflector used to fill in the shadow area, creates a balanced, overall type of lighting suitable for some portraiture.

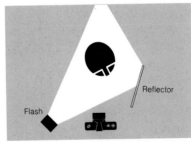 

An off-camera flash placed to the camera's left and behind the model produces an attractive highlight on her hair. A reflector softly fills in the shadows on the side of the model's face away from the light. Photos by John Menihan.

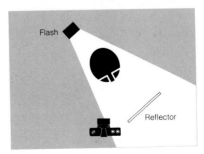 

Flash Photography

1105

FILL-IN FLASH—TABLE A

Subject Distances for Fill-in Flash with Blue Flashbulbs (Distances in Feet)

Flashbulb Type	Reflector Type	X-Sync 1/25, 1/30	X-Sync 1/50, 1/60	1/25, 1/30	1/50, 1/60	M-Sync 1/100, 1/125	1/200, 1/250	1/400, 1/500
Shallow cylindrical	AG-1B	3	3	2	3	4	4½	4½
Incorporated	Flashcube	4	4½	3	3½	5	5	5½
	Hi-Power Cube	6	NR	4	5	6	7	8
Shallow bowl	M2B	4	4½	NR	NR	NR	NR	NR
	AG-1B M-3B	4	4	3	3½	5	6	7
	5B, 25B	6	NR	6	7	8	10	10
	2B, 22B	7	NR	7	9	11	11	12
	3B, 50B	11	NR	11	NR	NR	NR	NR
Deep bowl	M2B	5½	6½	NR	NR	NR	NR	NR
	AG-1B M-3B	6½	7	4½	6½	8	9	9
	5B, 25B	9	NR	8½	11	13	14	16
	2B, 22B	10	NR	9	13	15	17	18
Studio	3B, 50B	15	NR	14	NR	NR	NR	NR
Shallow bowl	6B, 26B	FP-Sync		6	6	6	6	6
Deep bowl	6B, 26B			8	8	8	8	8

Reflector interior finish: all polished except studio (satin).
Reflector Sizes: Shallow Bowl—4″ to 8″.
    Deep Bowl—AG-1B: 2″, M2B, M-3B: 3″, 5B, 25B: 4″ to 5″, 2B, 22B: 6½″ to 7½″.
    Studio—12″ to 24″.
NR = Not recommended.

FILL-IN FLASH—TABLE B

Subject Distances for Fill-In Flash with Electronic Flash (Distances in Feet)

Output of Unit (BCPS, ECPS)	Unit Guide Number with ASA 100 Film Speed	1/25, 1/30	1/50, 1/60	1/100, 1/125	1/200, 1/250	1/400, 1/500
250	35	1½	2½	3½	5	7
350	40	2	3	4	6	8
500	50	2½	3½	5	7	10
700	60	3	4	6	8	12
1000	70	3½	5	7	10	14
1400	85	4	6	8	12	16
2000	100	5	7	10	14	20
2800	120	6	8	12	16	24
4000	140	7	10	14	20	28
5600	170	8	12	16	24	35
8000	200	10	14	20	28	40
11,000	240	12	16	24	35	48
16,000	280	14	20	28	40	56

Flash Photography

FILL-IN FLASH—TABLE C

f-Numbers to Use with Chosen Shutter Speed and Film Speed

Film Speeds	Shutter Speed (sec.)				
	1/25, 1/30	1/50, 1/60	1/100, 1/125	1/200, 1/250	1/400, 1/500
25, 32	f/16	f/11	f/8	f/5.6	f/4
40	f/19	f/14	f/10	f/6.3	f/4.5
50, 64	f/22	f/16	f/11	f/8	f/5.6
80	f/28	f/19	f/14	f/10	f/6.3
100, 125	f/32	f/22	f/16	f/11	f/8
160	f/40	f/28	f/19	f/14	f/10
200, 250	f/45	f/32	f/22	f/20	f/11
320	f/56	f/40	f/28	f/22	f/14
400, 500	f/64	f/45	f/32	f/28	f/20
640	—	f/56	f/40	f/32	f/28
800, 1000	—	f/64	f/45	f/40	f/32

NOTE: At apertures of f/16 and smaller, and at shutter speeds of 1/200 sec. and faster, the f-numbers are corrected for the increased exposure that blade shutters give.
Standard frontlighted daylight exposure based on 1/film speed (sec.) at f/16.

Alternating Current Operation of Flashbulbs

Diagram A shows an incandescent lamp in series with flashbulbs wired in parallel to protect the circuit fuse. The switch may be in either leg of the circuit. Diagram B shows flashbulbs wired in series with no incandescent lamp required for circuit protection.
NOTE: Use only flashbulbs listed in the article for ac flashing.

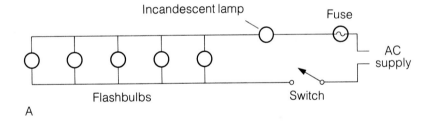

A

Number of Flashbulbs Wired in Parallel	Wattage of Incandescent Lamp
1	None
2	150–200
3	200–300
4–5	300–500
6–10	1000

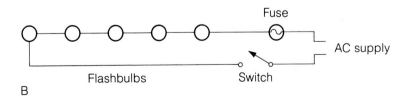

B

Flash Photography

Fill-in flash at the camera position effectively reduces the high contrast between backlight from the sun and the resulting heavy shadow on the side of the subject facing the camera. Flash should only lighten shadows, not eliminate them; too much flash causes unnatural illumination. (Near right) Photo taken with no fill-in flash. (Center) Photo taken with moderate fill-in flash. (Far right) Photo taken with excessive fill-in flash.

The basic exposures for fill-in flash are the same as for front-sunlit exposures, and they are given in Table C; they are based on film speed, shutter speed, and *f*-number. Varying the shutter speed and *f*-number to get equivalent exposures permits you to change the distance while maintaining the same lighting ratio. The tables for flashbulb and electronic flash fill-in usage (A and B) show the distances for each combination that results in a 3:1 ratio.

As in all flash photography, use the correct synchronization for the camera-flash combination. Most focal-plane shutter cameras equipped with electronic flash units have a limited range of distances within which fill-in flash can be successfully employed, because 1/60 sec. is usually the shortest exposure time that can be used (1/125 sec. can be used on some focal-plane shutters). A fairly large electronic flash unit used with a blade-shutter camera gives the greatest range of distances—a 2800 BCPS unit will give a 3:1 ratio fill at distances from 6 to 24 feet, for example, at different shutter speeds. Covering the flash with one layer of white handkerchief will permit dividing each distance given in the tables in half.

Procedure:

1. Find the proper line for the reflector and flashbulb type in Table A, or electronic flash unit in Table B.
2. Choose one of the distances given for the combination.
3. Find the shutter speed at the top of the column for that distance.
4. In Table C find the correct *f*-number for that shutter speed and the film speed.

5. Set the camera shutter speed and aperture accordingly, and take the picture with the flash unit at the distance selected.

It is also possible to determine fill-in flash exposures without use of the tables. With the sun as a main light from one side or behind the subject, flash at the camera is used to fill in the shadows to achieve a desired lighting ratio. (Electronic flash or blue flashbulbs are required with color films.) There are two methods.

Method A:

1. Determine proper exposure for the sunlight by taking a meter reading of the subject. Choose a speed suitable for the type of flash in use (for example, 1/60 sec. or slower is required for most focal-plane shutters with electronic flash). Set the lens to the *f*-stop called for at that speed by the meter reading.
2. Determine the guide number for the film-flash combination from the film data sheet, flash unit reference chart, or other source.
3. Guide number ÷ *f*-number set on lens = required flash-to-subject distance in feet for a 1:2 lighting ratio.

4. For other ratios, adjust the distance found in step 3 as follows:

Distance $\times$ 1.5 = Distance for 1:3 ratio
Distance $\times$ 2.0 = Distance for 1:5 ratio.

For color photographs use a 1:2 or a 1:3 ratio; for black-and-white photographs use a 1:3 to 1:5 ratio.

Method B:
1. Determine the *f*-stop for proper flash exposure by dividing the guide number by the flash-to-subject distance.
2. For a 1:3 ratio, set the lens one stop smaller. For a 1:5 ratio, set the lens two stops smaller.
3. Take an incident-light meter reading of the sunlight (or a reflected-light reading from an 18 percent reflectance gray card). Note the shutter speed called for at the *f*-stop to which the lens was set in step 2. If this speed is suitable for the flash and the kind of shutter in use, make the exposure. If it is not, change the flash-to-subject distance sufficiently to arrive at an *f*-stop in step 2 that will require a suitable shutter speed.

All of the above methods of finding the distance for the fill flash do not provide variations for the amount of fill provided by the open sky, which is not a constant factor. A method for particularly careful work that does take this variable factor into account is provided in Kodak publication No. R-28, *KODAK Professional Photoguide,* in 1977 and later printings. A reflection exposure meter is used to measure the conditions, and a dial calculator is used to find the flash distance for the right amount of fill-in light.

Recording Existing Light Plus Flash
When flash is used to take a picture in a brightly lighted room, the light from the flash will tend to overpower the room lights and cause a slightly artificial look. Our eyes are accustomed to seeing light come from the room's lighting fixtures rather than from an unknown source outside the picture. In the same way, flash pictures taken of a fire in a fireplace tend to look somewhat artificial because the flames look dim compared with other subjects in the picture—not at all the way our eyes see it.

(Left) This straightforward flash-at-the-camera picture has harsh shadows and lacks a sense of true depth. (Right) While the shutter was held open, a flash unit was fired at the top of the stairs to create this more provocative lighting effect. Exposure is always based on flash-to-subject distance, not camera-to-subject distance.

To take advantage of the existing lighting and give a more natural appearance to indoor flash pictures, use a slow shutter speed and a small flashbulb —an AG-1B, for example—or reduce the flash intensity with a neutral density filter over the flash unit (*not* over the camera lens). The reduced light will require a relatively large lens opening. The slow shutter speed will give the existing illumination more time to register on the film, resulting in a more natural-looking picture. Another way to get the same effect is to use bounce flash or reflectorless flash with a slow shutter speed. Both of these techniques require a large lens opening, which helps record the existing light; and the light from the flash reflected by the walls and ceiling is soft and glareless.

Open Flash

Flash pictures can be taken without synchronization by the open-flash method. The camera must be mounted on a tripod, and the scene or subject must be quite dark, for the shutter is open for a much longer time than normal. To make an open-flash picture, compute the required *f*-stop from the guide number and whatever flash-to-subject distance is convenient; use the guide number given for a shutter speed of 1/25 or 1/30 sec. Then, open the shutter using the "B" (Bulb) or "T" (Time) shutter-speed setting, fire off the flash unit, and close the shutter. Many flash units have a manual or test button to fire the flash when the unit is not connected to a sync circuit. Otherwise, use a paper clip or other metal object to short across the plug of the sync cord on the unit.

Open flash is good for recording dim light sources requiring longer exposure times than even the camera's slow shutter speeds provide. In photographing a lighted Christmas tree, for example, this would be the sequence: Open the shutter for a few seconds to let the tree lights register on the film, fire the flash to provide general illumination, and close the shutter. Or to photograph a jack-o'-lantern at Halloween, open the shutter, let the candlelight "burn in" on the film for a few seconds, and fire the flash to illuminate the outside of the pumpkin before closing the shutter. To get the same effect with synchronized flash, set the shutter on "B" and hold it open for a few seconds after the flash.

Painting with Flash

The open-flash technique makes it possible to use a single flash unit to light an area or subject much larger than the usual coverage of the flash. The method is to keep the shutter open while the flash is moved from place to place and fired repeatedly until all areas of the subject have been exposed. The most common way to do this is to use the "T" exposure shutter setting, or the "B" setting with a locking cable release. The lens is covered with a black card between exposures while the flash is moved from position to position. In cameras with between-the-lens shutters (in which the film is not advanced each time the shutter is cocked), it is possible to repeatedly open and close the shutter by means of a cable release. However, there is great danger of moving the camera slightly whenever the lens is cocked, causing details to be out of register when the overall exposure has been completed.

There are a number of obvious precautions in painting with flash. The camera must remain absolutely immobile. The light level of the scene or subject must be quite low so that repeated exposures do not build up unwanted density in some areas. An assistant is almost essential to move the flash unit while the photographer controls operations from the camera. The flash unit must be hidden from camera view by objects in the scene for every exposure, and

the assistant must never be between the flash and the camera—otherwise he or she will be recorded in silhouette. The flash must be at a consistent distance from the things it illuminates for each exposure. The *f*-stop to be used is determined by selecting a convenient flash-to-subject operating distance and dividing the guide number for a shutter speed of 1/25 or 1/30 sec. by that distance.

Although it takes some experience to be sure of good results, painting with flash makes it possible to obtain pictures under seemingly impossible conditions. Even experienced photographers find it useful to use instant print film to work out the number of exposures and the various flash positions required to cover a complicated subject or a large area.

Bounce Flash

A single flash turned so that the light bounces from the broad surface of ceiling or wall gives a diffuse light that minimizes shadows. This use of the flash can help to give a more even lighting for color photography. Since the light is indirect and diffuse, more exposure is required. White surfaces give the most efficient bounce light; colored surfaces may cause added color to shadows that will create prob-

(Below) This painting-with-flash photo was made with a slow film and an open shutter. Using the street lamps as fill lights, eight separate flashes were fired. (Right) Bounce flash gives even and diffuse lighting. A white card curved over the flash unit will direct additional light toward the subject.

lems with printing and interpreting color photographs.

This type of lighting is similar to the soft, hazy sunlight that makes possible pleasant pictures of people outdoors on overcast days. Bounce flash is especially appropriate for close-up pictures of people. When the flash unit is aimed at the ceiling, a wall, or a corner of a room, the light bounces down on the subject and produces soft, pleasing illumination. Light-colored surroundings reflect more light than dark ones and require less exposure.

Exposure depends on the size and color of the room, and on the total distance the light has to travel from flash to ceiling and back down to the subject. As a rule of thumb, use at least two stops more exposure for bounce flash than for direct flash at the same distance.

Although the exposure for bounce flash is difficult to compute exactly, it may be approximately found by the formula given below the diagram.

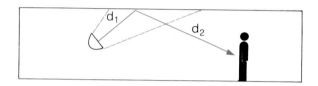

$$f\text{-number} = .7 \times \left(\frac{\text{Guide number}}{d_1 + d_2} \right)$$

The *f*-number equals .7 times the guide number divided by the sum of the flash-to-ceiling distance and the ceiling-to-subject distance measured along the center light beam from the flash.

If d_1 is 4 feet, and d_2 is 8 feet, and the guide number is 100, the aperture is *f*/5.6.

$$f\text{-number} = .7 \times \frac{100}{4 + 8} = .7 \times \frac{100}{12}$$
$$= .7 \times 8 = 5.6$$

This formula is for a relatively clean, white ceiling. For off-white or light-colored ceiling or walls, give one-half to one stop more exposure.

In order for this method to provide useful exposure data with bounce flash, it is important that a deep reflector is used, and that the flash unit is aimed in such a direction that *no direct light falls on the subject.* This is shown in the accompanying diagram by the dashed lines.

Bare-Bulb Flash

Another method of giving less directional light that softens shadows is the use of a bare bulb. Many flash units, electronic or flashbulb, permit the removal of the reflector. This allows the light to spread naturally in all directions. Thus the subject receives both direct light from the bulb and light that bounces from any reflecting surface. This lighting requires one, two, or even three stops increase in exposure, depending upon the efficiency of the reflector that was removed.

Umbrella Flash

A modified type of bounce flash is provided, usually for electronic flash, by silver, white, light blue, or amber-colored umbrellas made especially for photography. The flash unit is mounted on the handle of the umbrella, aimed at its inside center. The inside of the umbrella is then aimed toward the subject.

A guide number can be found for the flash-umbrella combination; with a clean, silver umbrella, the guide number is typically about .7 times the guide number for the flash unit used directly. Umbrella lighting is softer than direct flash lighting, but is more directional than bounce flash lighting. The article UMBRELLA LIGHTING has a fuller discussion of this technique.

• *See also:* ARTIFICIAL LIGHT; BOUNCE LIGHT; DENTAL PHOTOGRAPHY; ELECTRONIC FLASH; GUIDE NUMBERS; LIGHTING; MULTIPLE FLASH; PAINTING WITH LIGHT; RED EYE; SLAVE; UMBRELLA LIGHTING.

Further Reading: Bomback, Edward S. *Manual of Photographic Lighting.* New York, NY: International Publications Service, 1973; Cornfield, Jim. *Electronic Flash.* Los Angeles, CA: Petersen Publishing Co., 1976; Eastman Kodak Co. *Indoor Picture-Taking.* Rochester, NY: Eastman Kodak Co.; Edgerton, Harold E. *Electronic Flash, Strobe.* New York, NY: McGraw-Hill Book Co., 1970; Feininger, Andreas. *Light and Lighting in Photography.* Englewood Cliffs, NJ: Prentice-Hall, Inc., 1976; Mott, Verl. *Electronic Flash Equipment.* Indianapolis, IN: Howard W. Sams and Co., Inc., Subs. of ITT, 1974.